ADVANCES IN PRESENCING

ADVANCES IN PRESENCING

Volume 1

Edited by
Olen Gunnlaugson, Ph.D.
William Brendel, Ed.D.

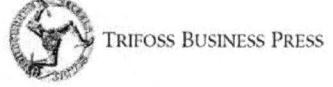 TRIFOSS BUSINESS PRESS

Dedicated to the emergence of presencing as a viable field of research and practice

About the Editors

Olen Gunnlaugson, Ph.D. is an award-winning Associate Professor in Leadership and Organizational Development at Université Laval (Canada) where he teaches MBA courses in leadership, management skills and group communications to managers, leaders and executives. With a research background in Leadership Development, Group Communication and Leadership Coaching, he received his Ph.D. at the University of British Columbia and did his Post-Doctorate at Simon Fraser University, Vancouver. To date, his work has been published extensively in books, articles and chapters in leading academic journals and books. He has presented and keynoted at numerous international conferences, received several teaching awards from universities in Canada and the USA and taught emerging leaders and executives at leading schools in Canada, USA, Austria, Sweden and South Korea. Over the past several years, he has been researching and developing Dynamic Presencing. As the focus of his upcoming book to be released in 2019, Dynamic Presencing introduces five journeys for transforming our existing presencing practices as an orienting way of being. For more information, visit www.dynamicpresencing.com

William Brendel, Ed.D. is an Assistant Professor of Organization Development and Change at Penn State University and is the CEO of the Transformative Learning Institute. William has over 20 years of experience as an organization development consultant, researcher, author and trainer. His publications on mindful leadership and organizational change span academic journals and popular press. His consultation and workshops have led to measurable transformations in organizational culture and performance across the U.S., China, India and Africa. William has previously held academic positions at Texas A&M, Temple University, and the University of St Thomas, where he has taught graduate courses in Organization Development, Leadership Development, Change Management, Talent Management, Group Dynamics, and Transformative Learning. William received his Doctorate in Adult Learning and Leadership, and Master's degree in Organizational Psychology at Columbia University in New York.

Table of Contents

CHAPTER 1

Reflections on Advances in Presencing

Olen Gunnlaugson and William Brendel

It is with great pleasure that we introduce the book series: *Advances in Presencing.* Over the past fifteen years Otto Scharmer and colleagues work with Theory U has played a vitalizing role in bringing together an international community of practice comprised of progressively minded organizations, communities and leaders who are committed to stewarding a more promising future for humanity. Since the last scholar-practitioner book on Theory U was released in 2013, there has been a growing collective interest in deepening and broadening the conversation with Theory U.

This three volume Series invites contributing voices from the Presencing Institute, independent researchers, scholar practitioners, consultants and many others into the conversation. Where the last research volume *Perspectives on Theory U: Insights from the Field* (Gunnlaugson et. al, 2013) focused more on the voices of academics and management scholar-practitioners, given how the Theory U community has grown over the past five years, we felt it was important to offer an updated practitioner focus on Theory U as a whole, with an interest in how this work, including the practice of presencing is being applied both individually and collectively.

As editors, we faced a number of thought-provoking challenges while developing this series. The first is that presencing presents a paradox. While it values a form of knowing beyond conventional thinking or downloading, in order to be considered a full-fledged paradigm of knowledge creation there needs to be some bracketing of its own conceptual real estate. In reading through the chapters in this book one will quickly discover that presencing as a practice, is in a phase of exploration, with no finite horizon or boundary informing its development. Intentional or not, presencing concepts and practices include and subsume neighboring practices and paradigms, most notably those of Buddhist, Existentialist and the consciousness-based wisdom traditions.

For instance, Vipassana or insight meditation tradition, which predates presencing by 2,600 years, is itself a methodology of letting go of the ego in order to let new insight into the nature of the self present itself freshly each moment. Not surprisingly, presencing resembles separate, modern Buddhist applications such as mindful leadership, which positions meditation as a secular inlet for organizational influence and creativity. Similarly, Theory U, for which presencing plays a central role, incorporates concepts from design thinking such as the use of empathy and rapid -prototyping.

Theory U practitioners also refer to presencing as a social field, which is very similar to the Buddhist concept of codependent origination, and what existentialists like Heidegger refer to as a field of care. Following from these observations, the question then becomes going forward, what essential differences distinguish presencing from its counterpart orientations and practices? What does presencing actualize and bring into being that these similar approaches do not? Given its growing significance in personal change, shared learning and social transformation projects across a wide cross section of fields, as academic practitioners continue to explore and develop upon their own sense and application of presencing, how might presencing begin to emerge as a field of research and praxis in the coming years and decades ahead?

One of the current values of presencing is how the aforementioned and other perspectives and practices are being woven together and updated in our current global context, an effort that is echoed through each of the three volumes of this book series. This has the effect of bringing these respective approaches to life in an experimental fashion, aligned with a growing collective human effort for a hopeful future versus a profitable quarter or immediate sense of stress reduction. How does presencing accomplish this? For one, scholars and practitioners have been compelled to upcycle English verb tenses and adjectives in order to describe particular nuances of learning in new ways with particular points of emphasis.

Those who are new to the concept of presencing often report a sensitivity to this shift in "languaging", and the same will be true for those who read this series; each chapter pushes the limits and limiting nature of the English language. This is necessary to the extent that presencing introduces concepts that the English language fails to describe. For instance, in drawing from Scharmer's distinctions in Theory U, presencing practitioners often talk about the connection of the head, heart, and hands as a more holistic framework for moving from a space of understanding to a space of knowing. In contrast, Sanskrit does not treat these concepts as separate and distinct, but rather, through the term "Citta" refers to a single heart-mind integration.

At some point readers may find themselves asking, is presencing a process that makes all other learning paradigms and activities more creative and useful, or is it the other way around? To navigate these conceptual challenges, this book series includes a tapestry of applications from a variety of contexts across the globe, spanning multiple languages, and accomplishing a variety of aims. It also honors ancient wisdom traditions from which presencing borrows and benefits, while at the same time cultivating emerging lineages and practices such as Dynamic Presencing.

To accomplish these eclectic aims, this three volume book series incorporates insight from both presencing scholars and practitioners, ensuring a balance of critical and creative perspectives that have been peer-reviewed, offering current perspectives on how Theory U is being adapted across a broad range of organizations, companies and contexts that are united in the deeper impulse of learning to shape and build a life-affirming emerging future for all stakeholders. By weaving these and other perspectives into the larger conversation of Theory U, we are of the mindset that these and other updates will ensure that the Series reaches a wider scope of reading audience and catalyzes interest across both the Academic and Practitioner world. Finally, we are at point in history where these two cultures intersect and it is our interest to shine the light on this intersection in a way that inspires a myriad of applications in the world with real projects and research efforts that are not only informed by this framework and but also practitioners capable of co-facilitating and co-leading and embodying these initiatives.

A guiding intention of this Series since its inception has been to raise further awareness of the applicability of critical and creative applications of Theory U to our colleagues, students, ULAB hubs, international communities of practice and beyond, further conveying how this body of work is informing, enriching, and sustaining new developments across a wide variety of disciplines. In effect, this Series will give a current pulse on the current scholar practitioner voices and perspectives on Theory U and presencing through featured writings on the experiences, challenges, and promise of this emerging field. It is our estimation that this work as a whole has the real promise to open up a new space of possibility for engaging a more coherent and resonant future for all concerned, which we know is not only possible but essential for humanity to shift its current course of risks that threaten our shared future in the twenty first century.

Inspired by the Theory U projects of Otto Scharmer and colleagues of the Presencing Institute, Theory U and presencing are approaching a tipping point as a viable, comprehensive praxis for stewarding change and global transformation. To illustrate and support this development, *Advances in Presencing* includes perspectives and applications by academics, researchers, teachers, change makers, consultants, community activists and thought leaders.

Overview of Chapters

Kelvy Bird's chapter, *Visual Presencing: A Practice, A Possibility, Visual Presencing,* explores the act of drawing within a social field – a tangible practice that can connect us across individual concerns, into a shared sense of order and possibility. As a graphic facilitator working for over twenty years to help people recognize their realities and envision their opportunity by reflecting their content through words and images, Kelvy reflects on her experience of what is involved with crafting visual maps born as a mental bridge to a collective coming to know itself. Visual Presencing introduces an additional dimension, or layer, of sourcing from an emerging future, helping bring the eyes of the practitioner and the eyes of a system alike – all eyes – opened to something never before considered. In this article Kelvy shares her practical experience and reflections through what she has experienced in her work as chief scribe for u.lab since its inception a few years ago.

William Brendel's chapter, *Sensing into the Future of Theory U: Catching up with Otto Scharmer and Adam Yukelson*, reveals some of the Presencing Institute's latest endeavors and challenges through exclusive interviews with Otto Scharmer and Adam Yukelson. Otto shares his perspectives on the newly launched Societal Transformation Lab (u.lab-S), and personally reflects upon ways greater well-being might manifest in everyday life. Adam Yukelson shares new learning opportunities and common areas of confusion that arise when people learn and practice *Theory U*. Adam concludes with an inside view of how the core PI team has naturally adopted its own practices as a way of being and working together. Inspired by these interviews, William provides additional commentary around ways the PI might: incorporate the lens of loosely coupled systems theory to help orchestrate its worldwide efforts; proactively manage naturally occurring intragroup dynamics and conflict in u.lab-S; and incorporate adult learning theory to better understand why participants often experience difficulty transitioning from the bottom of the U into stages of Prototyping and Crystalizing.

Olen Gunnlaugson's chapter, *Dynamic Presencing: A Journey into Presencing Mastery, Leadership and Flow,* offers a concise overview of Dynamic Presencing (2019), which is a new in-depth process method for developing our capacities for making the shift to presencing as an orienting way of being. Each of the five journeys build from the presencing theory and practices described in Theory U, introducing a set of in-depth practices, subtle distinctions and ways of engaging presencing that gradually bring to life an overall transformed understanding and lived into experience presencing. To this end, Olen begins by giving a brief overview of each of the five journeys in this chapter as a means to illustrate the possibilities of making a greater paradigm shift into learning how to live a dynamically presenced life.

Geoff Fitch and Abigail Lynam's chapter, *An Interpenetrative Application of Theory U,* describes an interpenetrative approach to the application of Theory U in an integral transformative development program that they have offered for the past 14 years at Pacific Integral. This approach emerged as they redesigned their program with the intent of finding a deeper integration of the tools and frameworks they had used for the purposes of social transformation. Over time, Geoff and Abigail began to see Theory U as a fundamental archetype for transformation in all aspects of their work; an archetype that is both timeless and unfolding in time, and that interpenetrates with the other frameworks they use. This chapter describes the evolution and distinctions of this interpenetrative approach to Theory U application as well as their experiences, lessons learned, and essential practices.

Mary Stacey & Reilly Dow's chapter, *Interweaving U: Releasing potential for personal transformation and global systems change at the Burren Executive Leadership Retreat,* shares their experiences with managing and leading an annual gathering of global leaders who are committed to developing themselves so that they can continue their generative change work in traditional power centers, and in next generation organizations that are cultivating human rights, sustainability, and post-patriarchal systems and ways of leading. Seeking to renew themselves and expand their reach, Mary and Reilly hear a call in the invitation to 'discover your next horizon'. In this chapter they explore how they interweave the U process in a planned and emergent way with other core elements such as Collaborative Developmental Action Inquiry (CDAI), the power of place, and creative process to support leaders in claiming the highest future potential of their leadership. They share the journey through the four-day retreat, including our engagement with what we call the *intense threshold* at the bottom of the U, offering the voices of participating leaders through their reflections: and excerpts from dialogue with poets, musicians, and visual artists.

Michael Schratz's chapter, *Leading System Transformation from the Emerging Future,* examines how educational leaders are often confronted with disruptive processes caused by incoherent policy measures, which pass on the pressures to perform according to government requirements. Michael explores how Theory U can support system transformation in moving a highly bureaucratic, strongly regulated education system by capacity building through a nation-wide leadership network towards more mutual understanding and professionalisation of leadership and learning. To initiate and sustain change dynamics, it connects educators in all sectors, regions, hierarchy levels and functions of the education system building on participation, shared responsibilities and dialogue. The chapter highlights how Presencing can help leaders to gain more ownership in dealing with the needs and expectations in their work context. Accounts of participants' experiences offer insights into how they collaboratively learn to identify with the overall goal of systemic innovation and translate challenges into innovative development processes by becoming agents of reform.

Markus Peschl and colleagues chapter, *The role of the shift from I-to-We and Theory-U* discusses the need for future-driven innovation approaches to address current challenges related to the rapid and disruptive societal and technological changes of the last two decades. Their claim is that three "illiteracies of the 21st century" render humans and companies alike unprepared to cope with these challenges. These include the inability to "see" and change perspective, deal with uncertainty, and anticipate novelty. Their diagnosis is twofold. First, these illiteracies are major deterrents in dealing with today's increasingly complex and unpredictable world. Second, a lack of socio-epistemological skills and attitudes in the domain of collective knowledge work/creation leads to these illiteracies. Markus and colleagues explore how Scharmer's (2007/2016) social technology of Theory-U provides a framework to facilitate the development of socio-epistemological skills and attitudes necessary for overcoming these illiteracies and may lead to thriving innovations. In addition, they focus on the shift from "I-to-We" (i.e., collectivization) as a key ingredient for successfully implementing the Presencing process. Empirical examples drawn from several Theory U-based innovation processes in a higher education context are presented. Based on these examples, Peschl and colleagues discuss several issues, such as a concrete process design, how to support a shift in attitudes concerning the "I-to-we", or the role of a facilitator for overcoming the 21st century illiteracies in an educational and organizational (e.g., HR) context.

William Brendel's chapter, *Beyond the Prism: What Ancient Wisdom Traditions offer Facilitators and Participants of the Presencing Process,* examines how Buddhist, Hindu and global Existential philosophies inform three movements central to the presencing process and its associated practices, including mindfulness, transformation, and transcendence. It begins with a concept shared between all of these wisdom traditions: the illusory nature of ego and its ill effects on individuals, organizations and society. William weaves together presencing practices such as Scharmer's Journaling activity with the philosophies of the Buddha, Heidegger, Jaspers, Kierkegaard, Nietzsche, Sartre, Schopenhauer, Unamuno, the Upanishads, and many similar offshoots. His chapter culminates in a case study of a small religious community that deepened its faith by transcending unhelpful habits of mind.

Kelly Becker's chapter, *The U Process and the Nile Project: Presencing with Music to address the water crisis in the Nile Basin Region,* looks at the Nile Project, a music collaborative formed in 2011 to address the mounting water crisis facing East Africa including limited water to serve its inhabitants, increasing population, and mounting conflict over distribution and use of the Nile River (Kameri-Mbote, 2007). Kelly discusses how the leadership of The Nile Project utilized the U process in their aim to move stakeholders from co-initiating to co-evolving, from low cooperation to high cooperation, from disconnected neighbors to connected neighbors, and from disengaged Nile citizens to engaged Nile citizens. The quotes and data shared in this chapter are from a qualitative, arts-informed research study on The Nile Project, which focused on how a group of musicians with different languages, musical traditions, and political views could collaborate to create music. Findings include how the organization effectively "changed the container" to create a conducive environment for this collaborative and transformational work.

Jackie Saldana's chapter, *Presence of Theory U in the Communities of Practice Process of Knowledge,* looks at Theory U as a reflective frame that industry practitioners can use to produce knowledge and innovation. She looks more closely at Communities of Practice (CoPs) as self-organized groups of practitioners that frequently engage in reflective practice to build knowledge, engaging in interconnected dynamics comparable to those of the Theory U. In this chapter, Jackie draws on a literature review of 110 CoP studies published between 2010 and 2016 reflecting knowledge creation in 20 countries and 20 industry fields reported the presence of Theory U dynamics. The review identified Theory U core elements among CoPs, such as co-initiating (joint enterprise), co-sensing (sense of common purpose), co-creating (innovation), and co-evolving (share repertoire). Saldana takes the view that Theory U provides opportunities for CoP members to interconnect with each other at deeper levels of understanding that permit the flourishing of creative ideas.

Kriyanka Moodley's chapter, *Using Inward Looking to Enhance the Facilitation of Theory U,* points out the importance of suspending our mental models as a means for accessing holistic intelligence and functioning. Kriyanka builds on the downloading stage and points out that it requires further exploration by looking inward, which provides a mechanism to recognize the psychological barriers of fear and separation, which can negatively impact the rest of the U-process by leading to excessive disconnection and fragmented interaction with others. By removing the barriers inhibiting us in a healthy way by quietening the mind, focusing on breathing and attention, and by moving the beam of attention inwards once we have identified what these habitual behaviors are, this chapter brings into focus the movement from ego-system awareness to eco-system awareness using Inward looking to facilitate the downloading stage of Theory U.

Florentina Bajraktari, Rosamund Mosse, Gabriel Neira Voto's chapter, *Transforming u.lab: Redesigning a Social Technology from a Strategic Sustainable Perspective,* addresses the Sustainability Challenges of systematically increasing socio-ecological unsustainability on a scale never experienced before. To address the Sustainability Challenge, u.lab's experiential response inspires participants to question their paradigms of thought and societal norms. By providing an approach that is systemic, participatory and emergent, u.lab enables solutions that are responsive to the dynamic nature of those interconnected challenges. In their chapter, Florentina, Rosamund and Gabriel address how they saw an opportunity to create a u.lab course specifically designed for sustainability that combines the strength of the U process and a strategic sustainable development approach. Using the Framework for Strategic Sustainable Development, designed to help practitioners to facilitate society's transition towards sustainable development, their research explores how u.lab can be re-designed in order to move society strategically toward a sustainable future.

Closing Remarks

In closing, a guiding intention of this Series is to raise further awareness of the applicability of Theory U and presencing to our colleagues, students, ULAB hubs, international communities of practice and beyond, further conveying how this growing body of work is informing, enriching, and sustaining new developments across a wide variety of disciplines globally. In effect, by showcasing current voices and perspectives on Theory U and presencing, this Series also seeds the participation of future critical and appreciative streams of research on the different methods of presencing, their respective communities of practice and the value derived from such scholarly-practitioner undertakings. In this sense, Advances in Presencing offers important guidance and inspiration to colleagues currently involved in this work. By encouraging not only further elaboration and refinement of the

Theory U framework and presencing approaches that are currently being explored and applied globally, this Series is also encouraging paradigmatic breakthroughs that may also provide new updates and prototypes to be followed and possibly further developed elsewhere. As a whole, Advances in Presencing affirms our convictions, and those of many of the invited authors, that this new, exciting, and extraordinarily important emerging field is one that has the promise to be of great service to humanity in the years and decades ahead.

CHAPTER 2

Visual Presencing

Kelvy Bird

Introduction

In some art forms, spirit drives the hand. This is the case in *visual presencing*, the act of two-dimensionally representing an experience of presencing. Presencing, as I consider it, means *being with* in order to access the potential of a moment. While being with, an artist opens themselves to a channel of spirit, which originates—like water from a well—in source. Source, as I experience it, is the pulse of life itself. It takes some slowing down to attune to the subtly of source, and to intentionally connect with the rise of spirit. Visual presencing, then, aids with this attunement, both for the artist during the creative process, and for those engaging with life force through a picture.

Creatives are familiar with the rhythm of back-and-forth toggle between inner and outer realms. Anyone who has tapped a beat on a table with a spoon or kneaded dough into a soft mound or skipped down a sidewalk is included in this broad term "creative." I believe that we are all born with innate creativity and the ability to make art; some people have simply cultivated physical expression more than others. Regardless of skill or talent, we each possess an ability to communicate in a way that cuts across divisions of culture and verbal language by using form. Visual presencing can help us revive our creative ability by emphasizing a connection with source over literal, objective representation. A visual expression born while presencing is depiction, instead, of a moment's truth according to the person receiving it.

My own path into this territory has curved through various creative contexts. Studying abstract painting in college, I learned to represent spirit through line, color, and shape. When I became a graphic facilitator—or what I will refer to as a scribe in this chapter—I learned to combine images and words to map ideas onto large, upright surfaces so that people could see what they were talking about. When I sat in dialogue circles for hours on end, I learned to take extensive, text-based notes to track the meaning coming through a collective, into a room. Participating in women's circles, I learned that to orient from the heart is to tap into an infinite and restorative resource. Now, alongside presencing colleagues and practitioners, I am learning to sense into a social field at any given moment, to facilitate how we see ourselves, others, systems and society. I am also continuing to practice, write about, and teach generative scribing.

In the following sections I will further define three forms of my current practice—scribing, generative scribing, and visual presencing—and end by sharing some experiments and possible applications of the later. My hope, and the incentive behind writing this chapter, is that readers will be able to identify ways that visual presencing could be part of their own path, on any scale, to bring forward their own unique gift of creativity, to manifest source.

Scribing

Scribing is a practice in which an artist listens to people talk and simultaneously draws a map of their ideas; those speaking can see a picture of their words unfold in front of their eyes. (See Figure 1.) The purpose of the drawing is to establish connections within content, aid with insight, and support decision-making. The weaving of words and pictures together facilitates group learning and cultural memory.

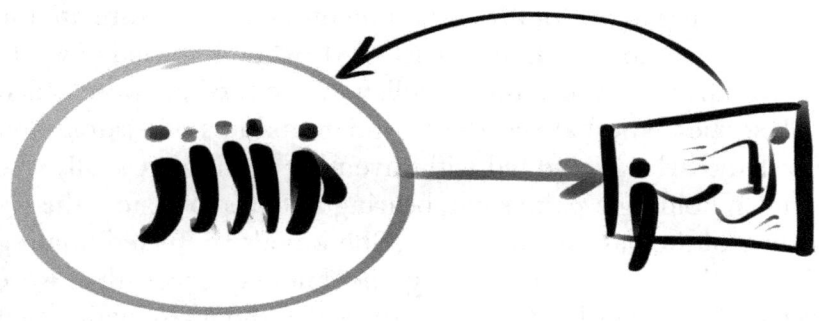

Figure 1: *The dynamic of scribing.*

Scribing (in its modern context) has its roots in the early 1970s in the San Francisco Bay Area. It is often defined as a practice that makes the unknown apparent through pictures, maps, diagrams, and models.[1] David Sibbet, founder of Grove Consultants International, originated the terms "Group Graphics"® and "graphic facilitation" to describe methods that use visuals interactively to facilitate group understanding in organizational contexts.[2]

There are many cousins of scribing, each of which slightly varies the live drawing approach. One is *graphic recording*, often a more literal pairing of words and pictures, with an aim to mirror verbal content. Other offshoots of the original practice have now-familiar terms such as sketch-noting, doodling, and mind mapping, and all have found unique uses, markets, and applications. And I would be remiss to omit the intersection of scribing with animation, motion graphics, cartooning, and even virtual reality, which have added dimensionality and access to the core profession in mind-boggling numbers.[3]

---

1 Robert Horn, "Visual Language and Converging Technologies in the Next 10–15 Years (and Beyond)," Paper prepared for the National Science Foundation Conference on Converging Technologies, December 2001.

2 David Sibbet, "A Graphic Facilitation Retrospective," http://davidsibbet.com/wp-content/uploads/2016/12/GF-RetrospectiveUpdated.pdf.

3 Andrew Park, the founder of Cognitive, invented the now ubiquitous whiteboard animation method, most widely known through the RSA Animate series that has received millions of views on YouTube. See the Cognitive website: www.wearecognitive.com.

According to one of my earliest mentors, Bryan Coffman, the term scribing goes back to at least 1981, when knowledge workers who drew on walls during collaborative sessions were called "wall scribes."[4] Seshat was the Egyptian goddess of wisdom and knowledge who is credited with inventing writing. "Usually, she is shown holding a palm stem, bearing notches to denote the recording of the passage of time . . . She was also depicted holding other tools and, often, holding the knotted cords that were stretched to survey land and structures."[5] I find it fascinating that the current role of the scribe has evolved directly from the original meaning. Scribes mark the passage of time and delineate structure within, and for, cultures—albeit with new methods. Each drawing maps territory the scribe is helping a social body to understand, whether it be a company's business strategy, a city's public land development, or a family's move to a new country.

Prehistoric cave paintings also recorded and charted the presence and activity of species. Native American medicine wheels, Tibetan Buddhist sand mandalas, and the dreamtime influence in Aboriginal art—along with many other ancient and contemporary co-created visual formats—include a spiritual approach to social art, recognizing the connection between the human species and source. I have gravitated to the term scribe to define what I am— and what I have actively practiced since 1995—because of this harkening back to something primordial, something that seems timeless and enduring, something that provides a service that cuts across any one lifetime or generation.

Scribes serve as artistic aids in shared seeing and human navigation. Scribes represent information, in as neutral a way as possible, to craft living artifacts. We draw, then document the work digitally, then let go of the original pieces by handing them off to

---

4 "Wall Scribing: One or two Graphics Team members listen to the conversation and draw what they hear. This is a form of instant feedback and visual translation for participants." *DesignShop Staff Manual, Athenaeum International, Version 3.3* (Boulder: MG Taylor Corporation, 1991), p. 37. See also Donald Frazer, *Hieroglyphs and Arithmetic of the Ancient Egyptian Scribes: Version 1.* "The profession at first associated with the goddess Seshat is the source of the Egyptian word 'Sesh,' meaning scribe."

5 Definition of "Seshat" from Wikipedia: https://en.wikipedia.org/wiki/Seshat.

clients; and sometimes we even erase our work surfaces immediately after a group ends their conversation. The process happens quickly, and the product is fleeting. The final digital images end up on people's smartphones, in documents, reprinted as posters, in reports, in library displays, and as handouts for those who were not in the room during the making of the piece. But the physical artifact is a mere echo of the primary value, which is in-the-moment collective sourcing and reflection.

Scribing is an inherently participatory social art form. The hoped-for outcome is that a group will see a course to take, find its direction. Thus the purpose of the scribe is to help people see what they are talking about, to aid in thoughtful, considered action. The painter Wassily Kandinsky viewed art as a liberating device that could bring the inner life alive through pure line, shape, and color.[6] Scribing, by going beyond an abstract two-dimensional plane, activates the inner life of the social field, the unseen—yet felt—territory of human interaction.

Scribing, as a social art, is an exposed, witnessed, feedback-dependent activity that only takes place in the presence of a group of people. It gives shape to human conditions in an organic way, in rhythm with what is voiced. It depends not on one artist's view, but on the input of many views that converge through the artistic act. I often refer to those in the room as a "participant-audience" to reframe the traditional interpretation of "audience" from passive receivers of an expression into active players in a co-creative act, even if the act is through one person's hands. When I work at a wall with a participant-audience at my back, then, my engagement is fully with both the substance of their conversation and their energy.

By responding immediately to what I hear and sense, live, in front of a group of people, I create a picture whose meaning they can quickly assimilate into the conversation. Discerning different vantage points in a group is a good starting point. I might hear some people speaking of aspiration and boldly write the word

---

6 Wassily Kandinsky, *Concerning the Spiritual in Art* (London: Dover Publications, 1977), republished from the original, *The Art of Spiritual Harmony* (London: Constable and Co., 1914).

"vision" on one part of a wall. I might also hear a faction speaking about limits and boldly write the words "conditions" on another part of the same wall. I might map comments around each main word to continue to highlight individual contributions and differences, while simultaneously listening for the voices that speak to the tension between the two camps. If these voices exist (and the possibility for them is not only in my mind) then I might add the words "creative tension" and most notably, draw some lines between the various areas of the board. (See Figure 2.) To note, underpinning this approach is the use of models, specifically Creative Tension from Robert Fritz, and Creating the Problem from MG Taylor.[7]

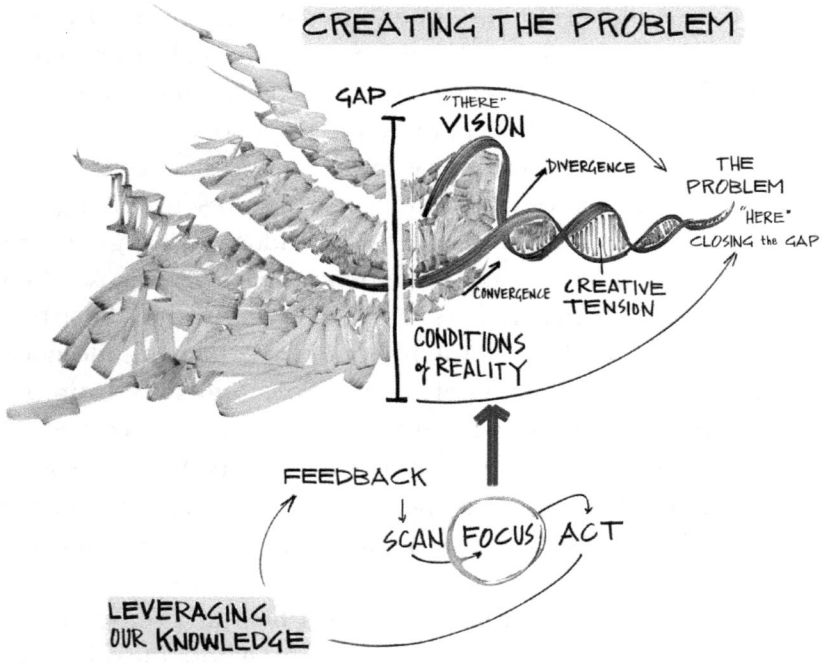

Figure 2: A representation of creative tension, drawn during a session for Columbia's Teachers College, ~ 2'x3', dry erase ink on white board, 2015.

---

7   Robert Fritz, *Creating: A Guide to the Creative Process* (New York: Fawcett Columbine, 1991), and Matt Taylor, Rob Evans, Kelvy Bird, *The Collaboration Code: Models, Frameworks for Transformation* (San Rafael: Imaginal Labs, 2019).

Thus, through its reflective mirroring, the drawing has the power to immediately structure, influence, and transform the thinking in a room. There is a reinforcing loop between the drawing itself and the receiving of the drawing; the loop expands the understanding that a room of people share and thereby can expand their sense of possibility. (See Figure 3.)

Figure 3: The dynamic of scribing as it influences thinking that then influences what is spoken and further recorded.

There is a cadence in the process that flows like this: I listen. I draw. You see. You speak. I listen I draw you see you speak. You see I listen you speak I draw. You speak I draw we see we listen. The words and the marks and the impressions and the thinking blend in and out of one another. The boundary between group and speaker and self and wall dissolves.

There are depths, or phases, of scribing that directly correlate with attention. Attention is informed by different levels of listening that can help us shift our awareness and sense of possibility. Otto Scharmer describes the four levels of listening as: (1) downloading; (2) factual listening; (3) empathic listening; and (4) generative listening. I apply each level of listening to the visual practice of scribing, as shown in Figure 4.[8]

---

8 C. Otto Scharmer, "Introduction" in *Theory U: Leading from the Future as It Emerges*, 2nd ed. (San Francisco: Berrett-Koehler, 2016). See also "Otto Scharmer on the four levels of listening," www.youtube.com/watch?v=eLfXpRkVZaI.

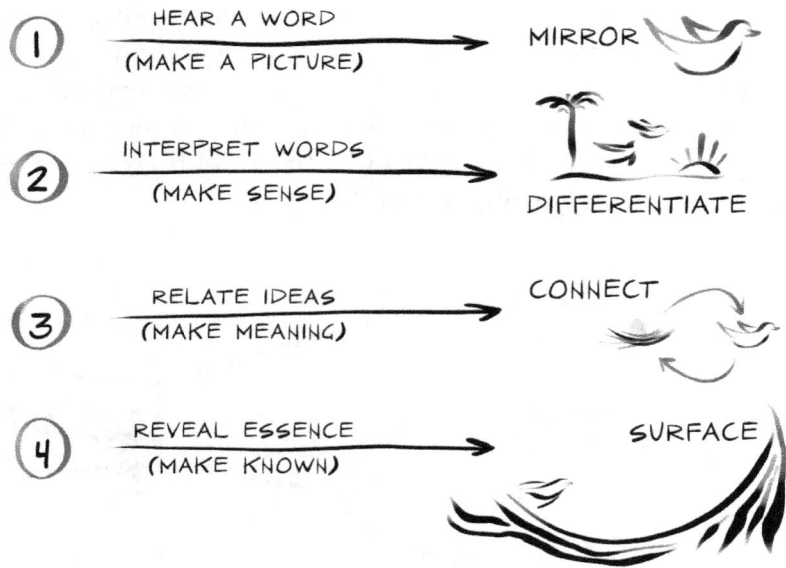

① HEAR A WORD
   (MAKE A PICTURE) ⟶ MIRROR

② INTERPRET WORDS
   (MAKE SENSE) ⟶ DIFFERENTIATE

③ RELATE IDEAS
   (MAKE MEANING) ⟶ CONNECT

④ REVEAL ESSENCE
   (MAKE KNOWN) ⟶ SURFACE

Figure 4: Levels of Scribing.

Level 1: Mirror. We hear a word and draw a picture from memory. Our image is literal; someone says "bird" and we illustrate a bird. This is object-oriented scribing, with a focus on naming individual parts.

Level 2: Differentiate. We interpret words and make sense of parts by expanding our vantage point. We draw what we hear in a factual context and organize parts into like clusters. "The bird is flying, then it reaches the coast and joins a flock" becomes a story.

Level 3: Relate. We connect ideas and make meaning by stepping back to see the entirety of a person or situation, seeking to understand relationships and structures in a way that encompasses the whole. We shift from noticing sequential movements to noticing dynamics from above, as if in a slice of time. The words are "bird" and "nest", and the scribing includes the feedback loop between the two.

Level 4: Surface. We reveal an emerging future potential by letting go of past conceptions and tapping into the true present moment. Once we sense the reality that wants to unfold, the essence that wants to be known, a drawing can help define the forces in play. What is below the bird? A gust of wind? A tide? A pending migration?

Generative Scribing

In level four scribing, "generative scribing," we sense into potential for the systems we serve. This requires being sensitive not only to the content that is obvious and clear, but also to the content that is fuzzy or faint—hesitations in a speaker's voice, long pauses between words, coughing that interrupts a sentence. We are fully receptive to all kinds of sensory and intuitive inputs: rain on the roof, a fly buzzing around someone's juice cup, the freshness or staleness of the air, the light, the shadows. As our aperture widens, we receive information with expanded awareness, attending to the unfolding nature of reality.

Generative scribing advances the visual discipline of scribing by extending the range of the artist to an entire ecosystem, "a system, or a group of interconnected elements, formed by the interaction of a community of organisms with their environment."[9] A generative scribe calls attention to an emerging reality that is brought to life by, and for, the social field in which it is created. No picture exists outside the context of the system—the interacting community—in conversation, and no system's comprehension of itself is complete without the reflective representation and aid that the picture offers. The relationship is participatory, reciprocal, and procreative.

My experience with this kind of work, starting from about 2003, leads me to believe that the key to generative scribing is sensing from the heart. It's piercing through to something essential, seeing clearly without fear of the result or consequence of what emerges. It requires trust in the complete blankness of things. It also demands personal vulnerability, which for me has meant softening to the situation and letting my defenses down,

---

9 Definition of "ecosystem" from Dictionary.com: http://www.dictionary.com/browse/ecosystem?s=t.

which sometimes is in conflict with needing to stay steady in order to produce! Most importantly, generative scribing can only happen when the social body (a handful or thousands of people) is committed to being together in place and time, committed to joining in the present.

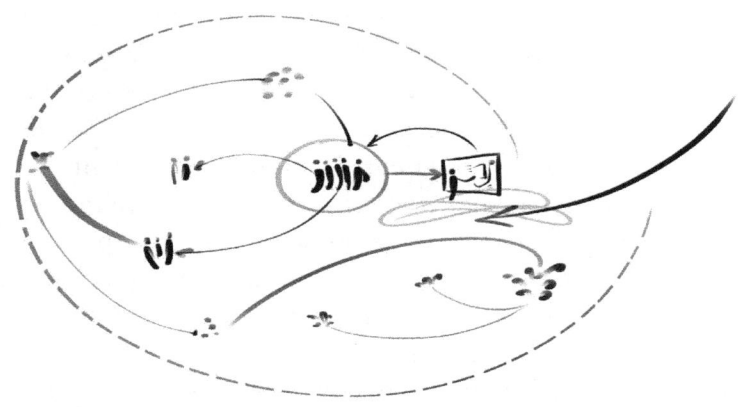

Figure 5: The dynamic of generative scribing.

The generative scribe must sometimes grope in the dark to find threads of meaning, then quickly get that out and up on a wall for others to see. Anyone who is able to see the drawing is actually an active participant in its creation. There is no "other." There is a hand that holds a marker, that leans forward from the extended arm of an upright physical body acting purely on behalf of the whole. I draw because we exist; I draw as a social act.

I have often wondered—especially in light of symbolic art, such as that of Indigenous peoples—about the true potential of generative scribing to cross physical and spiritual lines. Can a scribed image embody the dimensionality of past, present, and future in a larger timelessness, all at once? How far can we push the comprehensive limits of systems, and our own limits, to shift the place of understanding between known and unknown worlds? Can scribing generate a vibrational field that goes beyond literal words to transcend the moment?

As I continue to reflect on these questions, I choose an integrative approach to revealing unnamed wholeness, believing it presents as close an echo as possible to the complexity and inherent beauty of the natural world. Often this requires synthesizing multiple threads of content into one encapsulating picture. (See Figure 6.) It's an approach that deepens level three systems scribing, the value of which is in revealing interdependency. (See Figure 7.) It's also an approach that expands on the linear flow of level two story scribing, the value of which is naming parts that somehow could relate. (See Figure 8.) All levels have their place; none is better or worse! All scribing helps people see. A generative approach, quite simply, taps into an additional dimension of knowing.

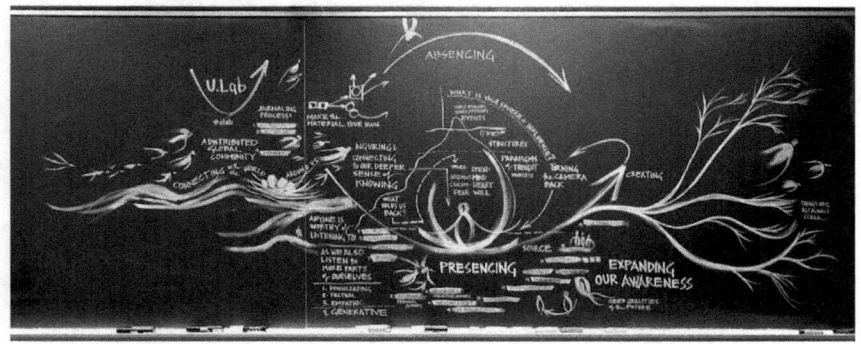

Figure 6: An integrated, generative approach to scribing.

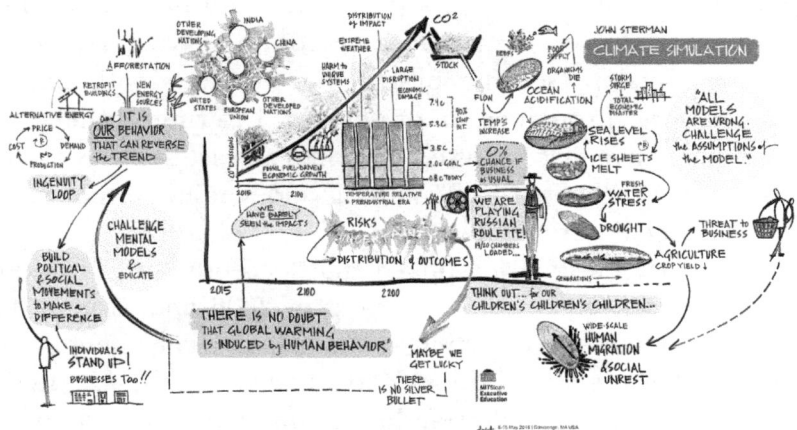

Figure 7: A systems approach to scribing.

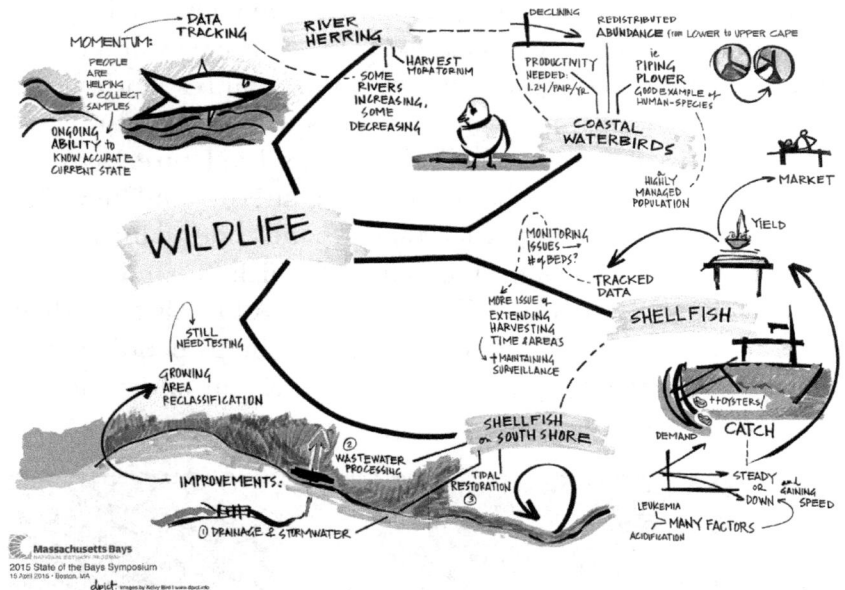

Figure 8: A story approach to scribing.

Visual Presencing

Like a seed in a pod that grows on an upward moving stem, visual presencing is inseparably embedded within generative scribing. It is a core capacity, a skill, for the generative scribe. But it does not need to serve a group or system; it can be a personal expression, practiced in private or in front of a group. In either case, the visual presencing practitioner connects with source, through spirit, through active presencing. Drawings come to life from a qualitative place of listening, when a practitioner is rooted in his or her authentic "self," sensing and serving an emerging potential. (See Figure 9.)

This is a capacity I've applied most recently, since working with the Presencing Institute starting in 2006 and scribing for u.lab and the u.ecology starting in 2014. I am still coming to understand what it is, what it represents when taking shape, and the impact it has on our understanding of humanity. In addition to tracking my own experiences with visual presencing, I have been experimenting with the method in a series of dedicated learning environments. In three specific workshops, I led similar exercises with slightly different conditions. These yielded consistent results, and has led me to believe that—regardless of artistic training or region in which a person lives—anyone who wants to experience visual presencing has it within reach.

Figure 9: The dynamic of visual presencing, originating in source, channeled through spirit.

Berlin

In Berlin, Germany, in July 2017, through a Visual Presencing Program, we attempted for the first time to stage a community visual presencing experience. The delivery team of Julie Arts, Angela Baldini, Aimee Aubin, and myself were experimenting with a way to embody level four listening through drawing. There were twenty-six participants in all: twelve graphic recorders and fourteen other familiar with Theory U but with limited, or no, scribing experience. We inserted the visual presencing experiment toward the end the second day, when we had been learning about the sensing phase of the U and were shifting into presencing. It followed this design:

1) Review the Levels of Listening framework.
2) Exercise with a hands-on experience to embody listening levels two and three. To practice the latter, we set up three-person groups around the room. In each group, one person shared a story, one person listened, and one person listened while scribing. We repeated this activity in rotation so that each person could practice each role.
3) Revisit listening level four and provide an overview of generative scribing.
4) Draw in front of a blank board—without any audio or video inputs—while connecting with source, within field awareness, attending specifically to level four listening and scribing.

As soon as we started, the sound of pen on paper pinned to cardboard was as loud as a howling winter snowstorm. After only a few minutes I paused the group, walked them through a short mindfulness moment intended to reconnect them to earth, sky, and heart, then rang a chime signaling that they could start drawing again. But some seeming urgency remained, and many participants continued drawing with gestural gusto.

Many other people did pause. Some sat. Some closed their eyes. Each found a rhythm within the social body that we had, and were extending, together. At the end of twenty minutes, we took a gallery walk to view and absorb the drawings. The pictures remained on the walls throughout the workshop, as a spiritual reminder and to serve as a container for other images and ideas still to come.

We did not talk about the experience as a full group because we had not included that step in the workshop design and were short on time. There would likely be much to learn from a follow-up reflection on what each person experienced in that short twenty-minute window, and from what they saw in the body of work they had shaped.

The general feeling in the room, though, was one of release, of freedom—where it seemed like people had been able to draw without the pressure of an expected outcome or need for the drawing to be literal or make "sense." Although the group's urge to draw had been very insistent, my memory is that they had achieved a sense of timelessness through the process and seemed more at ease with their own beings. I think we were all a bit surprised by the abundance of the visual outcome.

Munich

In October of the same year I collaborated with Svenja Rueger of the Value Web to deliver a Visual Practice Workshop in Munich, Germany. It differed slightly from the others in that the main framing was not Theory U but my own Generative Scribing model of practice. Instead of drawing to silence, people drew to the audio of Mary Oliver reading her poem "Wild Geese," with an intent to practice level four scribing. In this case, presencing was applied to visual practice (rather that visual practice applied to presencing, as in Berlin). Content informed the drawing, spirit informed the listening, and the hand united the two.

I took notes on people's reflections throughout the day. They included comments such as these:

- How has our container shifted and what is trying to emerge?
- This is poetry. I can let go. This is art now.

37

- How do I cope with the energy [coming through me]?
- How can I get to a level of trust with a client to be able to draw from my intuition?
- I would love to [draw like this] every day, but will anyone pay me for it?
- Something emerged from looking at someone else's drawing, and interpreting the drawings together. The two drawings enhanced the meaning of each one.
- The process of drawing, not the picture, carried the meaning.
- There are just lines and dots, but the whole world came together in that moment. It releases in myself a healing that I could never have predicted—that we have the ability to do that, that we have so much light in there, in what we draw.

Hangzhou

In November of the same year I co-facilitated a three-day residential Visual Presencing Program with Jayce Pei Yu Lee, Lili Xu, and Ripley Lin in Hangzhou, China. The design was similar to the one we used in Berlin: the first day dipped into capacities for opening (mind-heart-will) and perceiving (using the Iceberg model, see Figure 10) (Schein, Senge); day two focused on levels of listening and scribing, and day three on discerning and project application.

One large difference between this program and the others was that everything I said was translated from English into Chinese after each one or two sentences. The dedicated translator, Chloe Gao, had already attended two of my previous workshops and knew the material well. But it's hard to know how my tone and emphases may or may not have come through. While the other three facilitators could tell how well the group was following the process and understanding what we were trying to convey, I felt two steps behind. The drawings were also in Chinese, and it was difficult to find feedback on the learning process without directly understanding what people were writing.

The venue was in an eco-park called XiXi Wetlands outside Hangzhou, where we were able to walk through low-lying areas of water on carefully maintained paths. The access to nature and the fact that the entire group ate every meal together added a dimension to our level of connection. While the in-room delivery was a challenge, the warmth of the convening was quite clearly felt by all.

On day two, Lili delivered the section on four levels of listening, and we had participants engage in an exercise with a leaf to experience level four. Lili encouraged us to "regard the leaf as a representation [of energy]. The dynamic movement is the reality. See with the heart." And she referenced Goethe: "Every object, well contemplated, opens up a new organ of perception within us."

Instead of providing large markers for each person, as we did in Berlin and Munich, the local team found Chinese brushes and ink. This was a brilliant choice, as the thick brushes with fine points lend themselves perfectly to energy moving through the body, arm, and hand. While markers have plastic casing and a nib where ink comes out, the brushes had wooden handles with fiber bristle. These natural materials, I believe, allowed for a stronger connection to culture, place, and source. We worked on undyed, brown paper. I mention these things because each step in the process, each choice of location, staging, tools, and even how to handle the verbal language affected the quality of experience.

Despite the variety of conditions across these three unique cases—Berlin, Munich, and Hangzhou—it seemed that each person was able to access source in some personal way and apply that authentically through their own hand. No one abstained or did not draw. There was no copying of someone else's style. There was no better, no worse. No expert, no beginner. Each brought forth an energy they had connected into through our collective presencing experience. All growth was in the direction of yes.

Personal experience

I have so far described visual presencing as something that happens in a group context. But there is a personal side to it too, that I have examined more intimately by working directly alongside Otto Scharmer and, as mentioned, with our online course and platform u.lab: Leading from the Emerging Future. Sometimes I have planned out the skeleton of a drawing on a wall if our core team has a clear enough sense of the content. Sometimes I start with an entirely blank slate, quite literally, working on a well-used old blackboard surface. Sometimes I use markers loaded with chalk ink. Sometimes I use a brush with the same ink.

When a visual presencing element comes into the work it might be captured in one small feature of the drawing that the participant-audience would never recognize, since it happens through the making and is not easily noticeable in the final picture. Sometimes a bit of ink will drip down from a mark, no matter how careful I've been in my application. Sometimes a texture results from drawing with a certain repetition or directionality in a rhythmic sort of state. Sometimes a large arc I've drawn is crooked and has a bend to it midway, a bend that does not make sense from the large gesture my arm has made. These features are all unexplainable in the moment, and I notice them, and let them be. It is in these fractions that I feel the presencing coming through, the letting come. And my own letting go is the acceptance that the marks wanted to be there just as they showed up. (See Figure 10.)

Figure 10: Ripley Lin, practicing visual presencing in the Hangzhou program

As in the workshops, where a consistent structure yielded similar and surprising results, in u.lab the format is almost always the same. Timing, team, room, wall, camera across from me, inks, chalks, wipes, remote audience participating from their local settings, some known content that fits within a design, much unknown content that emerges in the moment. But one thing I realize now as I write is that my interior state must always be open. That is a defining characteristic of visual presencing. When I am stuck in thought or am feeling too much or am concerned about how legible my writing will be, I am closed off. It is necessary to be open in the heart and to allow the hand to be guided from *that* place. Not from the mind or the will, but from a place of pure generosity where outreach and intake meet.

At this point, you might be wondering how visual presencing differs from any other kind of art-making. I wonder too. I think a key difference is creative intent. With visual presencing, the intent is to guide some intangible sense or spirit—inside and out-side—into form through the act of drawing. It is not about an artist's idea or view or self-exploration that the artist projects into a work; this is the case with many 20th century painters, including Abstract Expressionists, for example. In my experience, it's not personally about the artist at all, beyond the sensibility and will-ingness of the artist to serve as a "guide" for a new potential to take form. Thinking and ego only get in the way of that.

Figure 11: A burst of pigment about 2" wide, that came to represent an eye, a portal for seeing. u.lab. Pigment and chalk ink on blackboard, 2018.

I still wonder at the mysterious way that spirit takes shape. During the programs I mentioned above, the freeing potential for individuals and the collective was undeniable with each swirl, each ink blotch, each arc, each tilted head, each breath in and out that I witnessed in others, and that I have felt in myself. As I was stirred, the drawing stirred, the energy stirred, the field stirred.

Humanity faces existential challenge with the environmental breakdown a consumptive part of our species (myself and at least 3 generations of my ancestors included) has caused.[10] Functioning from "I" will only perpetuate this destructive cycle. How to shift it? Reinforce, instead, the goodness of the human spirit and revive a lost will to care for the well-being of the whole, of the planet and of all living creatures. Visual presencing could be one aesthetic way to know ourselves more truthfully and tap into our deeper humanity, in the face of these transitions.

The result of visual presencing, as applied within generative scribing, is that the eyes of the practitioner and the eyes of a system—all eyes—are opened to something they have never before considered. The nascent is brought to light, offered through the hand, through conscious intent. Because one individual is willing to function as a channel for spirit, spirit is able to find its way into this earthly realm.

There is power in visual presencing, too, for the individual who draws alone. Being able to locate our truest self and tap into an energy that is larger, more long-lasting, and deeper than that of our minds, hearts, and hands alone—that would be something on its own! Imagine all the people who now say "I can't draw" shifting their mindset to "The drawing that comes through me provides insight and is a gift that will be useful as my life goes forward."

Certainly with our global society in the midst of great transformation, the more we can connect to an inner place of authenticity that gives guidance, the more our actions will come forward with a quality of rootedness. Visual presencing is one art form to

---

10 Laurie Laybourn-Langton, "It's no longer climate change we're living through. It's environmental breakdown" in *New Statesman America*. February 12, 2019. https://www.newstatesman.com.

aid in this great turning, shifting us from an outside in to an inside out way of being.

CHAPTER 3

Sensing into the Future of Theory U:

Catching up with Otto Scharmer and Adam Yukelson

William Brendel

Introduction

I recently had the unique opportunity to sit down separately with Otto Scharmer and Adam Yukelson of the Presencing Institute (PI) to learn more about their unique perspectives regarding recent advancements and initiatives. My dialogue with Otto, the institute's Founding Chair, began with a preview of some of PI's latest work, including the surprising scale and progress of the Societal Transformation Lab (u.lab-S), a worldwide innovation network that pools their energies to facilitate greater well-being around the world. We also talked about what greater well-being looks like and how it might manifest in both ordinary and profound ways. Finally, we explored the ways we must change our relationships with technology and education to make these shifts sustainable. My dialogue with Adam, who co-leads the design and delivery of PI's large scale innovation platforms, focused on learning opportunities made available by PI, not only for individuals but also groups and teams, as an attempt to bridge the gap between theory and practice. We also discussed how scholars and practitioners can collectively work to clarify common areas of confusion that arise when people learn *Theory U*.

Lastly, we talked about how the PI team bends the U process inward to guide their own strategic planning and day to day work. While my dialogue with Otto and Adam took slightly different paths, they both confirmed that PI is poised to bring its original intention to life in a time when the world seems increasingly disconnected and ego-driven.

Later in this chapter, PI's depiction of a better future will likely remind you of similar well-being efforts by other organizations. What is strikingly different however, is the extent of thoughtfulness amongst the PI team to: 1) thread their sense of purpose throughout even the most mundane, technical and structural components of their operations; 2) position PI uniquely, not as a transformation effort in and of itself, but rather as connector and amplifier of all change efforts that share the contours of the Theory U philosophy; and 3) maintain faith that a critical mass of humanity will indeed evolve during a time that may seem hopeless.

Weeks after our discussion I found myself thinking about what PI could do currently, given context of its programs and planning, to sustain the rigor and relevance of its initiatives well into the distant future. As a thought experiment I fast-forwarded ten years, imagining various scenarios for this rapidly scaling effort. This exercise generated three substantial areas of additional exploration in this chapter.

My first commentary employs research and practices for managing loosely coupled systems and analyzing social networks (Burke, 2014, Orton & Weick, 1990, Weick, 1976) to explore ways in which PI may effectively balance centralized control with decentralized empowerment of their network. My second commentary focuses on proactively managing intragroup dynamics and conflict (Gaertner & Dovidio, 2000) between PI and the myriad of societal transformation organizations it is bringing together as part of u.lab-S. My third commentary focuses on the critical influence of adult learning style preferences (Kolb, 1984; Kolb & Kolb, 2005; Kolb, 20007), which may lend insight into why people experience difficulty transitioning from the bottom of the U into stages of Prototyping and Crystalizing. Although these commentaries are not exhaustive, they are meant to spark further conversations within PI and its broader network. Later, particularly in the section focusing on Adam's work, I bring these commentaries together to produce strategic learning solutions that may help PI sustain its global efforts.

Catching up with Otto

My conversation with Otto began by aligning our attention with intention, specifically the original intention of PI and its connection to u.lab-S. Otto framed this original intention as "linking spirituality and science with practical societal evolution and change." Otto threaded this ambitious statement through the institute's evolution, a journey through the U process in its own right, up until present day. As PI has clearly strengthened its capacity to continuously invite and connect individuals across the world, according to Otto, the next movement of evolution involves supporting broader, "networked infrastructures of teams that feel deeply connected to the original intention of Institute." To scale its efforts worldwide PI has been very planful in its approach, given many other similar well-being initiatives that have gained traction. The idea is not to compete, but rather to connect and provide holding environments for further innovation between teams, many of whom stem from these organizations. Operationalized, u.lab-S is a "multi-local innovation journey for teams who are coshaping more sustainable and equitable social systems worldwide" (u.lab-S Website, 2019).

In addition to cultivating a global infrastructure, Otto suggested that another condition for the success of u.lab-S initiative that has emerged recently is a strong, authentic desire from the social field. Humanity is reaching a type of critical mass, according to Otto, approaching an outcome of what he characterized as the increased noise of Absencing versus Presencing. As a result, interest in PI and u.lab-S are at an all-time high. While u.lab-S originally attempted to launch their work with 100 teams they received 350 applications. Otto shared that they will now likely start with 250 teams. It is clear that while PI itself is small in comparison to its global aspirations, the primary drivers of change will include its network of teams. One of the application criteria to become a u.lab-S team helps to fill in this influence gap: "Conveners / teams should be in a position to influence some element of the system you want to transform (either as a grassroots activist, an institutional leader or through some other mechanism of change (e.g., public opinion)."

Given the impressive scale of u.lab-S at its very inception, after my discussion with Otto I found myself wondering what it will take to sustain this network over the next ten years. In contrast to the speed at which this initiative will likely spread, the size of PI's central operations seems disproportionately small. Over time, could the quality, rigor, and original intention of PI fade? While Theory U is designed to accommodate a wide array of cultures, leadership styles, spiritual orientations and other contextual anchors, teams and individuals must still be familiar "enough" with central tasks and mature enough in grasping its deeper intention. Evidence of such a bar or standard became apparent in our call for chapter submissions to this book series. While a great deal of submissions demonstrated a strong level of experience, proficiency, and maturity, a few did miss the bar.

Developing strong teams with a master-class understanding of Theory U, as Otto and his team continue to accomplish, is a critical step in sustaining and aligning the process and intent of u.lab-S across distance and time. These teams will serve as critical hubs for clarification, continuous learning and even local recruitment. What more can PI do? As an Organization Development consultant, I am brought back to the question: given its unique context and intention, how much should PI balance its structure and span of control (tightening) with empowerment and flexibility (loosening)? Literature and research on *Loosely Coupled Systems* (Weick, 1976; Orton & Weick, 1990; Burke, 2014) or LCSs, provide a helpful starting point for addressing this question.

Karl Weick (1976), known for his work on loose coupling, as well as mindfulness and sensemaking in organizations describes LCSs as "a situation in which elements are responsive but retain evidence of separateness, in terms of logic, physical nature and identity" (p. 3). He later wrote that "loose coupling is evident when elements affect each other suddenly (rather than constantly), negligibly (rather than significantly), indirectly (rather than directly), and eventually (rather than immediately)" (as referenced in Orton & Weick, 1990, pp. 203 – 204). Weick notes several advantages of such systems, which (1) lower the probability that the central organization will have to respond to every slight change in the environment; (2) heighten sensitivity to changes in the environment and therefore know their situation better than a tightly coupled organization; (3) adapt to unique local needs in an economic and sustainable fashion in a way that strict standardization does not allow; (4) retain a greater number of novel solutions; (5) remain "sealed off " from deterioration in in other parts of the system; (6) greater agency and efficacy with local actors (i.e. facilitators and teams); (7) reduce the amount of money and time that is typically required of tightly coupled systems.

Still, consistency in intention, action, and feedback – all critical success factors for Otto and his team - are necessary to prevent an LCS from fraying too much. Over time and distance, it is likely that some components of the Theory U process itself will be taken out of theoretical context, repackaged around a different social theory, utilized as a tool within a different transformation framework, or locally customized to the point that it loses its essence. Weick (1976) offers the following advice:

> Given the ambiguity of loosely coupled structures, this suggests that there may be increased pressure on members to construct or negotiate some kind of social reality they can live with. Therefore, under conditions of loose coupling one should see considerable effort devoted to constructing social reality, a great amount of face work and linguistic work, numerous myths (Mitroff and Kilmann, 1975) and in general one should find a considerable amount of effort being devoted to punctuating this loosely coupled world and connecting it in some way that can be made sensible (p. 13).

With regard to the u.lab-S's intention to steward a multi-local innovation journey, Burke (2014) offers helpful advice for managing changes that will naturally arise. From time to time as changes occur internally and externally to an LCS, Burke suggests it is important to know what should be tightened and what should be loosened, through *Social Network Analysis*, a process that identify gaps in networks, the specific types of roles members play that impact change management, and tools for large systems interventions. This analysis would require members of the PI network to,

> respond to a brief questionnaire asking them to identify people with whom they interact within the organization. The interaction can be identified as information exchange, informal relationships, simply as those one works with most closely, and so on...The typical outcome is a computer-generated picture or map with small circles or dots depicting organizational members and lines between the circles that show who relates with whim and perhaps how often (p. 429).

I believe that additional value to Social Network Analysis can be realized when developing strategies for targeted educational opportunities in spaces that promise greatest impact to the network, as opposed to educational opportunities that impact an area of the network that has little if any connection. This will be a crucial step for strengthening PI and the u.lab-S network.

In addition to upgrading institutional infrastructures to support u.lab-S and tapping into growing interest, Otto shared that,

> As a community we are now at a point where we can really have a positive impact on many other networks and initiatives of change. This next year will really shift the field for us because we will – in even greater fashion – directly deliver on our original intention.

According to Otto, these teams will build their shared goals around seven levers of that drive comprehensive social impact: Democracy and Governance, Farm and Food, Finance, Health, Education, Business, and a Cross-Cutting category that bridges ecological, social, and spiritual divides. Collectively according to Otto, these levers serve to influence healing, health and well-being, while closing spiritual divides.

Creating a vision and strategy for u.lab-S is a labor of love on its own, but how does one get the process rolling? According to Otto, PI recently held a space with 12 other co-convening organizations. These included Ashoka, League of Intrapreneurs and other similar organizations. Otto described this as a process of reaching out and creating a more collective holding space: "The way you build a platform is to model what you want to see, which is a kind of collaboration, co-creation, and shared sense of ownership of the larger platform that is to be formed." While we discussed this experience, I was immediately struck by the caliber of participants, all key players in their own right with well-defined agendas, markets, strategies, and stereotypes cast upon them by other well-intentioned non-profits. I found myself thinking about what might be done to manage conflict that will likely arise during and following the convening approach that Otto described.

Despite their designation as non-profits, participants will likely need to quantify the value of participating in u.lab-S in relationship with the cost. This return on investment is not always self-evident, and will become more important later on when participant organizations decide who primarily drives and invests in what is created. This is a heretical thought given the collaborative ethos of PI and other organizations listed, but still, responsible non-profits will be motivated at some level to quantify their direct social impact in relationship to the time and energy they invest. While good internal and shared intentions exist between u.lab-S participants, successful stewardship of this effort by PI will address natural conflicts before and as they arise.

While intergroup biases cannot be completely suspended, efforts like u.lab-S might consider incorporating proactive processes up front. One activity that u.lab-S already includes is the development of superordinate goals, which are shared goals that cannot be realized without balanced cooperation of all groups that comprise the STL. While this is a common step for framing shared intentions and outcomes, three additional activities – *Decategorization, Recategorization and Mutual Differentiation*

– are shown to save time, effort and potential heartache (Gaertner & Dovidio, 2000). To decrease stereotypes and outgroup biases, Decategorization involves getting-to-know-you activities at a more personal and individual level, versus framing participant discussion around the way each identifies themselves as a member of their organization. Individual differences are appreciated and the validity of stereotypes and outgroup biases begin to dissolve, and sometimes immediately. Recategorization involves defining group categorization at a higher level of "category inclusiveness"; that is to say that participants come to learn that they are in many cases members of the same group, such as a school of thought or superordinate groups. Lastly, Mutual Differentiation,

> encourages groups to emphasize their mutual distinctiveness but in the context of cooperative interdependence. Also, by dividing the labor in a complementary way to capitalize maximally on each group's relative superiorities and inferiorities, the members of each group can recognize and appreciate the indispensable contribution of the other. (Gaertner, Dovidio et al, 2000, p. 10)

Decategorization, recategorization, and mutual differentiation not only make logical sense, but are relatively easy to integrate and stylize given the processes and underlying intention of u.lab-S.

Moving from strategy to outcomes, Otto and I began exploring the broader context in which u.lab-S's are being conceived. I wondered out loud whether our society is experiencing birthing pains, and asked Otto what types of societal transformation are waiting to be born? Specifically, I asked about how transformation would manifest in every day events, "What might we see and experience that indicates the type of change you envision? When you turn on the news, or talk with someone on the train, what do you suspect we will see or hear?"

Otto's reply:

Yes, a pain related to giving birth to something that wants to be born" Otto agreed, "that's actually exactly the case. The crisis is one of letting go and letting come, from one established way of operating to another one. I think in terms of the framework and message in *Leading from the Emerging Future: From Ego-System to Eco-System Economies* (2013) book as well as the closing chapters of *The Essentials of Theory U: Core Principles and Applications*, which describe the societal evolution that we are in. It's a birth pain for what? In terms of Theory U, I would say birth pain until I go into 4.0 on these various systems levels for farmed food, education, health, finance, business. It's spanned out but you can see the same evolutionary shifts in all of these fields, which is exactly what the five or six initiatives we are launching in the next few months we are referring to.

In terms of what we might be seeing, Otto shared:

In general, we would see awareness, consciousness, people paying attention to each other, to themselves, and to the natural environment as well. We would have economic mechanisms that focus more on well-being for all, so that levels of inequality would decrease. We would learn to not only live, but also co-evolve with nature so that we get a much deeper appreciation of what she is for us and what we can be for her. To some degree, that's happening. We'll be moving into society where for more and more people, there will be much higher degrees of freedom. The reality is, if much of the work is being done by machines, which is what we're moving towards, it means that the jobs that are left are basically social, and call for empathy, well-being, the human interface, and the creative realm.

Knowledge of these shifts, according to Otto, will be important, but what emerged in our dialogue as even more important is the level of responsibility each of us assumes. When I think about societal transformation, I am reminded of a couple of ways in which they take place. Sometimes they evolve incrementally. In other cases, which may characterize the transformation Otto is speaking of, change occurs with the speed of an epidemic.

In *The Tipping Point*. Malcolm Gladwell refers to this moment of change-unleashed as a "moment of critical mass, the threshold, the boiling point" (2006, p. 12). What this might look like locally and globally, both in person and through the web, is hard to say. While the change will likely not be driven by any one specific organization, the smaller scale changes developed by PI's hubs and laboratories will be a key. Gladwell describes the paradox of the epidemic: "that in order to create one contagious movement, you often have to create many small movements first (2006, p. 191). In fact, the design of u.lab-S meets this criterion as it describes itself in promotional literature as a structure for activating and amplifying "a locally anchored, globally connected net-work of hundreds (and over time thousands) of cross-sector change initiatives that are working to build new economic infrastructures that generate well-being for all." For more on how to accomplish this, one can refer back to the work of Burke (2014) who integrates Gladwell's specific change agent roles (Connectors, Mavens, and salespeople) into social network analysis and epidemic change.

Otto continued to explore what this new world will require of the public at large:

A lot more people will have to reinvent their own lives because many of the basics are already taken care of. We will need a new educational system that supports that. We will need to use technology in a much more mindful way. A nutshell summary of the 20th century can be found in Rachel Carson's *Silent Spring,* which addresses the unintended impact of technology on nature. In the 21st century, the story that's unfolding now, is that we see the unintended impact of the use of technology on the mind, on our interior dimension. Moving forward 10, 20, or 30 years further, hopefully we will be a lot more education around that. Of course, we will still use technology, but we'll use it in a way that interferes less with our own inner growth and evolution and in a more organized in a way that is helpful rather than an obstacle in that journey.

Later I had a chance to read the work of Rachel Carson, and it is clear that the inroad she suggests for change is greater presence. According to Carson, "The more clearly we can focus our attention on the wonders and realities of the universe about us, the less taste we shall have for destruction" (Carson, 1962, p. xix).

As we concluded our discussion, Otto shared what might be a defining characteristic of societal transformation:

> For me, maybe the main characteristic of the society of the future we are talking about is that we succeed in protecting our own humanity which is at risk at this point. Protecting our planet and protecting our social relationships which are in the process of falling apart. That is nowhere clearer than here in the U.S., but it's happening all over. Societies are falling apart.

Recalling Otto's sentiment sometime after our discussion, I reflected on the concept of dialectic, from the great German philosopher Hegel, which suggests that society will continue to fall apart and reassemble collectively over and over again, as if in a social spin cycle, but all in the direction of some kind of perfection (Fox, 2005). Whether or not you agree with Hegel's philosophy of progress, one cannot disagree that the world is facing crises like never before, particularly with regard to the physical harm being done to our planet, and the sad irony that despite our greatest achievements in technology, children continue to starve, terrorism continues to flourish, and political corruption seems all but inevitable. I believe the point Otto makes above constitutes two invitations for the reader. First it intimates an existential question not only for the world but for the individual: what role will you play? Or in PI parlance, what type of footprint do you want to leave behind for humanity? The second is that Otto seems to be inviting us to address the greater well-being of mankind not as individuals, but as part of a social fabric. In PI parlance, this is often referred to as a social field.

> Otto's next comments entertained the possibility of society being unwound entirely.

> If we want to have a society moving forward, we need to rebuild these foundations. It's not good enough to fix the old stuff because it's already dead in most cases. We need to learn how to activate really generative social fields. That's the most scare resource I would say exists in this century. And that, at its essence, is what Presencing and Theory U are helping you to do.

As you may suspect, my discussion with Otto at times felt like jumping from mountain top to mountain top with little time spent in the details. However, this conversation pattern makes an important point as we were able to ground our thinking but at the same time leave space for further reflection. It reminded me of a meditation activity conducted by Arawana at an institute retreat I attended several years back. We focused on how we are rooted, centered and connected to our planet, before shifting our attention upward to the infinite. Holding both of these orientations at once is the trait of transcendent leaders. Otto modeled this well.

Indeed, the process that is written all over the work of PI is learning, or adult learning to be more specific. It is a balance between the tensions of what theorist David Kolb (1984; 2005) calls concrete experience and abstract conceptualization, and between active experimentation and remote observation. My conversation with Adam demonstrates how PI is managing these tensions by providing learning opportunities that complement the presencing process. I elaborate more on these important tensions in the context of PI next.

Catching up with Adam

Unlike Otto, who I had met previously, this would be my very first conversation with Adam Yukelson. Given my background in adult learning, I was eager to hear more about Adam's supporting role at the institute and specifically u.lab-S. When I asked him to describe his current work, Adam shared that his primary role includes creating 'online to offline' infrastructures for communities of individuals and organizations around the world to teach themselves theory. He continued,

> What I've been primarily been involved in has been the U.Lab and now newer initiatives that build on theoretical principles. The basic idea is that while you can learn about our work by reading and understanding the theory and having an intellectual understanding, learning primarily comes alive through practice.

This struck me as a natural maturity process for the institute, which is now looking into the use of technology to enable learning from experience, or what Dewey once referred to as a Genuine Education, which exists in the moment. Dewey himself remarks, "cease conceiving of education as mere preparation for later life, and make it the full meaning of the present life" (Dewey, 1893, p. 50).

Here we also have a classic tension in adult learning described by Kolb, between the value of abstract conceptualization (thinking) in which we run scenarios and thought experiments about how we might apply an approach, and concrete experience (feeling) or meaning-making in real-time, a value unto itself (Kolb & Kolb, 2005). Adam spoke directly about the related importance of bridging theory with learning from experience and active experimentation:

> The approach that we have taken with u.lab is to create learning environments where people can learn by doing. My involvement includes creating conditions that make it more likely for people to step in, have some sense of what

these methods and tools and frameworks are like, and then learn them by actually going out and applying them.

David Kolb does in fact list active experimentation as a critical approach to adult learning, but lists three additional drivers, which PI might use to develop a more comprehensive approach and to analyze the most effective forms of learning for each team. The following learning style preferences yield numerous insights into the balance required for in-depth learning. These include (Kolb & Kolb, 2005):

1. *Concrete Experience:* learning from specific experience, being sensitive to feelings and people
2. *Remote Observation:* Observing before making judgments, viewing issues from different perspectives, looking for the meaning of things
3. *Abstract Conceptualization:* Logically analyzing ideas, planning systematically, acting on an intellectual basis
4. *Active Experimentation:* Learning through "hands on" activities, dealing with people and events through action

The web can be leveraged in ways that allow PI to offer comprehensive learning opportunities that engage learners from the inside-out; that is, in a fashion that is learner-centered and grounded in adult learning theory and practice.

I wanted to hear more from Adam about where in the theory most people get stuck or have a misunderstanding. I asked, "Sometimes when I teach theory, there tends to be a common area of confusion or misunderstanding. With Theory U, what do you typically see as a primary source of confusion?" Adams response was very telling, as it focused on two particular areas of misunderstanding. The first pertains to how the first three levels of listening are more readily understood than the fourth. To refresh, Level One listening refers to *Habitual Listening*, where your focus is on confirming the thoughts and opinions you already have. Level Two includes *Factual Listening*, where you listen for something new from the actual person, which might in fact disconfirm what you already know. Level Three, *Empathic Listening*, occurs when you truly begin to see the situation from the other person's view, utilizing your heart to feel into where they are coming from. Level Four, which Adam believes may be the most difficult to comprehend includes *Generative Listening*, which occurs when, "Your listening happens from and holds the space for something essential to become present or to manifest. Time slows down, and the boundary between you and the other begins to collapse" (Scharmer, 2018, p. 12). Adam shared,

> It seems to me that people in ULab tend to have a little confusion around the levels of listening and particularly the articulation of the deeper levels; level four especially. We created a listening self-assessment on our website where people reflect at the end of the day on how much time they spend in each level of listening. What often comes up is people say said that they spend 25% of their day in level four listening. To me level four listening is about a complete shift in identify. So, if you just break it down – that's like four hours of waking time where you feel like your identity is maybe fluid and shifting. So I don't think that level four listening is fully understood. The good thing is that people are beginning to understand a distinction in how they pay attention; and that is really more important than how much time you spend in each level. What's important is that you can learn that there are different ways of paying attention. But in terms of where confusion happens, Level Four listening may be more of a rare phenomenon than people think it is.

A second area of confusion becomes evident when people begin transitioning from the bottom of the U into prototyping.

> To me one of the most intriguing parts of the U process, as I understood it through my own experience when I first got involved ten or so years ago and still to this day, is

this transition from the bottom of the U up into prototyping, crystallizing, and actually taking action in the world. Otto and Ken Wilber did an interview one time back around 2003, in which they discussed the transition between the experience of Presencing and action in the world. Their emphasis was more about bringing the future into the present. What I've seen happen is that people go through a deep inner transformation journey, where they start to connect with a new sense of possibility and then… old frameworks, old mindsets, the old ways of being tend to reestablish themselves. PII think this distinction about staying in tune to what is wanting to happen and how to actually do that is one of the most interesting parts of the U process, and a part that I feel is often underemphasized.

Here is where my previous reflection on Loosely Coupled Systems and Adam's discussion around the impact of scaling come together to produce a potential solution. In any functionalist or capitalist society, it may be said that there is an imbalance between learning by doing and learning by thinking, with a stronger emphasis on doing. A productivity focus may compel Theory U practitioners to skip or skimp on transition from the bottom of the U, where abstract conceptualization is emphasized, and rapid prototyping, where active experimentation and concrete experience are emphasized. On a large scale, one way to encourage practitioners to dwell at the bottom of the U might be melding a learning diagnostic tool like Kolb's *Learning Style Inventory* (Kolb, 2007) with Social Network Analysis (Burke, 2014), to determine which teams in PI social network are more likely to have difficulty with transitioning from the bottom of the U. This would allow for PI to provide targeted educational opportunities to particular members of PI community that are more likely to experience difficulty not only during this transition, but at any transition point in the U process.

I also thought it would be interesting to ask how people who run PI turn the U process inward upon themselves for strategic planning and improvement. I asked Adam "At some point your team must engage in the U process itself. So, what is it like to sense into the future on your team? What is arising for you at this moment in the advancement of your work?" Adam replied: It's an interesting question. I mean the answer might surprise you a little bit. We certainly do use the practices and methods as they are written out. But also, in reality the process is more fluid than that in terms of how we use it internally. And where we are, at least in my work that I'm helping to oversee and lead, is at an interesting place. I guess one way of framing it is not how we support innovation within social systems, but what are the infrastructures that are needed to actually transform the systems themselves. And there isn't really a clear roadmap for how to do that or how to even build a project or initiative that supports that. So our process on the inside can often feel kind of chaotic and emergent. We engage in an interplay between sensing into what we feel is needed in the world and what needs to happen and then putting quite a lot of things out there and seeing where the feedback comes from. Where our key partners have energy. What's really resonating with that?

Thinking back on Adam's answer, I thought about how this group of people shares a very unique set of characteristics. Those that come to mind are that 1) they are all expert-level practitioners with a deep grasp on the U process; 2) perhaps more than any other team, they practice presencing informally, across everything they do (perhaps to the point where it is habitual); and 3) their charge, unlike other U teams, is to steer what they refer to as Mundo level initiatives, in which ambiguity looms large. If anyone outside of the institute were to be a fly on their wall the process may indeed seem chaotic. This drums up a question around whether there is a unique, implicit team development process that PI leaders have experienced. It would be fascinating to tap into that tacit knowledge and incorporate it as a lesson in how teams can move from a more mechanical application of the U process, to one that is more embodied, ever-present and emerging. It is hard to imagine that this would come easily for most people who require greater structure.

Adam continued,

If we put ten ideas out there, maybe there are three that people really latch onto and say, 'Yeah, this is what's needed.' We then tend to move toward amplifying those ideas. Within a team, it's challenging to work that way because it can feel like there's a sort of lack of structure, such that what we were playing with last week is no longer relevant this week. But that's the challenge of working emergent programs into the emergent needs of the world. How do we balance that dynamic of seeing what key partners have energy around and also looking at our own internal capacity to deliver on that?

With regard to key partners and what is currently resonating, I asked Adam about what types of energies are sprouting up for the Presencing institute. Adam shared, It's recognition that given the urgency of the environmental and social challenges that we face there's a need to move beyond team-based projects to innovation ecosystems. Maybe we don't have quite the perfect framing for it just yet. What does it actually look like in practice to help people collaborate across boundaries or work towards a greater common good while still being mindful of and working towards the objectives and needs of their own organization? So there is a sort of sense that we have to collaborate in new ways. We have to create these ecosystems and transformations locally in different parts of the world but how to do that feels like a frontier. It is unclear to many people.

Given my earlier reflections around developing superordinate goals and setting conditions for healthy intragroup dynamics, principles such as Decategorization, Recategorization, and Mutual Differentiation can be applied to the online case studies that demonstrate how people connect their collaborative objectives with those they need to satisfy in their organization. It may also be helpful to translate these processes into a toolkit.

Adam concluded by sharing the way programs are serving a greater sense of purpose.

The programs I'm currently working on ask: "how do we actually begin to work less from our own kind of organizational and personal boundaries and more kind of on behalf of something that is the greater good?" The sweet spot is not to stay utopian and idealistic, but where the rubber hits the road and things become practical. We're also still trying to figure out how best to design these programs. It's an evolving, iterative process.

As Otto, Adam and others at the Presencing Institute continue to champion Theory U and cross-organizational initiatives such as u.lab-S, what is clear that we must all strive to engage in presencing throughout all of our interactions, perhaps to the point where, paradoxically, it becomes habitual. Teams and larger connected initiatives, if appropriately diagnosed and sustained as Loosely Coupled Systems will help the Presencing Institute contribute to a society that strikes a balance between universal and local appeal. As most global change initiatives require a balance between standardization and customization for local needs, a core strength that must be exhibited is one that Otto, Adam and the rest of their team already embody: the ability to weave the original intention of the institute through everything they do and building this social field outward, strategically, and with patience. It would be one thing for Otto and Adam to ask that readers trust in the process. What is more powerful, clearly, is their ability to model this trust.

References

Burke, W. W. (2014). Changing loosely coupled systems. *The Journal of Applied Behavioral Science*, *50*(4), 423–444.

Carson, R. (1962). *Silent spring*. Houghton Mifflin Harcourt.

Dewey, J. (2008). *The Early Works, 1882-1898: 1882-1888. Early essays and Leibniz's new essays concerning human understanding* (Vol. 1). SIU Press.

Fox, M.A. (2005) *The accessible Hegel*. Prometheus Books.

Gaertner, Samuel L.; Dovidio, John F. (2000). *"Reducing Intergroup Conflict: From Superordinate Goals to Decategorization, Recategorization, and Mutual Differentiation"*. Group Dynamics: Theory, Research, and Practice. 4 (1): 98–114.

Gladwell, M. (2006). *The tipping point: How little things can make a big difference*. Little, Brown.

Kolb, D. A. 1984. *Experiential learning: Experience as the source of learning and development*. New Jersey: Prentice-Hall Kolb, A. Y., & Kolb, D. A. (2005). Learning styles and learning spaces: Enhancing experiential learning in higher education. *Academy of management learning & education, 4*(2), 193-212.

Kolb, D. A. (2007). *The Kolb learning style inventory*. Boston, MA: Hay Resources Direct.

Orton, J. D., & Weick, K. E. (1990). Loosely coupled systems: A reconceptualization. *Academy of management review, 15*(2), 203-223.\

Scharmer, C. O. (2018). *The essentials of Theory U: Core principles and applications*. Berrett-Koehler Publishers.

Scharmer, C. O., & Kaufer, K. (2013). *Leading from the emerging future: From ego-system to eco-system economies*. Berrett-Koehler Publishers.

Societal Transformation Lab: u.lab-S Website (2019): https://www.presencing.org/s-lab

Weick, K. E. (1976). Educational organizations as loosely coupled systems. *Administrative science quarterly*, 1-19.

CHAPTER 4

Dynamic Presencing:

A Journey into Presencing Mastery, Leadership and Flow

Olen Gunnlaugson

Introduction

This chapter offers a brief overview of Dynamic Presencing (2019)[1]. As an apprenticeship into mastering the depth dimensions of presencing, Dynamic Presencing focuses on five phenomenological journeys that bring forth a new language and approach for assisting practitioners in presencing their work, lives and moment to moment experience. To build the energetic and attentional capacities to attain this aim, each journey of Dynamic Presencing uncovers a nuanced embodied movement of presencing as it interfaces with and opens the pathway for a presenced way of being, knowing, perceiving, communicating and leading. In this way, each journey introduces an inner core movement that is designed to activate and support emerging ways of engaging presencing amidst our day to day experience. As practitioners move through these journeys, initially as a training and then more as second nature once the territory is sufficiently em-

---

1 Gunnlaugson, O. (2019). Dynamic Presencing: A journey into presencing mastery, leadership and flow. Trifoss Business Press.

bodied, this opens the prospects for a gradual unearthing of a series of shifts in understanding of how to orient from presencing in our immediate experience[2].

In briefly sketching out the five journeys here, the intent of this chapter is to share possibilities for how presencing can grow into a transformative way of re-orienting our experience from a more in-touch, in-depth and dynamic moment to moment experience of presencing. In this way, Dynamic Presencing uncovers possibilities for a deeper shift from understanding presencing as a practice to engaging presencing as a fundamental way of experiencing.

The journey of primary presence

The initial journey of primary presence introduces a method for transforming our relationship to the underlying ground of presence that informs and supports our existing presencing practice. Following the world wisdom traditions, within the Theory U literature presence has been regarded as a byproduct of being present to our experience in the moment. In primary presence, we uncover the underlying ontological ground that we actively draw our presence from and establish a basis of sustained inner felt contact with it. By redirecting our attention to this primary experiential ground, we learn to connect with the energetic source of our presence, which draws upon the innate wisdom and intelligence that resides there. From the standpoint of leadership and communication, learning how to skillfully access this ground plays a critical role in determining the quality of our presencing as well as our overall capacity to sustain presencing in our awareness amidst day to day work and life. To this end, primary presence works with developing the capacity to effectively uncover, activate and embody the generative ground of presence that closely informs and guides our presencing nature amidst action.

---

2 Dynamic Presencing based trainings online as well as an upcoming ICF-certified Dynamic Presencing Coaching training program are currently being developed. Further information will be available at www.dynamicpresencing.com

By shifting our attention from the byproduct (i.e. presence) to the underlying cause (i.e. source ground), the journey of primary presence introduces an in-depth method for activating the fullness of our presencing nature. To assist us in this aim, primary presence also introduces a core movement (Figure 1.0)[3] through four lifeworlds: being real, being witness, being essence and being source. Each lifeworld serves as a generative site from which we excavate and apprentice directly with a key dimension of our overall presencing nature. As we make our way into the core movement, there is a gradual uncovering of the specific ground of presence that assists us in reclaiming our presencing nature from the inside out.

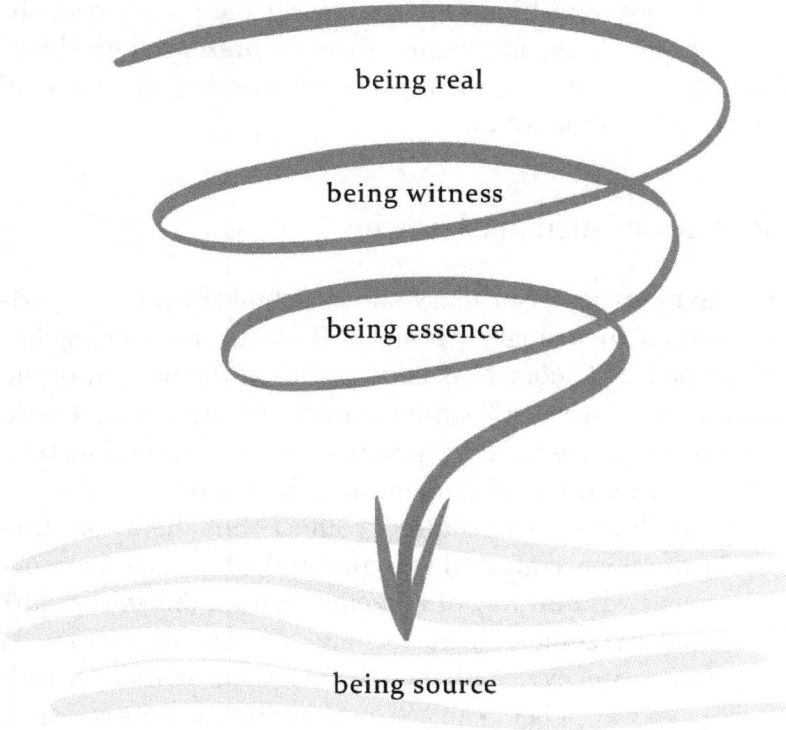

being real

being witness

being essence

being source

Figure 1.0: The core movement of primary presence

---

3 All Dynamic Presencing illustrations have been drawn by Reilly Dow.

As a transformative journey, primary presence initiates a phenomenological rediscovery of the underlying ground conditions of our presencing nature. As each ground level of presence is re-integrated and re-inhabited, it begins to play a role in shaping and guiding the quality of our presencing awareness. This assists us in cultivating a more sustained capacity for presencing. By learning how to actively resource our presencing from these four grounds, the journey of primary presence helps us build and reclaim an active foundation of presence as our in-the-moment source point for engaging presencing action. By reconnecting us immersively to the generative ground that supports our presencing self, this initial journey lays the foundation for a transformed understanding of how to catalyze and sustain presencing as a way of being. By distinguishing and reclaiming these four core dimensions of our presencing nature, primary presence introduces a path and process for supporting and empowering our presencing nature in any situation.

The journey of primary knowing

The next journey of primary knowing builds from the territory uncovered in primary presence. To date, presencing has been described in Theory U as taking place at the bottom of the U between the gestures of letting go and letting come. Inside primary knowing (Figure 2.0), practitioners are invited to connect with a third hidden wisdom gesture, letting be.

Letting be brings us into direct contact with the actual textures of the ontological ground that guides the Dynamic Presencing process as a wisdom way of knowing. Why is this important? Two principal challenges in performing presencing involve 1) learning how to uncover and then stabilize our awareness with presencing as a way of being and 2) learning how to access a presencing way of knowing from this ground. In the journey of primary knowing, the new gesture of letting be serves us by supporting both functions.

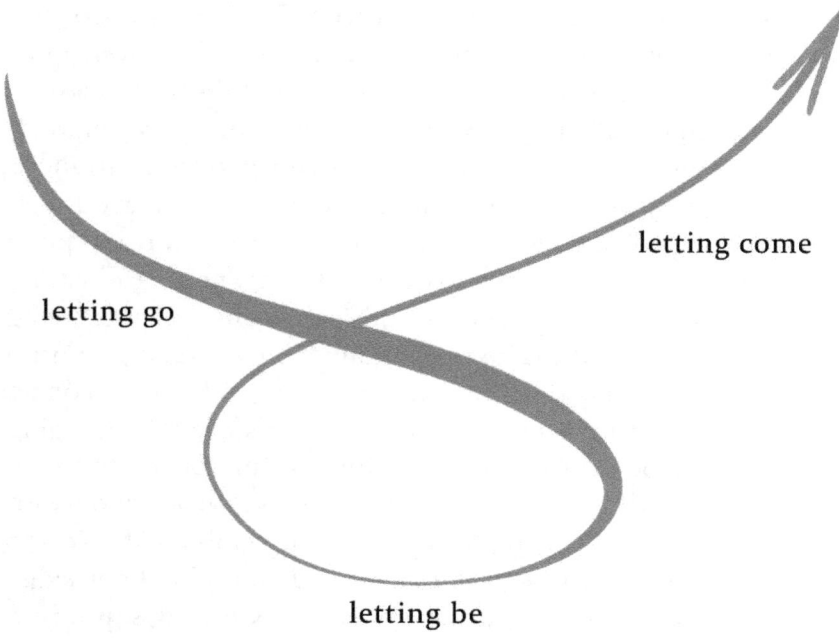

letting come

letting go

letting be

Figure 2.0: The core movement of primary knowing

In Theory U, the main presencing injunctions (i.e. letting go into letting come) are generally interpreted as a performative leap across the presencing abyss[4]. With the introduction of letting be, we explore a subtle scaffolding and new ontological pathway down into it. Mindfully journeying into the abyss instead of leaping over it uncovers a new embodied wisdom means from which we learn how to re-orient presencing from. It also reveals a new excavation site through which presencing can be uncovered, directed and led from directly as a way of knowing.

Because the gesture of letting go requires a shift in the habitual nature of our self, letting be provides supportive bridging conditions to make this transition from our ordinary everyday self into our emerging presencing self. Letting be assists our senses in acclimating interiorly to the liminal experience of presencing, giving us a phenomenological footing and subtle

---

4   Scharmer, C. O. (2007). Theory U: Leading from the future as it emerges. SoL Press, Cambridge, MA.

ground of consciousness to connect with. This helps uncover a trustable felt-based means and focus point to redirect our new-found presencing awareness. In this way, letting be provides a wisdom path of learning how to 1) become more stably embod-ied within our presencing self and 2) access a more continuous presencing way of knowing from this deeper wisdom ground.

As our presence grows to become a resilient ground and place from which we can know directly from, the new gesture of letting be helps stabilize our awareness interiorly from our presencing nature. Given that the Theory U injunctions of letting go into letting come do not provide our presencing self the adequate space or time to indwell with presence and discern the emerging future, letting be provides a new means for supporting this pro-cess. By promoting a more depth attuned synchronization with presence, primary knowing brings us a fuller embodied access to our presencing nature as it unfolds us and emerging knowledge in real time. Overall, the journey of primary knowing supports a transformed understanding of presencing as a presence-guided wisdom way of knowing. Where primary presence helps us access the ground of our presencing self, primary knowing shows us how to optimally engage a wisdom way of knowing from this emerging self directly.

The journey of primary perceiving

Primary perceiving, the third journey of Dynamic Presencing brings us a level down from the core movement of primary know-ing. It reveals to us a path that uncovers a new way of engaging presencing at the level of our direct perception. A typical edge for most presencing practitioners is the challenge of keeping our perception embodied and adequately connected with our pres-ence. In primary perceiving, we work with expanding our exist-ing presencing practice into the subtle location where our em-bodied perception meets the inner dimensions of creative emergence and not-yet manifested reality.

As a central journey of Dynamic Presencing, primary perceiv-ing offers us important perceptual scaffolding by stabilizing our presencing perception at the very granular levels of our felt-embodied experience. Moving down a level from the second journey of primary knowing, in the transition from letting be to letting come, we explore the core movement of Primary perceiving.

The core movement here is a fluid process that draws us into felt perceptual contact with the arising new. This helps make the emerging future more accessible and immediate at the level of our felt perception. By introducing a process to connect with and sustain our connection with presencing perceptually, primary perceiving gradually reveals a new presencing way of seeing. Like a magnetic attractor, the generative ground from which we access presence makes it possible to move into felt synchronization with the arising new[5], helping it take shape in ever new forms and expressions. The core movement (Figure 3.0) of primary perceiving supports practitioners in attaining a richer perceptual relationship with the subject we are inquiring into, ourselves, one another and the world around us.

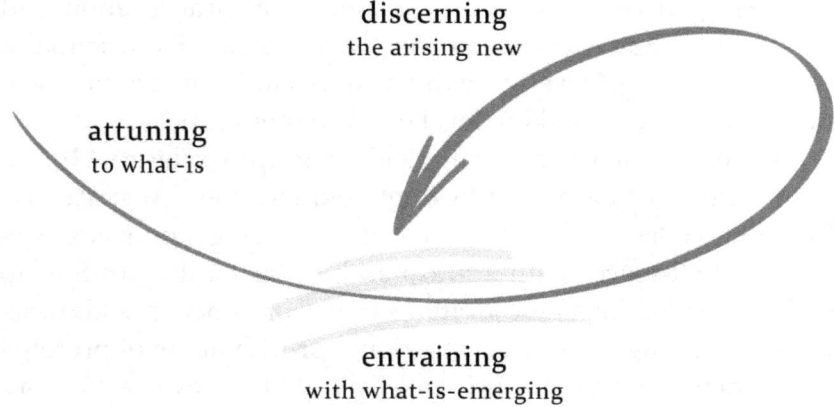

discerning
the arising new

attuning
to what-is

entraining
with what-is-emerging

Figure 3.0: The core movement of primary perceiving

---

5 The *arising new* is the *Dynamic Presencing* term for the emerging future. As a phenomenological reference point, unlike the emerging future, it fosters a more immediate in the moment discernment of new emergence as it unfolds.

Each of the three phases of primary perceiving brings our perception into a fuller felt embodied contact with both the Source of emergence and its particularities. This brings about an immediate perceptual clarity, a felt-embodied cognition and an active renewal of our seeing from Source. By working with improving the quality of our discernment, we engage a presencing-led seeing that helps us more effectively notice and sense the seeds of the emerging future in real time. Learning to be in touch with our experience at these finer levels of granularity helps distill further precision with the presencing process as it makes its way into unfolding our very perception.

The journey of primary communicating

The journey of primary communicating builds from the Theory U rendering of presencing as a single social field to include four distinct yet interconnected presencing locations or generative spaces for engagement within the presencing field. Each presencing space represents a phenomenological location and specific geography within the presencing field. Experientially, each location helps us engage the field dynamics of presencing at the subtle felt-sensemaking level of our experience.

Within this new presencing field geography (Figure 4.0), we are introduced to a new individual field location or i-space and three new collective field locations of presencing: you-space, we-space and all-space. With a grasp and understanding of how to work with these four new locations in the presencing field, practitioners can engage a more situational-precise mode of presencing in their day to day work and lives. This gives rise to more differentiated presencing field dynamics and a new presencing field awareness that can be explored in different ways and contexts where presencing is being applied.

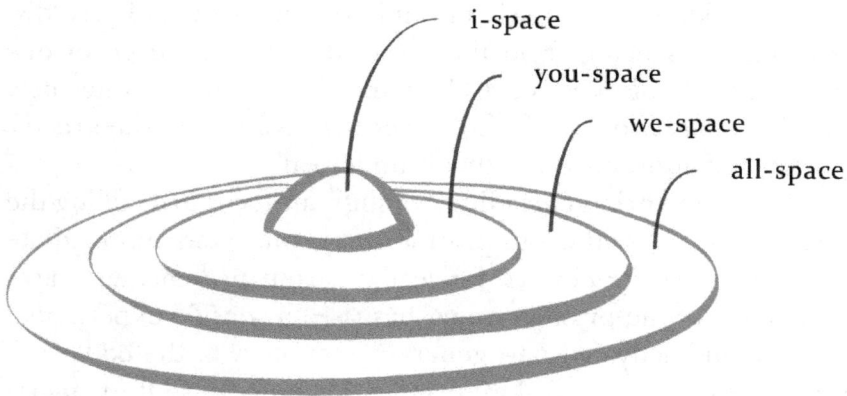

Figure 4.0: The core movement of primary communicating

Each presencing field location connects us to a region in the presencing field where we can develop a more relationally precise and contextually aligned presencing process. As practitioners learn to engage presencing in unique and varied ways across each field horizon, this increases our overall awareness and capacity for a fluid engagement of presencing inside and across various workplace and life situations. Because organizational life in the twenty-first century increasingly asks for our participation and leadership in these four locations, there is a growing need to develop our presencing field mastery in this new way. As each field location contains a set of spatial and relational reference points for engaging presencing in context, practitioners benefit from the updates of primary communicating by developing an increased field acuity and capacity for working with presencing in different situations. Overall, the four fields help Theory U practitioners foster greater awareness of how our emerging presencing self interfaces through the particular presencing field we are engaging.

The journey of primary leading

Through each of the initial four journeys we have uncovered direct means to experiencing presencing as a primary form of presence, knowing, perceiving and communicating. By re-dis-covering presencing from the inside out through each of our main faculties of experience, Dynamic Presencing activates new insights, realizations and discoveries that assist us in the greater presencing apprenticeship that is underway.

Turning to primary leading, we shift our focus to distilling the essential aspects of the four prior journeys into a more immediate and actionable framework for leading from presencing aware-ness. Each of the prior journeys has shed a specific experiential light on and activated new generative territory at the bottom of the U. As we turn to explore primary leading, we shift to engag-ing the presencing process in individual and collective contexts of leadership.

The core movement (Figure 5.0) of primary leading brings us into contact with the subtle region of our inner body where our presencing self interfaces with the presencing field. From our stillpoint, we explore connecting to our source ground of pres-ence as a basis for leading from presencing awareness with great-er precision, attentiveness and ease. The three-phased core movement of primary leading engages our presencing experi-ence as it emerges in the situation we are in the middle of.

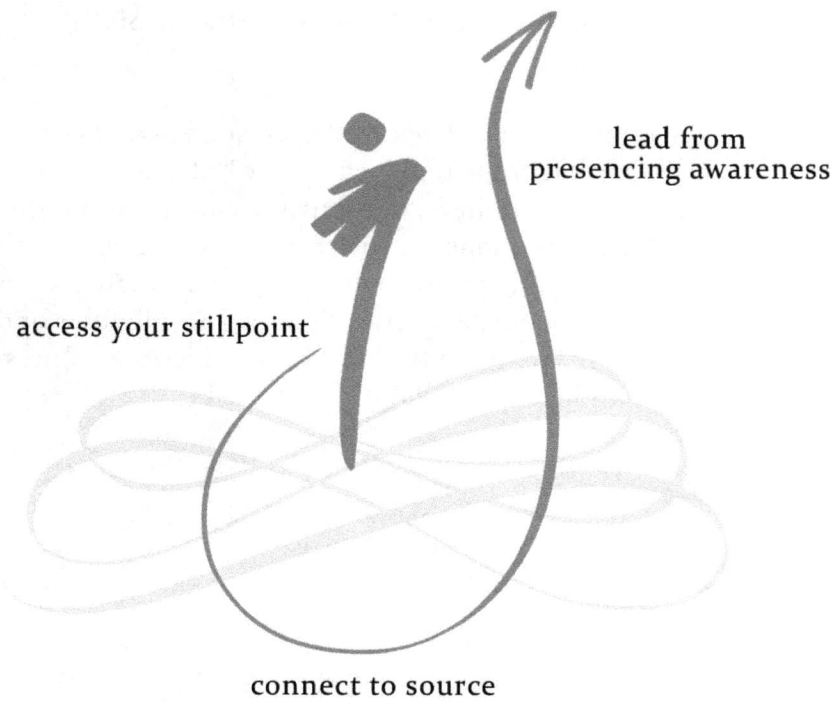

Figure 5.0: The core movement of primary leading

primary leading addresses the practitioner need for an actionable way to engage presencing in the moment. Learning to lead from presencing awareness in real-time is the focus of primary leading, which opens a pathway to presencing in situations where we are under-resourced, under-supported and in need of a way forward. By developing the capacity to draw from the dynamism of presencing awareness in action, primary leading opens the way for a new form of presencing leadership to reveal itself more spontaneously without recourse to relying on the U movement to generate presencing awareness.

Journeying to the far shore of presencing mastery, leadership and flow

As an emerging lineage, Dynamic Presencing joins Theory U initially by setting out from the "near shore" of one's existing presencing practice. From here, our journey moves out into the open water, where practitioners explore new inscapes and horizons beyond their existing presencing practice. Through a series of five transformative journeys, practitioners gain glimpses and eventually begin to experience the "far shore" milestone of presencing mastery, leadership and flow.

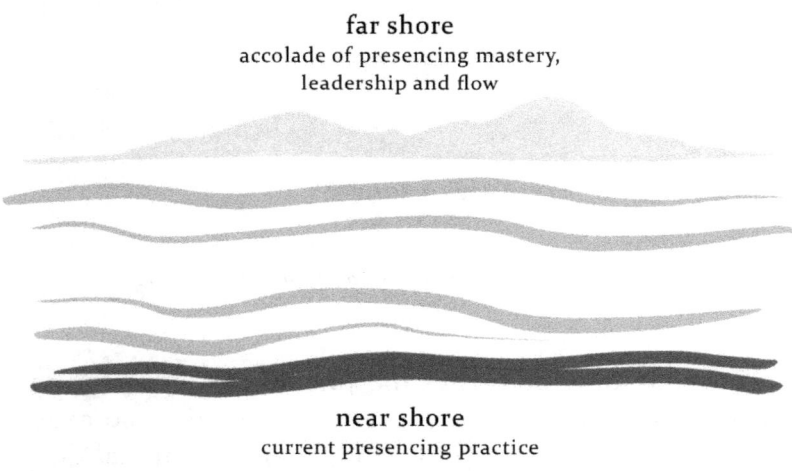

far shore
accolade of presencing mastery,
leadership and flow

near shore
current presencing practice

Figure 6.0: The far shore of Dynamic Presencing

In introducing a series of new core movements that support an overall development of presencing as an in-depth, dynamic and sustained way of orienting our presencing experience, Dynamic Presencing reveals new territory and opens new horizons for what is possible with presencing as a practice. At these foundational levels of our humanity, new inscapes emerge through which presencing can flow through anew, illuminating unforetold insights and revelations. In this sense, Dynamic Presencing is about helping us open and develop our core faculties as presencing instruments in service of learning to live from a place of emerging wisdom and generativity.

For presencing to grow to serve our professional lives and communities of practice at more foundational levels, it must extend beyond the current landscape in which it is understood more functionally as a tool or practice for bringing forth new knowledge. What has been needed for some time now is a rethinking of how to more effectively engage and access presencing as an in-depth, dynamic and sustained path of leadership, mastery and flow that is available to everyone, anywhere, anytime.

Building from the presencing framework introduced in Theory U, the five journeys of Dynamic Presencing reveal a series of new core movements and elements that support the overall development of presencing as an orienting way of being. Through an in-depth immersion into each journey, new discernable pathways for presencing grow, guiding our work in ways that have little historical precedent. While the descriptions of the core movements shared in this chapter touch upon the subtle interior dimensions of presencing, applied in a more cognitive way, they invariably miss the mark. Because the essence of the work of Dynamic Presencing is presence-grounded and awareness-based, it is uncovered gradually through insight, embodied realization and immersion into these five journeys as a transformative leadership process into a transformed understanding of how to access and live directly from the territory itself.

As an updated practitioner method, Dynamic Presencing breaks the glass ceiling of prevailing conceptions of what is possible with presencing as a practice of knowledge creation. When authority is given back to our innate presencing nature at these foundational levels of our humanity, new possibilities open through which presencing can flow through anew, illuminating unforetold insights and revelations.

In this sense, Dynamic Presencing is designed to support practitioners in opening up and developing our capacities as embodied presencing instruments for emerging wisdom and generativity that draw from the living depths of our individual and shared interiority as well as the greater presencing field as core interwoven dimensions of who we are.

CHAPTER 5

An Interpenetrative Application of Theory U

Geoff Fitch & Abigail Lynam

Introduction

This chapter describes an interpenetrative approach to the application of Theory U in an integral transformative development program that Pacific Integral has offered for the past 14 years (Ramirez, Fitch, & O'Fallon, 2010, 2013; Fitch, 2016). The term interpenetration indicates two aspects of a phenomena (such as an individual and a collective or the left and ride side of the "U") that are both distinct and paradoxically co-exist and are inseparable. This approach emerged as we redesigned our program with the intent of finding a deeper integration of the tools and frameworks we made use of. Over time, we began to see Theory U as a fundamental archetype for transformation in all aspects of our work; an archetype that is both timeless and unfolding in time, and that interpenetrates with the other frameworks we use including integral theory (Wilber, 2006), constructive development theory (Cook-Greuter, 2002, O'Fallon 2011), integral polarity practice (Murray & O'Fallon, 2010) and others. The chapter describes the evolution and distinctions of this interpenetrative approach to Theory U application, as well as experiences, lessons learned, and essential practices.

Pacific Integral has been exploring, facilitating, and researching transformative change in an integral, developmental context, through its Generating Transformative Change program, its own organization, and other communities of practice it has convened and participated in. We have convened, facilitated, and engaged with dozens of different integral developmental collectives, involving over 300 individuals, and over durations ranging from nine months to several years. The core of this exploration has been the Generating Transformative Change program (GTC), which enacts and facilitates a new way of being and action in the world grounded in later, more subtle states and stages of consciousness that we refer to as Causal Leadership (Ramirez, Fitch, O'Fallon, 2013). Part of Pacific Integral's learning and evolution has been to ground our work in research, through an ongoing longitudinal study of the developmental growth and experience of participants, before, during, and for years after they complete the programs.

Theory U is a central framework through which we engage our work. We are also deeply informed by integral theory (Wilber, 2001, 2006), leadership development and action inquiry (Torbert, 2004), ego development theory (Cook-Greuter, 2002; Loevinger, 1996; O'Fallon, 2011), dialogue (Bohm & Nichol, 1996; Isaacs, 1999), organizational learning theory (Argyris, 1999), subject-object theory (Kegan, 1998), insight dialogue (O'Fallon & Kramer, 2008) and several other bodies of work from Eastern and Western spiritual paths and traditions. A foundational orientation to our leadership and organizational work is a developmental understanding that spans the concrete, subtle, causal, and non-dual worlds in which our conceptions of individual and collective transformation evolves.

Through an interpenetrative approach, we endeavor to consciously hold multiple perspectives on our learning process. Further we aim to engage thoughtfully from those perspectives while acknowledging that all perspectives on the process are co-arising and co-creating the moment. This approach is distinct from an integrative method, which starts with models and distinctions and moves to reconcile them through editing, framing, and modification into a new, sensibly mapped model. An interpenetrative approach arises out of the view that a deeper wholeness exists - a process beyond our mapping - with which we are participating.

From this perspective, we hold the tensions and paradoxes that exist in and between our models and our perspectives on them. Sensemaking is contextual, provisional, and often paradoxical, and is coincident with witnessing and an openness that allows novelty to emerge.

The following is an example of an interpenetrative approach applied to the recognition that transformative change is an individual and collective phenomenon. An interpenetrative view understands that this separation is in a sense arbitrary, that both co-create each other and co-evolve together, and yet looking at each separately offers insights on different dimensions of change. Both of these perspectives are available at any time and can often point in different directions, yet in any social system there is a unified occurrence that is unfolding, with complexities and a wholeness beyond our ability to map it.

Another way to understand interpenetrative is to examine the four stages of a polarity which are: 1) no other, 2) either/or, 3) reciprocal or both/and, and 4) one within the other, paradoxical, or interpenetrative (O'Fallon, 2010b). Stages three and four can be seen as different degrees of integration, where both/and is an early form of integration from the perspective of separateness and interpenetrative is a deeper intermingling of opposites, seen from the intuition of unity. The fourth stage, which is interpenetrative recognizes that you simply can't have one without the other, that indeed one half of a polar pair actually enacts and depends on the other pole. For instance, in the individual and collective polarity, individuals are shaped by collectives and couldn't exist without them and collectives are made up of individuals. In GTC we engage in individual *and* collective development; separately, together, and interdependently. What this means in practice is that we engage in deep interpersonal work and support the conscious development of the collective to support an individual's healing and development, and vice versa. And in terms of the integration of different theories and models, each is held as distinct and unique, and efforts are made to preserve the integrity of the approach, as well as worked with interdependently. Developmentally, interpenetration begins with later subtle stages of consciousness (O'Fallon, 2010b) and further evolves in the later transpersonal stages as the vantage point be-comes awareness itself. At these later stages, one is able to take or witness a more holistic view of phenomenon, which includes an understanding of the limits of distinctions in language.

Our application of Theory U includes the use of the frame-work as a directional path towards transformation, with the parts of the U process held as distinct and sequential, and an approach that recognizes that the left, bottom, and right side of the U are always present and co-evolving, such as the territories of Open Mind, Open Heart and Open Will (Scharmer, 2007). In an inter-penetrative approach, these frameworks are recognized as both distinct and precise in their own perspectives, while also inter-twined and pointing to analogous realities. In our experience, this has revealed new power and depth in Theory U as it can in-form and be informed by other perspectives and offers a novelty to how it can be applied. By engaging and integrating these mul-tiple perspectives, the U practice is deepened and accelerated.

The chapter describes our intentions, theoretical orienta-tions, experiences, and learning with our experiments in the ap-plication of Theory U in our transformative work, with a particu-lar emphasis on the benefits, challenges, and questions arising out of this deeply paradoxical approach.

Background on Generating Transformative Change

In order to engage a long-term developmental process in the Generative Transformative Change (GTC) program, as well as in-the-moment practices, we integrate the use of Theory U as both a process as well as an ongoing, in-the-moment, dynamic way of being and doing (Fitch, Ramirez, O'Fallon, 2010). This occurs by practicing specific Theory U-based processes, as well as integrat-ing the U process and its constituent elements into a non-linear, holistic framework for the development of capacities and enact-ment of practices for transformative change. For instance, by rec-ognizing that all the points on the U are ever-present, we can en-act them in a moment and simultaneously – open the heart, mind, and will, ground in source and enact the emerging future in an instant.

The application of Theory U as both a process as well as a way of being and doing, integrates two core intentions of GTC. First, the participants individually and collectively learn to understand, engage, and embody transformative processes in themselves and in the systems in which they work. Second, the participants individually and collectively develop their inner capacities and potentials as leaders and as people.

In addition, the GTC program brings together a diverse array of implicit and explicit intentions. We often describe GTC as a leadership development program, designed to support people growing and expanding into transformative leaders. Our organizational programs similarly aim to increase the capacities to effectively and transformatively engage with an organization's vision and mission. While these descriptions create a context of leadership, a more complex set of intentions is at play. Participants bring their own intentions for their own development: expectations, goals, plans, and visions for the future. The explicit intentions are complemented by implicit intentions arising out of the developmental, emergent process itself. In other words, if there is a future that wants to emerge, beyond our preconceptions of it, we can conceive of this future as an intention that in a sense, life wants for us, and it is to be discovered. From the outset, we invite participants to listen for this future that wants to emerge (Scharmer, 2007); their next stage of leadership and expression in the world. The intention of GTC is to be an incubator for this future, and to invite participants to imagine and sense into what that future might be. As designers and facilitators of GTC, it is our intent to discover the developmental unfolding in each participant (and each cohort), rather than to predict it or impose a particular form of development on groups or the individuals as transformative programs consciously or unconsciously might tend to do. We also encourage participants to continue to reveal their own implicit intentions for growth and transformation through their own responses and actions. This is a process of discovering and uncovering intentions, as well as consciously creating intentions for growth and development.

Ultimately, the provocation to leadership offers a learning opportunity with the intention to expand creativity, impact, and service in the world. Through all of our GTC work, we attend to the question, "What greater form of consciousness and action is emerging in the individual/collective and how can we participate in and support that emergence?" One can do so only through one's particular "map of the world," which includes our present sensemaking in models of adult development, state development, and organizational and social transformation. However, the limitations we place on our presencing of the ever-present Mystery or ground of being finds a home in the U model, which gives us a process for exploring and evoking that Mystery in its next form in practical ways.

We launched our initial GTC cohorts around the time of the first publications of Theory U (Senge, Scharmer, Jaworski, & Flowers, 2005). After the first two cohorts, we began to comprehend the transformative process that the participants and cohorts engaged in, through the lens of Theory U and began to explicitly integrate and experiment with the theory in the program. We also engaged the Integral framework (Wilber, 2001, 2006) as well as other models, and had the intent to integrate and synthesize these perspectives into a unified approach. We were initially influenced by a conversation between Scharmer and Wilber (Scharmer & Wilber, 2003), in which they made a connection between the stages of the U-based processes and states of consciousness, and between the process of presencing and stimulating developmental growth through stages. Together they drew a connection between the three levels of the U – Open Mind, Open Heart, and Open Will, and the three states of consciousness and domains of reality – gross, subtle, and causal, and their relationship to fostering development. This helped us connect the process of change inherent in Theory U, with capacities and structures in the growth of consciousness and leadership. As we deliberately integrated these approaches and made similar connections, the conversation between Wilber and Scharmer encouraged our experimentation, research, and action, and in particular it stimulated a more interpenetrative view. While the domains of Open Mind, Open Heart, and Open Will represent movements of a process through time, the territories pointed to by Wilber are

84

states of consciousness that reveal ever-present aspects of reality or territories of depth. We recognized that presencing is something that occurs specifically in time and also, paradoxically, is always happening.

The Evolution of GTC

Our integration of Theory U involved several stages of evolution of the program. We began by learning about Theory U and then drew connections and points of integration with other theories and practices incorporated into GTC. We then designed and integrated a U-based process that cohorts engaged with during the second half of the program, starting with the third retreat. This process emerged as a pivotal point in the program and began to be referred to as the "heart of GTC." This process involves a 4 and a half-day retreat working with a variety of practices to open the mind, heart, and will of the cohort. It includes consciously revealing collective facts and the cohorts' interpretation of them, patterns of interaction, communication, and leadership, patterns of judgments and type-casting, and so forth, to help the cohort release each other and the collective from these potentially limiting habits. The process supports the cohort to let go of who they have been to discover who them might be together, individually, and as a collective – to source their cohort anew from a deeper ground of being. From this, the cohort engages in prototyping new ways of being and acting together.

We began to recognize Theory U as one of the central frameworks of the GTC experience. Simultaneously, we started to integrate Theory U in a deeper way into our own organizational and transformative practices. Each cohort, each retreat, the program itself, and our own organization were held as an emergent future and the capacities, tools, and processes of Theory U were brought to bear.

The GTC program has continued to evolve through an emergent process. Some elements have remained consistent: it utilizes an intimate cohort model that involves intensive retreats every three months, inter-session work online, and group and field work. However, it has also varied in length from nine months to nearly two years and the curriculum has evolved substantially over the fourteen years it has been offered.

As GTC continued to evolve, we started to integrate the core theories and practices of GTC within Theory U in a more inter-penetrative way. For example, the arc of the whole program was designed as a U process, as were each of the retreats. There is also an explicit U process as a component of each retreat. The first two retreats involve a U process to discover and design individual intentions and prototypes that are enacted during the intersession; then during the third retreat, the cohort engages in the collective U process mentioned previously. In addition, the tools we offer and the capacities we aim to cultivate are more explicitly oriented to develop the participants' and cohort's capacity to navigate the transformative territory of the U, as they progress through the program.

The principles that guided the design of GTC were that it be integral (encompassing as much of reality as possible), developmental (not merely asserting a single worldview, but situated in an ongoing, evolutionary trajectory), and motivated by universal compassion (serving to reduce suffering and increase fulfillment in the largest span and depth imaginable). These principals were integrated in a variety of ways; from concrete mapping and multi-disciplinary learning designs, to a deeper inquiry on their interpenetration, which then revealed new approaches that transcended and included the particulars of each practice.

The key capacity development elements we integrate within the U process are 1) individual and collective stages of development, 2) various practices of state development, including meditation, awareness practices, and subtle energy work, 3) a relationship to polar opposites and paradox as a key dimension of cognitive development (Murray & O'Fallon, 2010; O'Fallon, 2010b), 4) moral development by stimulating and reflecting on a wider span and depth of care, 5) complexity of thinking by working with systems and their relationship to one another, 6) psychological and interpersonal practices to develop capacity to work with shadow, projection, and relationship dynamics and 7) action learning prototypes to integrate, embody, and practice what participants have learned.

Questions Prompted by Theory U

The introduction of deep, transformative processes based on the Theory U framework prompted a number of questions for us. First, it provided a way to distinguish and talk about the territories of transformation, by seeing the domains of Open Mind, Open Heart, and Open Will (Scharmer, 2007) as territories of depth, i.e., different levels of subtlety at which change is occurring. These distinctions stimulated inquiry into other aspects of the program. We inquired into where we could we go deeper by engaging the following questions: Where had change opened but not been sustained? How could we more fully activate the depth of presencing (openness to more coherent but unconceived-of potentials)? How does personal and collective shadow relate to our ability to move through the transformative process? How does the transformative process reveal shadow? How do individuals and collectives transform together? Second, we began to see the practices and processes we engaged in, both in the program itself as well as in our own organizational and facilitation practices, through the lens of the Theory U's transformative framework. For example, the arc of the U became a core design principle for retreats; we came to attend to the voices of judgment, cynicism, and fear throughout the learning process; etc. These shifts in perspectives challenged us to redesign our conception of the program in light of Theory U.

As mentioned previously, we began to sense the potential for a deeper cohesion in GTC's design and sought to find a more powerful integration of the other frameworks and practices we employed. At a theoretical level, we drew connections between the frameworks and practices that we hadn't seen before. The more we proceeded with this integration, the more we recognized that the different frameworks we applied interpenetrated, and the more we began to see it as a whole. This process mirrored our own personal and collective development to a more

universal, holistic perspective taking that foregrounded the uni-
tive whole that we were engaging with and backgrounded the
process of negotiation and integration of difference.

Theory U as an Interpenetrating Archetype

We began to see Theory U as a fundamental archetype for
transformation, present in all aspects of our work; it draws on the
timeless dimension as well as unfolding in time and it interpenetrates with the other frameworks we use. Theory U's technology
of social transformation can be seen to articulate not just a process, but to point towards domains of existence and change that
are in constant relationship as an identity, a movement, and a si-
multaneity. These territories interpenetrate, which is to say they
paradoxically exist distinctly and co-exist in the same time and
space. They form each other and are in a continual dynamic relationship to each other. In our personal experience, they can be
seen as aspects and dynamics of consciousness and form, which
we are engaged in discovering, integrating, and enacting with
ourselves and the world. This is important to our approach as we
have found that holding awareness on this interpenetration allows for a deeper coherence and experience of wholeness to come
to light, as well as more spontaneous and novel directions and
solutions to emerge.

Thus, we refer to this approach as interpenetrative. This
term is significant in the STAGES developmental model (O'Fallon, 2011), but points to a perspective in awareness that is found
in many contexts. In the STAGES model, it indicates a pattern
in development of how we hold polar opposites, where the tension is held in paradox and deep interrelationship and interdependence. In polarity theory, interpenetration can be thought
of as one step beyond both/and thinking – an understanding of
the deep interrelationship between and co-creative aspect of
two opposing dimensions (Murray & O'Fallon, 2010; O'Fallon,
2010b). In Buddhist philosophy, 'interpenetration' points to the
deep interconnectivity of all things and of all dharma. In Chris-
tianity, the notion of 'perichoresis' refers to the dynamic inflow-

ing and interdependence of the three elements of elements of the trinity. In developmental psychology, Kegan (1998) pointed to the fifth order consciousness capacity to see self in other and other in self. Interpenetration is sometimes symbolized in the Taijitu, or Yin/Yang symbol, by the small dot of the opposite color in each sides of the symbol, which remind us of the emptiness of duality, or ultimate non-duality of opposites.

In GTC, we hold the frameworks we use, such as Theory U, as perspectives on the present moment and on the dynamic unfolding at multiple levels. As such they reveal, enact, and enable something unique to the circumstances. The practice is to embody the perspectives as deeply as we can, to let them go, and let them come as needed, through the design, facilitation, and response to the moment. We endeavor to stay present to the enactment of our sensemaking and to take wise action based on the needs of the process unfolding through the moment. This has paradoxically led to both a deep integration of Theory U into our work, as well as a very light holding of it as a framework.

In the following sub-sections, we consider interpenetration along three different dimensions: within elements of Theory U itself; between Theory U and other models and frameworks; and between essential tensions or polarities that arises in the context of its application in transformative change. The vantage point of interpenetrative awareness will be explored through each of these categories, as a way to illustrate and evoke the perspective and its application.

Interpenetration of the Elements of the Theory U Model

Let us look more closely at some of the elements of the Theory U framework, which has served as a rich map of the transformative process for GTC and examine how we might see these from an interpenetrative point of view. First, we can differentiate territories of depth (of greater subtlety and complexity): Open Mind, Open Heart, and Open Will. In the context of Theory U, these territories represent movements through the social transformation process. But these are also roughly analogous to the domains of depth of being, variously referred to as gross, subtle, and causal; or in colloquial terms, body, mind, and spirit. The term *gross*, also known as *concrete*, refers to the world of the senses, of ordinary perceivable matter, and of individuals and groups in their concrete appearances. The *subtle* is the world of mind, with its conceptions, emotions, constructions, and contextualization; the world of imagination and subtle contexts and systems. The 'causal' is the domain of awareness of awareness itself, of the un-conditioned mind, full and empty, the witness and the manifest phenomena of all concrete, subtle and causal realities, as well as the very subtle content of mind that is present at this level. At this very subtle level, we touch into what is sometimes called the Source, the primordial ground of Being, which is paradoxically empty and also full of creative potential. It is at this point, the bottom of the U, where we are no longer downloading anything from the past and have the clearest potential to step into a new future (Ramirez, Fitch, & O'Fallon 2013; O'Fallon, 2011).

From the perspective of the bottom of the U or Source, we can recognize that the territories in Theory U are not just stages of a movement, but ever-present aspects of reality. The U process guides us to practice moving through these domains. At the same time, there are many frameworks that have distinguished these domains and articulated practices for working with them. Psy-chological models and contemplative traditions lay out bodies of work for realizing facility with them. Adult stages of development unfold ability to see and work with the content at these levels (O'Fallon, 2011). Thus, we can see these territories as transited by a process, such as Theory U poses (a path to follow), but also see them as potential capacities to develop, as we grow and develop, as well as potentially ever-present aspects of experience. The bot-tom of the U is ever-present, as is every other point along the trajectory of the U.

As referred in the previous paragraph, we can also take an ever-present perspective on the stages of the U process, which appear to proceed from 'left to right.' Each of these stages repre-sent a kind of archetype of the transformative journey; a capacity, a pattern in being, and an aspect of the self. These archetypal patterns are appropriately enacted at each stage of the U process when successful. But they are also ever-present potentials and when seen in this light we can acknowledge they interpenetrate with the entire U process itself (as all tensions or polarities ultimately co-create and unify).

For example, in the act of crystallization (as one moves up the right side of the U), we are letting come a future that wants to emerge, standing in it, and giving voice to it. This future crystallizes or comes in to very subtle form in our consciousness and by giving voice to it becomes an attractor for that future, however inchoate. At this point, the felt sense of this future is often very strong and clear, while as of yet unformed. To give voice to this is an act of daring and courage – the act of faith in the voice of a prophet. If we begin to imagine the capacities, stance, and identity of this perspective on Theory U as a kind of universal archetypal structure, we see that it can be (and ultimately must be) present in some form throughout the process. From the beginning, wholehearted participation in the U process is a kind of apriori faith in an emergent future. It is a kind of declaration of that future, without content. Deepening our capacity for prophetic faith (as with all the other archetypal patterns of the stages of the U), strengthens our engagement with the U process, especially when it apparently 'fails' us.

Similarly, as we move into enacting through experimentation and prototyping, we initially engage with the future as something unknown, complex, and emerging. At this point in the process, it is too soon to know with any precision where we are heading but, nevertheless, we are captured by a sense and vision of the future, so we experiment to engage with that emergent future. Experimenting is described in exploratory, playful terms - such as 'explore divergent alternatives' or 'fail early and often' (Scharmer, 2007). Effective engagement in this stage requires a kind of serious play. We must stay connected to the heart (and source) of our vision, while at the same time not hold it too tightly or become attached to images of what it might eventually look like. We can see that this is not only a requirement of this stage, but a kind of archetypal pattern, a quality, capacity, and aspect of the self. If we imagine who would be needed to bring about the early stages of a nascent vision, we can begin to imagine the qualities and capacities of this self – social connection, creativity, novelty, wholistic sensing, trust. If we approach the whole U process (and perhaps all of experience) with this quality of serious play, with lighthearted enthusiasm, the experience can be infused with wonder and joy, and our willingness and engagement deepened.

These examples show how the elements of Theory U can be seen to interpenetrate with each other and not merely be held in a static model and process. There are numerous other ways to see essential patterns in the elements and structure of Theory U itself. For example, by identifying the polar tensions inherent in the model itself, such as Open and Closed, Reflection and Action, and so on, each are held in awareness, as a play in time, as a paradox, a dynamic tensegrity, and an expression of a whole that is infinitely greater than our ability to distinguish it.

Interpenetration of Theory U and other Frameworks

The deeper more universal patterns in the elements of Theory U are also suggested in other frameworks, while at the same time enacting distinctions and actions that are foreign to Theory U. As such, you can explore the interpenetration of these frameworks with Theory U.

As previously mentioned, Wilber and Scharmer noted the coherence between the territories of depth in the Integral framework (gross, subtle, causal) and those in Theory U (Open Mind, Open Heart, Open Will). In integral theory, these territories are both states of consciousness (interior) and domains of reality (exterior). A developmental perspective is a fundamental component of integral theory and O'Fallon's STAGES developmental model (developed in part through experience with the GTC program at Pacific Integral and influenced by the patterns inherent in Wilber's Integral model), integrates an understanding of states and stages as well as the territories of depth pointed to by integral theory and Theory U. In Theory U, we transit territories as we presence and enact a new future, i.e. as we move down the U, we enter awareness of more complex and subtle realities until potentially letting go into the ground of awareness itself. In integral theory, they can be seen as ever-present realities and states of consciousness (which we can say we are touching into and provoking through the U process). In the STAGES model, they are also developmental structures, which emerge over time in individuals. We can then say that Source is an ever-present dimension of reality, which we let go into and presence with, *and* that this is a kind of state experience that is more or less available to us as a conscious enactment, depending on our level of experience with it. This is what makes Theory U possible and deepened through facilitation that supports a process of letting go and letting come to and from Source.

While the connection points one can draw to other frameworks is probably endless, the key for us was to recognize and see our work through the deeper structure of Theory U. Some frameworks are not as comprehensive as Theory U but still integrate a deeper structure. An example of this might be Torbert's Action Inquiry, which incorporates a model of single-, double- and triple loop learning that is similar to the territories of depth in Theory U (Torbert, 2004). The analogy between triple loop learning and Theory U's presencing was drawn in a 2005 paper by Starr & Torbert.

Other frameworks include these territories of depth or process with different contexts, emphasis, or interpretation. Snowden's Cynefin framework of complex systems provides a useful view of systems at different levels of complexity that relate to the levels of the U. At the level of 'Downloading', Snowden's notion of 'Known' or simple systems applies, in which we are free to operate with known solutions, i.e., to download. At the level of Open Mind, 'Knowable' systems, where analysis (suspending) is important, but cause and effect are still clear. At the level of Open Heart, 'Complex' systems are at play, where cause and effect become less accessible. At the complex systems level we are part of the system and experimentation or probing is the appropriate action.

In Theory U this leaves the domain of Open Will, letting go, presencing and in Cynefin, the Chaotic system. Snowden interprets this from the more conventional perspective of something requiring crisis management, a state in which there is high turbulence and unpredictability. In Theory U, the goal is to achieve a kind of unpredictability, a sense of liberation from the predictability of past patterns. We might do well here to evoke the Greek's original meaning of the term Kaos, "the primordial state that precedes Creation. Chaos is an emptiness, but a fertile emptiness, a nothingness that contains the mysterious seeds of all that is, a vast and formless potential capable of bringing forth all form into expression" (Golabuk, 2012).

Seeing the elements of Theory U as archetypal patterns naturally draws us into more universal and traditional frameworks that elucidate these patterns. We see the elements of the U in the Hero's Journey, in the rhythms of change identified in the I Ching, in the patterns of the seasons, of the day, and of the breath. We see it in our language and culture. The territory of Open Heart is suggested through commonplace wisdom expressions such as "be the change you want to see in the world" and "you are the world." The human experience of letting go and letting come is suggested in statements like, "it is always darkest before the dawn" and "change comes in the 11th hour." Even the words, "f**k it," have something to say about the U process. The goal again is not to integrate these distinctions piecemeal or merely frame them in a larger metacontext, but to hold them simultaneously and lightly, while foregrounding awareness of the whole of the process. This allows for them to inform the work, to hold contradictions and tensions gracefully, and intend the action most conducive to openness and insight.

Interpenetration of Tensions Inherent in the Transformative Process

Theory U can also be viewed through the inherent tensions that are at play in the model and in the transformative process itself. Some of these are explicit in the model itself, such as the tension of reflection (the left-hand side of the U) and action (the right-hand side of the U). Other tensions such as individual/collective, interior/exterior, idealism/realism are implicit in the model. Some exist at multiple levels of depth such as individual/collective, which is explored in greater depth below (Fitch, 2016). In GTC, we work with polar tensions at the concrete and subtle levels as well as very subtle tensions revealed at the causal level, such as transcendence/immanence, awareness/form, and part/whole. As we engage in the process of transformative change viewed through the U, these polarities are at play, both inherently in our growth and our relationship to each other and the moment, as well as specifically in how the framework provokes the polarities.

For example, Theory U implicitly challenges us to exercise our relationship with the tension between realism and idealism. The invitation of the right-hand side - to engage with and lead from the future that wants to emerge – is a powerful call to idealism, while carefully inviting us to enact it through prototyping and emergent practice. We are also invited to let go of the excesses of realism such as judgment, cynicism, or fear. At the same time, the left-hand side is a profound call to realism, to withhold our temptation to jump across to the other side of the U, until we have had the courage to fully encounter what is at its depth. To suspend our judgements and sense into an issue or challenge, is to face reality deeply. We can hold this tension as a kind of rhythm or both/and context throughout the U, but we can also see the deeper interpenetrative nature of this tension. Human experience includes transformation and movement towards a more enlightened future. This is real. We can only fully embrace a more idealistic future, the future that wants to emerge, if we actually conceptualize it as real. Likewise, our most enlightened visions of the future inherently include greater openness, acceptance, and embrace, i.e., greater willingness to be with reality as it is.

In GTC, one of the most significant tensions we have explored and integrated is that of the individual and collective. No other tension is more deeply connected with our experience of being human and the dynamics of transformative change. We started our work in GTC with a focus on individual development but quickly came to see how collective development was deeply connected to individual development (Fitch, 2016). Collectives both liberate and constrain their members, and vice-versa. Our learning community work then grew to include transformative change at a group level, recognizing that it needs to be enacted consciously by all of the participants. Further, we came to see the tension between the individual and the collective to be fertile ground for growth. Engaging the tensions between the individual and the collective calls us to confront our own limiting patterns formed in group life and affords an opportunity to step into a more open, paradoxical relationship to both. Smith and Berg's work on the *Paradoxes of Group Life* identifies a rich and complex set of distinctions for this work (1997). Taken from a deeper perspective we can come to see that there is one transformative movement occurring and that individual and collective levels are perspectives that highlight unique dimensions of it.

As a practice of Theory U, these individual and collective perspectives are always at play. There is an individual and collective through line in all experience. Each individual who participates in a collective U process is driven by unique intentions and patterns. They have their own unique transformative unfolding that is a potential that may or may not have anything to do with the collective future. Likewise, groups have identities, potentials, and a call for involvement in the future they are working toward. All engagement with the transformative experience is ultimately a kind of symphony of collective and individual movements, jostling and provoking each other in their own way and their own timing. To integrate individual and collective transformation and growth in GTC, we include practices and processes for both. An interpenetrative perspective on this tension calls us to hold this whole symphony of movement, including our own individual and collective parts, as both witness and responsible actors. As we move through the U and presence the self and work that wants to emerge, we engage in growth through the dialectic inherent in these tensions, building causal capacity to hold both sides from a still point, and working with the transformative change that occurs in the dynamics of these tensions.

Thus, Theory U reveals itself not just as a process of social change, but one seemingly informed by a deeper architecture, which when seen shows the 'U' as pointing to a kind of mandala of being and becoming. It points to and provokes the underlying polarities through which we rest in our experience and move towards greater expression and allows us to situate them as a greater whole, which rests dynamically in its tensions, while being empty and unlimited in possibility. In other words, it is both a path for development and transformation, for becoming, and it is a reminder of the ever-present ground of being, the bottom of the U, our fundamental nature of being, as are all points on the U. Letting go of the illusion of the fixed self, we see that who we are and what is next is continually arising from the fertile, groundless ground. In a moment that we *are not* in touch with that realization, the U process, is an enactment of it and an awareness practice that supports our experience of it. In a moment where we *are* in touch with that realization, we can see the U process as a kind of ritual that animates what is already happening in its own time and way, and that can help us remain faithful to and in integrity with it.

Practical Applications

In this section we review the practical applications of Theory U in the GTC curriculum after shifting towards a more interpenetrative approach.

While previously the U Process had a couple of specific applications points in the program, we first began to look for additional opportunities to apply Theory U and added new U processes to the curriculum. Next, we began to design an architecture for the application of Theory U in the program with both an individual and collective track. We saw that the individuals and collective(s) were going through different U processes simultaneously. For example, a team might be engaging in prototyping while one of its members is letting go of her will in relationship to her evolving role in groups. As we saw both happening, and at different rates, we began to more consciously design for and to support these multiple and varied individual and collective U process. Third, Theory U entered our lexicon more deeply and we began to see each part of the program as a kind of U. Each retreat was designed in consideration of the U process; as was each segment of the retreat. Fourth, as we deepened our openness to the transformative process, we came to see that we are limited by our own projections on it. With this in mind, faculty come to the retreats expecting the unexpected. In this sense, there is a transformation that wants to occur that is independent of our design for it, for the whole, and the individuals. So, one could say that there are indigenous U processes that are at play in the historical occasion. In addition to our designs for the process, we are open to discovering what they are and what really wants to happen. We are part of the whole that is being transformed. Fifth, we began to apply Theory U internally at Pacific Integral, to frame our own work around it, for example by distinguishing what parts of our work are at which stage of the U and by deliberately apply a U process internally when needed. In the context of GTC, we see ourselves as we design, produce and facilitate as presencing ourselves and our work, constantly, and in our own transformative discovery. And finally, the awareness of capacity development in the context of the U had us seeing the different parts of the program as relating to phases of the U and offering learning opportunities to support our ability to navigate those territories.

To illustrate some of these changes, we'll look at part of the design of GTC. As was reviewed previously, in the first two retreats participants are exposed to a variety of experiences that build capacity, connection, and history with each other at a collective level. But in this part of the program the U process is largely focused on the individual. Each session participants are guided on an individual U journey and presence, out of the context of the transformative learning they have been immersed in, the future that is emerging in them personally. This U process includes a review of the learning participants have experienced during the retreat, an examination of the contexts of their own life and work, a holistic sensing that emerges out of individual shadow work, letting go meditations, nature walks, journaling, and dialog with other group members. Meditations include guided visualization, emptiness meditation, breathwork, and movement that facilitate the letting go process. Participants are introduced to the practice of prototyping and set up and engage in this work in the inter-sessions.

In retreats three and four, collective U processes are introduced and integrated with the individual U processes. The cohorts go through powerful journeys to discover and enact what is emerging at a collective level, working with collective shadow, paradoxes of group life and collective presencing, while also paying attention to their own individual emergent process. This represents a significant turn towards collective evolution and transformation but builds on the knowledge of the U process and the individual capacities they have been building. In the third retreat, the U Process provides a deep integration of their collective experience to date with a focus on presencing the potential practice and contribution of the collective itself. The movement of the left-hand side of the U is a progressive and challenging self-examination of the cohorts' experience of itself and of each member. It includes an examination of the reality and results of the cohort to date, as well as a collective shadow process that helps unearth the patterns of meaning making, assumptions, and projections that have been present in the group. This practice builds the capacity and norms of collective self-awareness, as well as prepares the cohort to presence the group's future being and work together.

In the current form of GTC there are many aspects of the U processes that are in a stage of institutionalization. They are well understood and designed. There are also aspects of it that are quite emergent – more in a stage of experimentation. In recent years, for example, we have brought in more exploration of cultural contexts and identity. This is new and we 'fail early and often' with it and enjoy this process with the understanding that it is a place of complex emergence and new learning.

At the same time, in recent cohorts we had a shift in the diversity of participants from a cultural and identity perspective. This has sparked challenging and unexpected turns in the evolution of the two most recent cohorts. While we have offered GTC for 14 years, with over 25 cohorts held on three continents, there is a degree to which we see the process as a kind of unknown unfolding.

In holding the process as it unfolds both predictably and unpredictably, we endeavor to return to our own presencing and ask at the deepest level, what is happening? How are we a source of it? What are we blind to? What is self and our work?

Benefits, Challenges, and Questions from an Interpenetrative Approach

On the whole, the interpenetrative approach to applying Theory U has had some significant benefits for our work. As we made our transition to this approach, we were driven by the intention to deepen the power and impact of the program. We shortened the length of the program but also intensified the process. We see this interpenetrative approach as instrumental in this change. It allowed us to keep the practices of transformation more present and alive in every stage of the program and to work with the transformative potential in each moment. Additionally, the focus on development of individual and collective capacities in support of the presencing process, served as a positive feedback loop on the use of Theory U. As the participants progress through the program, they become more able as individuals and as a cohort to engage and work with transformation. And as we at Pacific Integral conceive of everything we are doing as a kind of transformative process, with greater access to the distinctions and capacities to enact that perspective, a kind of transformative energy and intent was released that deepened the power and impact of the work.

We also observed a deeper coherence emerge that opened up our own exploration of trans-conceptual collective intelligence (the emergence of coherent movement in the collective not dependent on our conception of it). As we hold a meta-integrative perspective, we could sense and experience a movement towards deeper integration and intelligence, that transcends the ways we make narrative sense of the process. GTC cohorts are developmentally diverse and we consciously avoid reducing the space to a normative interpretive framework, allowing for a deeper integration in the tension between sensemaking and the paradox of meaning. Likewise, holding a meta-integrative perspective creates potential for integration between polar opposites such as that of the individual and collective, action and reflection, engagement and detachment. In short, we aim to hold space for individual and collective movement through multiple simultaneous 'U' processes, where participants make different meaning about the experience but share an open reflective awareness/presence and a meta-cognitive curiosity that allows for a sensing of the greater whole within which the process is held. There is something deeply graceful and magical about what can unfold in this space of openness.

At the same time, there are challenges to this approach as well. One challenge is unleashing so much complexity and nuance so that occasionally a needed simplicity gets missed or we get sidetracked in a dead end. We have come to recognize subtle attachments and confusions that have contributed to this. For example, the U process challenges us at every step of the way to see and evolve patterns of consciousness that are artifacts of the conventional mindset. An example of this is the tendency to view prototyping through the frame of project management. It takes time to understand the frame of reference with which to see a complex system and the kind of probing and experimenting that is at the foundation of prototyping. Likewise, much of the U process can be driven by intent and will – except of course the process of letting go, which can be encouraged, but is not fundamentally an act of will but of willingness and grace. Therefore, if we hold the U too tightly or too loosely, we can lose the dynamic relationship with the creative evolutionary unfolding and the process can become inert. Finally, there are times to not take the interpenetrative perspective – for example to foreground the individual over the collective exclusively or vice versa, rather than holding a deeper integration, which may not always be what is called for in the moment.

With this perspective on the U, each 'stage' of the U takes on a kind of archetypal form to it. This learning has been to discover the real nature of these dimensions of ourselves, to learn about our relationship to them – our aversions and attachments – and to re-own and integrate them in ourselves in a way that they can be expressed with agility and effectiveness. For example, let's consider sensing, presencing, and crystalizing. The sensing self, the observer, committed to truth and with an Open Mind, can emerge tainted with our personal history of the emerging rational consciousness and its conflict with the collective order. We may be afraid to express the truth, to admit it, for fear of hurting each other. Or maybe we are attached to our sensing self, retreating to the observer position for safety. At its essence, the sensing self is the Witness, the knowing nature of awareness and our journey to reintegrate this into the self may have us face traumas related to freedom and detachment that are qualities of this self.

The presencing self is our self at the bottom of the U, which is at home with the Source, the ground of Being, having let go of our very will and open to receiving. At the heart of embodying this self is discovering and letting go of where we don't trust and of finding a deeper trust in Life. Befriending the bottom of the U is a profound journey and once open to it, we may become subtly attached to a conception of what it is to be 'let go' and surrendered, which might lead one to be 'stuck in the bottom of the U' or have them view any challenge as a prompt to return to the U, rather than to address it as an adaptive challenge or simply feedback (failing early and often) in the crystallizing process. The true integration of the connection with Source is to discover how it is just as present in every stage of the U, in every manifestation of the self as it is in presencing.

The crystallizing self is the voice of the higher self, of the future that wants to emerge; it is a place of deep faith and leadership. To integrate this self, we may have to challenge our traumas and aversions to giving voice, to standing out, and to idealism. Likewise, we may be attached to idealism and faith and avoid the deeper integration of idealism and realism needed to practically enact the future. Reintegrating this self is to see the faith innate in the entire process and to be willing to give voice to it at any time; to be a representative of the heart's truth.

The interpenetrative approach has required in some sense that we each internalize the process at a deeper level to have greater agility with it, as we cannot rely as much on a pre-scripted form to the U.

Conclusion

To presence all of this subtly and complexly for the purpose of illustrating our approach to applying Theory U is to obscure something: the simplicity and humor with which we ultimately hold the process. The deeper stand to take in all of this is to let go or at least hold very lightly our theories and practices and to stand in presence with each other and with all that is happening, and to Love, to support, and to nudge a greater clarity, reverence, and communion into light. The foundation of the interpenetrative view is the still, luminous, and blissful being, holding the apparent opposites we can allow to come together.

In practice, transiting and working in the territories defined by Theory U can be challenging and require an intentional holding of the process. At the same time, this is a holistic transformative process, which means we are part of that process and can't know exactly where it is going. This challenges us to paradoxically hold a loving container for the process, to be open to deep integration, and to be a mutually vulnerable participant in the process. As an interpenetrative archetype of transformation, Theory U offers a developmental practice, a transformative process, and a way of being.

References

Argyris, C. (1999). *On organizational learning*: Blackwell Business.

Bohm, D., & Nichol, L. (1996). *On dialogue*. London: Routledge.

Cook-Greuter, S. (2002). *Ego development: Nine levels of increasing embrace*. Unpublished manuscript : Wayland, MA.

Fitch, G., Ramirez, V., & O'Fallon, T. (2010). *Enacting containers for integral transformative development*. Paper presented at the Integral Theory Conference.

Fitch, G. (2016). *In, As, and Towards the Kosmic We*. from Gunnlaugson, O., Brabant, M. (2016). Cohering the Integral We Space: Engaging Collective Emergence, Wisdom and Healing in Groups: Integral Publishing House.

Golabuk, P. (2012). *Field and Fate Workshop*. Philosophy Center.

Isaacs, W. (1999). *Dialogue and the art of thinking together: A pioneering ap-*

proach to communicating in business and in life. New York : Currency.

Kegan, R. (1998). *In over our heads: The mental demands of modern life.* Cambridge, MA: Harvard University Press.

Loevinger, J. (1996). *Measuring Ego Development.* London.

Murray, T., & O'Fallon, T. (2010). A Perspective on Kesler's Integral Polarity Practice. *Integral Review, 6*(2).

O'Fallon, T. (2010). *The collapse of the Wilber Combs matrix: The interpenetration of state and structure stages.* Paper presented at the Integral Theory Conference, Pleasant Hill, CA.

O'Fallon, T. (2011). STAGES: Growing up is waking up--interpenetrating quadrants, states and structures. Retrieved from Pacific Integral website: http://pacificintegral.com/docs/StAGES_OFallon.pdf

O'Fallon, T., & Kramer, G. (2008). Insight dialog and insight dialog inquiry Retrieved June 20, 2008, from: www.pacificintegral.com

Ramirez, V., Fitch, G, & O'Fallon T. (2013). *Causal leadership: A natural emergence from later stages of awareness.*

Paper presented at the Integral Theory Conference, San Francisco, CA.

Scharmer, C. O. (2007). *Theory U: Learning from the futures as it emerges.* San Francisco : Berrett-Koehler Publishers.

Scharmer, C. O., & Wilber, K. (2003). Mapping the integral U - a conversation between Ken Wilber, Otto Scharmer Retrieved December 15, 2011, 2011, from: http://www.presencing.com/dol_content/docs/KenWilber-OS2003.pdf

Senge, P. M., Scharmer, C. O., Jaworski, J., & Flowers, B. S. (2005). *Presence: exploring profound change in people, organizations, and society.* Doubleday.

Smith, K., Berg, D., (1997). *Paradoxes of Group Life.* Hoboken: Jossey-Bass.

Starr, A., Torbert, W. R. (2005). Timely and transforming leadership inquiry and action: Toward triple-loop awareness. *Integral Review 1.*

Torbert, W. R. (2004). *Action Inquiry: The Secret of Timely and Transforming Leadership.* San Francisco : Berrett-Koehler Publishers.

Wilber, K. (2001). *Sex, ecology, spirituality: The spirit of evolution.* Boston, MA: Shambhala.

Wilber, K. (2006). *Integral spirituality: a startling new role for religion in the modern and postmodern world.* Boston: Shambhala.

CHAPTER 6

Interweaving U:

Releasing potential for personal transformation and global systems change at the Burren Executive Leadership Retreat

Mary Stacey and Reilly Dow

> The time is right for the artistic imagination of each of us to co-create the leadership that the world most needs and deserves. – John O'Donohue, *Beauty: The Invisible Embrace*, 2004

The Burren Executive Leadership Retreat (BELR) is an annual gathering of global leaders, based in the west of Ireland. It is also a community that leaders can return to when they want to renew their energies, expand their capacity, and encounter diverse, yet like-minded peers. The BELR grows out of our vision of leadership as a creative act in a rapidly changing world, as well as our view of leadership development as the process of building the personal and collective capacity for such creative acts in order to thrive in the midst of increasingly complex conditions.

Each summer we welcome approximately twenty-five culturally and generationally diverse participants, whose professional lives take place in corporations, the arts, the sustainability and social justice sectors, non-governmental and religious organizations, entrepreneurial fields, political and academic life, and through roles such as CEO, Secretary General, National Party Leader, University President, Student, Artist, and Coach.

The four-day gathering unfolds at the intersection of artistic and leadership practice, as participating leaders join poets, musicians, and visual artists in exploration of their work. Our stance is that the role of both leaders and artists includes risking themselves into the unknown for the sake of expanding what we can collectively envisage as possible. Our design aims to create conditions which liberate the transforming potential of the environment, so that participants come into greater contact with their authentic selves and a higher future potential for their work, in a movement toward what Scharmer calls presencing: the capacity to sense what wants to come forth and then allow it to come into being (Gunnlaugson, Baron, & Cayer, 2013; Scharmer, 2009, 2016; Torbert, 1978). This capacity is similarly known as triple-loop awareness, the capacity to be fully present and exercise revisioning, frame-changing timely leadership (Nicolaides & McCallum, 2013; Torbert & Associates, 2004; Starr & Torbert, 2005); negative capability, the ability to surrender creatively and engage the unknown and the unknowable in ways that support creative emergence (Hebron, 2014; Omer, 2017; Keats, 1817) and in the Irish, the *neart*, the life force of creativity aligned with the underlying patterns of life (Condren, 2010).

The chapter offers a look inside the BELR container, "a nested set of spaces within which inquiry, learning, and meaning making can take place, and the potential and possibility of a group can unfold" (Corrigan, 2015, p. 291). Inside the container, we interweave the U process in a planned and emergent way with other core elements: Collaborative Developmental Action Inquiry (CDAI) (Nicolaides & McCallum, 2013; Torbert, 2013; Torbert, 2017); the Power of Place (Gomes, 2005; Jones, 2014; Weiner, 2012); Creative Process (Jones, 2006, 2014); and Generative Facilitation (Bird, 2018; Bushe, 2010), thereby creating the conditions where participants can individually and collectively undertake transformative learning that shifts their perspectives, perceptual lenses, core beliefs, schemas, mental models, emotional landscapes, and mindsets and thereby expands their capacity to engage complex challenges that will later emerge in their systems change work (Cranton, 1996; Mezirow, 1981, 2000; Omer, 2017; Stacey, 1998).

To offer readers a sense of how the BELR supports participants in expanding their presencing capacity and in moving toward the highest future potential of their leadership, we will:

- Make visible two patterns we see emerging for today's leaders and leadership itself, which have led us to design the BELR as a retreat space for artists and leaders.
- Explore ways that interweaving U contributes to the transforming power of the BELR experience and also enriches and expands the horizons of the U process. This will include an exploration of the Intense Threshold, a space of fecund messiness we perceive at the bottom of the U, with its invitation to hang out in a raw place of ambiguity and complexity rather than avoid the unbearable tension of staying in the unknown (Beck, 2017), which can be present in a U process and manifest in the desire to quickly move toward projectifying the experience.
- Travel through the BELR's U process, bringing in the written reflections of participants at various stages of the journey and excerpts from their dialogue with artists to offer a glimpse inside the container, *"An alchemical experience, difficult to articulate, that requires trust."*

The Context for Leadership

We live in a time where each one of us will be asked to reach deeper, speak more bravely, live more from the fierce perspective of the poetic imagination. – David Whyte, *Letter from the House,* 2016

The environment in which today's leaders serve is highly complex and becoming more so every day (National Intelligence Council, 2017). The now ubiquitous acronym VUCA foregrounds the interconnected volatility, uncertainty, complexity, and ambiguity that globally-minded leaders navigate as systems collide and collapse more visibly every day. They carry the burden of this complexity at every level of scale—personally, in their relationships, and in the communities and organizations where they focus their energies (Yeyinmen & Stacey, 2018).

In our decades of international work in leadership development we have noticed the emergence of two patterns that have led us to create the BELR. The first is that even mature leaders who have the capacity to transform organizations and systems can get caught in the net of trying to ameliorate VUCA conditions by creating the PAID environment of relentless *pressure*, being *always on*, with *information overload*, and *distraction* (Hougaard, 2016; Torbert, 2017; Yeyinman & Stacey, 2018). In this intensity leaders can find themselves regressing: falling back to earlier reactive stages, feeling in over their heads, stressed, overwhelmed, and less effective, with a loss of confidence and capacity, and in a state of fight/flight/freeze caused by being under near-constant neurological threat (Joiner & Josephs, 2007; Kegan, 1994; Leitch, Rooke, & Wilson, 2016; Livesay, 2015; Rooke & Torbert, 2005; Wickremasinghe, 2018). These leaders, having seen themselves at full capacity and knowing that they are not currently approaching situations aligned with that potential, sense that the BELR is a place where they can reclaim their centre of gravity creativity, authenticity, choice, and flexibility. They arrive at the retreat in deep contact with the VUCA/PAID experience, *"I can see how much we're all carrying and how much we need to put down to reach into the unknown, not knowing what we're reaching for."*

We've noticed the emergence of another pattern: the world is becoming a less hospitable place for those who seek to place leadership at the center of their lives, who aim to lead with integrity through an ethical use of power, and toward the sustainability of human life and the planet. It is a vexing time for those of us who believe in the rights of artists, leaders, and ordinary citizens to push boundaries and take risks and so, at times, to change the way we see the world. Artists and scholars who might, in other eras, have been celebrated for their originality and independence of mind, are increasingly being told, "Sit down, you're rocking the boat" (Rushdie, 2013). As with artists and scholars, so too with leaders.

In an environment where the individual leader and leadership itself are both under threat, heroic forms of leadership and competency-based executive programs cannot create the communities that will help leaders thrive or prepare them to engage with the future that is emerging. "Whatever leadership used to be—it used to be. Now it has to be something different. Now we all have to be more than we were" (Bateson, 2017, p. 2).

The BELR is our way of responding to an urgent call to cultivate the kind of leadership that is 'able for' the future that is emerging, with an individual and collective capacity to be resilient, hold clarity of purpose, and exercise capabilities that are well-matched to VUCA conditions, which, in their very nature, are attuned to the dangers and opportunities of systems edges and thresholds (Omer, 2017).

The BELR Container: Interweaving Elements

As a hosting team, we begin our container-building work in the months before each retreat so that when we arrive, we can be prepared to facilitate in a multi-dimensional way, through a timely and amplifying interweaving of the U process with other core elements. The BELR creates the conditions of a complex systems challenge (Omer, 2017) and a catalyst for development. It is a holding environment (Kegan, 1982; Nicolaides & McCallum, 2013) where the ratio of supports and challenges is kept in such a balance as to assist participants in operating from their least defended, highest functioning selves and to inhabit more complex and emergent ways of being and leading.

In this section we explore the BELR container elements that work both visibly and invisibly to support participants in sensing the future that is in need of them and to come closer to the questions: "Who is my self? What is my work?" (Scharmer, 2009, 2016)

Collaborative Developmental Action Inquiry and Presencing

CDAI is a lifelong process of transformational learning and a disciplined leadership practice that encourages us to work more vulnerably with feedback and to use power in ways that support our own and others' development. With practice we become better able to simultaneously inquire and act in response to what is unfolding on a moment-to-moment basis at the individual, relational, and systems levels (Torbert & Associates, 2004; Stacey, 2011). Like the U process, CDAI is intended to increase our capacity to enact integrity, mutuality, justice, and sustainability for ourselves, our communities, organizations and systems and to expand our range of awareness and intention (Nicolaides & McCallum, 2013; Scharmer, 2009). Both the U process and the practice of CDAI weave individual, group, and structural elements together to enact deep and generative change.

We have noticed that leaders who are attracted to the BELR have the capacity to reflect on past actions and modify them to accomplish a goal in the future (single-loop feedback), to reflect on and modify the assumptions, blind spots, and strategies that are guiding actions (double-loop feedback), and, at full capacity, to pay attention to and revise their personal intention and/or a shared vision (triple-loop feedback and awareness) (Nicolaides & McCallum, 2013). Scharmer (2009) describes triple-loop awareness and learning in terms of presencing, which involves dropping the individual and collective ego.

Triple loop awareness is a temporary state of personal and collective consciousness necessary for traveling the U process, and for consciously and willingly allowing an un-predetermined future to emerge at the bottom of the U. It is through this attention that we can we begin the journey toward intentionally, rather than habitually or accidentally, generating timely action, action that does not merely conform to existing norms of timeliness, but can also transform existing norms

(Nicolaides & McCallum, 2013). By interweaving the U process and CDAI during the retreat, we discover a mutually amplifying relationship that powerfully supports the opening of mind and heart and a movement toward a state triple-loop awareness, the capacity to be fully present and exercise revisioning, frame-changing timely leadership (Starr & Torbert, 2005) and a disciplined vulnerability to the emergent future (Nicolaides and McCallum, 2013).

During the BELR's four days, we invite participants to travel the U while deepening into a spiral of personal, interpersonal, and systems learning and inquiry in action toward a state where vision/intention, strategies, actions, and outcomes can be explored and transformed through:

- First person attentional practices (such as journaling, meditation, and silent walks), which increase the capacity to hold inner awareness and choice in the midst of ambiguity and uncertainty
- Second person interpersonal practices (such as trio coaching, Open Space conversations, and studio practice), which increase the capacity to build trust, to co-resolve dilemmas, to test assumptions in the midst of action, and to take committed collaborative action
- Third person systemic reflection (circle reflection, dialogue with the artists, scribing, and time in the landscape), which, when sustained over time, increases the capacity to design and lead systemic transformation (Torbert, 2017).

As illustrated in Figure 1, the practice of CDAI yokes inquiry and action across three levels of inquiry (me, we, it), four territories of experience (vision/intention, strategy, action, outcome), and three levels of feedback (single-loop, double-loop, triple-loop) toward transforming action.

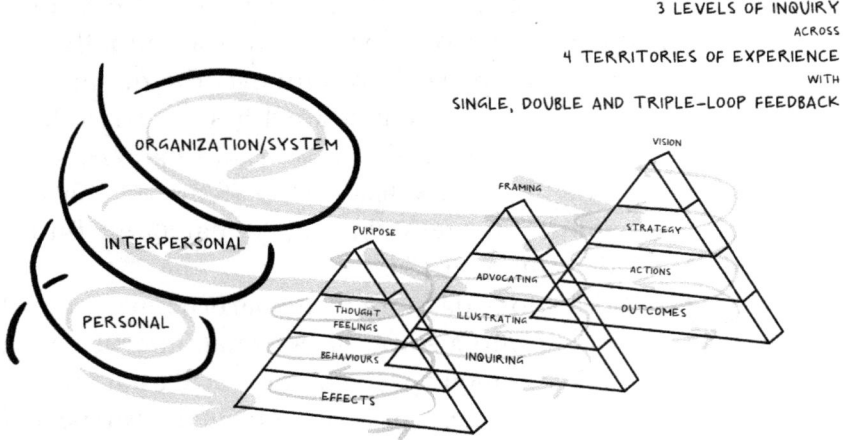

Figure 1: The three levels of inquiry in CDAI, across four territories, with single-, double- and triple-loop feedback.

By interweaving CDAI practice and U process, we offer participants a powerful process to support them in accessing more expansive states while they are in the retreat, and a lifelong practice for engendering more personal and organizational transformation in turbulent environments and with greater efficacy and sustainability in the long term (Torbert, 2017).

The Power of Place and Presencing

It is intentional that we gather in the "thin place" that is the Burren landscape. From the Irish *An Bhoireann*, the Burren literally means a rocky place. Uniquely on the planet, Arctic, Mediterranean and Alpine plants grow side-by-side while acid and alkaline loving plants abide in close proximity. Everywhere paradox and surprise are the norm. The presence and unflinching beauty of the place is palpable. Few can fail to be touched and awakened by its primeval force (Hawkes, 2018).

In Celtic mythology, thin places are threshold spaces where the visible and the invisible world come into their closest proximity (Gomes, 1996). In a thin place, "the walls are weak, and a luminous quality remains that allows us to catch a glimpse of the something larger than ourselves. We are jolted out of old ways of seeing; feelings of belonging and homecoming are evoked (Blanton, 2014). They transform us—or more accurately, unmask us. We let go and become our essential, or more authentic selves (Weiner, 2012; Scharmer, 2013). In a thin place we have a better chance of accessing what Scharmer (2013) calls the blind spot and what Thomas Merton called a hidden wholeness (Hare & LeBoutillier, 2017). With careful attention to facilitating safe and trustworthy space, by embodying our daily encounters with the landscape as a pilgrimage, we support BELR participants' encounters with what lies at the threshold of the thin place that we find in the Burren. Jones (2014) asks us to consider, "What stories can this place tell us that may shape our own sense of who we are and how we lead?" (p. 94). Envisaging these larger unknowns sets us on a pilgrimage, a path that poet Antonio Machado (2003) says can only be laid by walking.

Our local hosts, stewards of the Burren, welcome us with hospitality that supports a sense of tradition, and our evenings in village life invite a sense of playfulness. Our morning circle creates space for ritual and intimacy. Using Humble Inquiry (Schein, 2013) we are invited to speak in first person and listen into the center for the voice of collective wisdom emerging from the whole (Hayashi, n.d.). An Open Space session is a place to inquire into our big questions about leadership, and our peer trios are a place of slowing down, deepening truth and intimacy, and arriving at an understanding of that which was previously beyond our reach. Place based container elements and facilitation choices that support presencing include:

- The thin place that is the Burren landscape
- The hospitality of the local community
- Circle as a place of ritual, intimacy and listening
- Small group spaces such as Open Space and trio peer coaching sessions
- Indigenous poetry and music
- Framing time in the landscape as a pilgrimage
- Silent, meditative walks to ancient sites

Creative Process and Presencing

Figure 2: Scribing fragment from 2017 reflecting dialogue between artists and leaders.

We view leadership in the same way we view painting, acting, or drawing: as a creative act that flows from and is supported by a creative process and disciplined practice. Reframing leadership from a directive and rational task to an imaginative and improvisational practice allows us to work with creativity not explicitly linked to technique, but rather as a capacity for engaging with the world and responding to our surroundings, for embracing encounters with the unknown, and for holding the intensity of and opening to what is wanting to emerge (Beck, 2017; Hirshfield, 2015; Scharmer, 2013; Taylor, 2012).

Creativity, like presencing, cannot be scheduled or controlled and made to play by rules; both need a container (Hayashi, n.d.). Interweaving U with creative process enhances both and strengthens the BELR container, so that artists and leaders can come together in exploration of their work, and also come into contact with the two root questions of presencing: Who is my authentic self? What is the higher purpose of my work? (Scharmer, 2009, 2016).

If the essence of creative process is in the craft practice, rather than the flash of creative insight, the BELR offers participants an embodied experience of a carefully curated set of practices that integrate the mind with heart and body (Jones, 2014; Taylor, 2012).

Hospitable Space

The BELR is designed to be a multi-cultural, multi-generational gathering. Many years four generations gather from four continents. Grounding all of our activity is the metaphor and practice of hosting—in conversation spaces and tangible places at all levels of scale (the Burren, the local community, the circle)—through expression of hospitality, inclusiveness, diversity, and generosity.

Engaging in Dialogue

Each morning artists and leaders sit in circle to invite listening, empathy, shared understanding, and to create bridges that unite whatever has been divided in and between us (Jones, 2014). We let go of usual roles and status and sit as peers learning to become present in a group space, a field of authenticity where we can be liberated from shadows, projections, and other limiting constraints (Beck, 2018; Torbert & Associates, 2004). A section of the visual reflection is shown in Figure 3. We connect with the generative field through our non-linear, self-organizing, emergent dialogue and, on embodied level, experience how complex life really is. Our scribe catches the emotions, new perspectives, and ideas that make their way into our dialogue and change the way we see, feel, and understand. We listen for the moment when our dialogue is complete, and then move on.

Small Group Inquiry

Small group inquiry invites intimacy that allows us to be vulnerable with one another and discover possibilities for generative action (Beck, 2018). We gather in trios to share our intimate leadership questions and dilemmas and to access the wisdom of our peers. We explore the big questions of leadership through Open Space (Owen, 2008), where participants follow their energy and interest to self-organizing conversations.

The Arts: Poetry, Music and Painting

The arts invite us to places in our experience where words cannot go; they create images and metaphors that expand our awareness. Art that is not offered as a performance or entertainment brings our humanity into the room and a willing, undefended meeting with whatever arrives (Hirshfield, 2015).

The retreat faculty includes master artists whose professional lives unfold at the intersection of leadership and artistic practice. Poets call participants to rediscover the poetic imagination in leadership, guiding us toward "questions that have patiently waited, questions that have no right to go away" (Whyte, 2003, p. 4). The poetic spirit clears away the old order to open the space for the regenerative force of life to flow though (Jones, 2014). We draw on the Celtic wisdom traditions that, as Condren (2010) writes:

saw poets as not simply wordsmiths. They played an important role in inaugurating and legitimizing kings, and could overthrow them, should they not live up to their duties, and challenge unjust law. The Celtic understanding was that all things are born in darkness. Facing into the darkness, including the darkness in themselves, poets were uniquely positioned to call a community to integrity to defend the weak, to pronounce judgements on false decisions, and to puncture the pretentiousness of rulers and despots. Three things were required of them: knowledge which illuminates, a cultivation of their own intuitive powers, and making manifest hidden wisdom from within their own bodies or within the collective unconsciousness. (p. 10)

Musicians bring us home to feeling, and to the heart and mystery of life. Their music renders the invisible visible and transports us back and forward in time (Jones, 2014). They embody a finely tuned presencing capacity and speak improvisationally into the present moment, staying in music as a metaphor for leadership: "I've learned about courage, the need for freedom, the need to be spontaneous, and the need to be present, more than anything. I feel there's a wisdom in knowing what is all around you, and playing that" (M. Hayes, personal communication, February 11, 2008).

Excerpts from the Dialogue Between Artists and Leaders, and participant view of the outcome include:

"We are creatures made to live in all three tenses at once, to hold past, present and future together, but in every human life there are those thresholds and those hours that seem to carry within them a very specific invitation."

– David Whyte

"Even when it wasn't making any sense I had to keep listening, and then it came through. If one is open and listening with the heart, and at the same time one is open and giving—if these two moments intersect, it's incredible."

– Martin Hayes

"The poetry and music open you in very powerful ways to new feelings and insights"

– Participant

"A transformative space, a creative place of risk taking where questions emerge, stories are shared, and the power of the arts allows us to move beyond the rational."

– Participant

Studio practice

On the third day of the gathering we invite participants to create a painting while holding an inquiry into the future of leadership. It can initially feel daunting to those who have never engaged in this form of practice. They are confronted with what they perceive to be their own limitations as they make gestures into the unknown. As the question connects them to something, they discover, *"A deep way to get to the real meaning of leadership without masks, and a way to recover our own creativity"* (BELR participant).

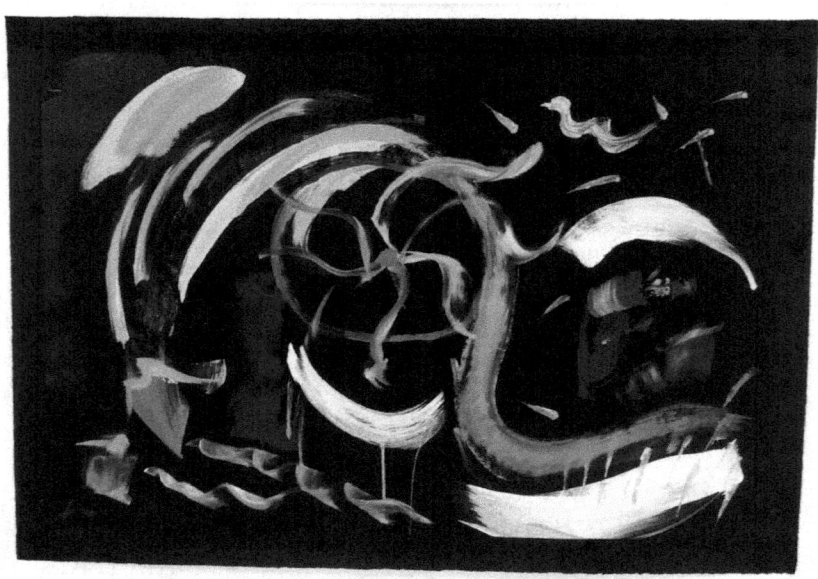

Figure 3: Participant painting from BELR studio practice in 2017.

Generative Facilitation and Scribing

Beginning with our container building work we practice negative capability, which the poet Keats (as cited in Hebron, 2014) first described as "to be capable of being in uncertainties, Mysteries, doubts, without any irritable reaching after fact and reason." More recently, negative capability has been described as "the ability to surrender and engage the unknown and unknowable in ways that support creative emergence" (Omer, 2017) and an essential capability for leading in complexity. By taking this stance, we embody and model an essential capacity for intervening in timely moments and presencing the place where genuine creative energy flows, while allowing the elements in the container the freedom to do their work: combining mysteriously to uniquely support the transformational learning of each participant.

We pay particular attention to the threshold between the visible and the invisible through aesthetic dimensions such as beauty, spaciousness, emergence, and coherence, which Guttenstein, Lindsay & Baron (2013) notes as a key factor in presencing. We hold ourselves in such a way that we can *be* the container, an embodied presence that can create safety, absorb anxiety, provide a sense of continuity, enable authenticity, free up and channel energy, create ritual-transformative space, and support the manifestation of intention (Bushe, 2010). Select examples of participant views of the outcomes of generative facilitation include, *"Readiness to dance, let go of the plan, an incredible gift for listening into the moment, following the thread with intuition, and proposing a move."*

Generative scribing (Bird, 2018) is used as a visual reflection to help participants see their emerging learning through the eyes of the scribe. The graphics are a living memory of our time together; images and metaphors make our system visible to itself and help us create shared meaning. As Bird (2018) writes, this form of scribing is not solely focused on content or outcome but the internal, tonal processes of a group coming together and the scribe's presence: "love, as a base note, is the ore, and order, of the container" (p. 39). In this context the scribe moves between levels – mirroring, differentiating, connecting and surfacing

(Bird, 2018) – often focusing on the third and fourth spaces, to connect with and make visible what is emerging. Participant interaction and responses to the graphics are integral to the scribing process and inform the conversational and shared nature of this art form in the room.

Journeying Through Our U Process

An invitation to participate in the BELR co-initiates and activates the social field, as illustrated in Figure 4, creating a unified focus with its call to *discover your next horizon*. We arrive on Sunday evening, and the unfolding begins as we cross the threshold of a 17th century castle for our opening. We slow down and hold space for creative breakthrough, so that participants can discover *why* they are there, *while* they are there. We encourage them to join us in letting the elements do their work, which is a first act of surrendering to what is wanting to be born.

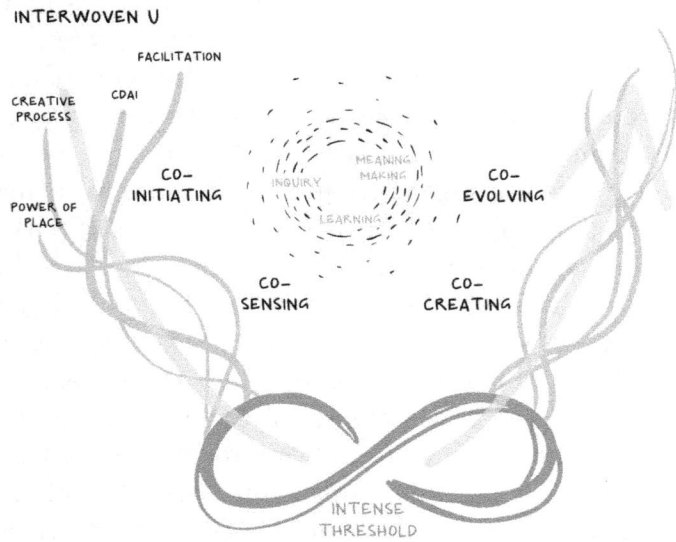

Figure 4. Interwoven U model of the BELR.

We go outside our usual boundaries, co-sensing a larger context in a new way through poetry and music, and during silent pilgrimages to sacred sites in a landscape with the power to blow the heart open (Heaney, 1998). In our daily circle, we share personal experience and listen to what is emerging from the whole including, *"This is a place without an agenda to change you but, at the same time, providing a setting with poetry and music that invite you to consider your relationship with yourself and others as a leader."*

Slowing down, staying in inquiry, our evaluative minds fall away and we come into contact with a subtle power of the collective field. Between Monday afternoon and Wednesday morning, we come to the bottom of the U through a repeating pattern of morning Circle, dialogue between artists and leaders infused with poetry and music, peer inquiry, and time in the landscape. We work in Studio Practice, making gestures into the unknown, and are surprised by what emerges in shape and colour. This facilitates letting go and letting come *in its own time*, and supports our capacity to "stay in this place until the current of the story is strong enough to float you out" (Whyte, 2006, p. 288). In this place, we learn to hang out in the eye of the storm of ambiguity and uncertainty, in (rather than *at*) an Intense Threshold, a multi-contextual, multi-layered space of fecund messiness, with its implicit inquiry: can we be poised here, in the not knowing of a myriad of factors, trusting our intelligence, our imaginative minds, our compassionate natures? This way of being at the bottom of the U contrasts the enthusiasm that that often emerges and leads to a desire to ameliorate the unbearability of being in the unknown. Can we stand that we don't know where our questions will lead us? (Beck, 2017). Staying in this place and allowing the elements to do their work is a creative space that supports deep inquiry into the questions: Who is my self? What is my work?

In a container spacious enough to hold this tension, we spiral again into solace through poetry and music, during times of solitude and meditation, in the intimacy of coaching trios, and circle reflection—all of which evoke cognitive, emotional, and spiritual encounter, and support us in letting go of our habitual ways of being.

We work with the energy that asks us to "pass through the eye of the needle, letting go of everything and offloading baggage that isn't essential" (Scharmer, 2013, p. 22). We surrender to what is wanting to come in its own time, cultivating a deep and wide state of awareness (Torbert, 2004), presencing what Scharmer calls "the moment when we reach a point of melt-down, and we have a choice: we can freeze and revert to our deeply ingrained habits of the past, or we can stop and lean into the space of the unknown, into that which wants to emerge" (Scharmer, 2013, p. 29). By honoring that the elements will combine Mysteriously to meet each participant in the Intense Threshold, we experience a U process that does not insist on prototyping before the time is ripe, and which acknowledges that we need to allow space for intention to crystallize in its own time, as "the process of connecting to our Self, to our highest future possibility, and moving toward action can be a sequence we go through in an instant or over a period of many years" (Scharmer, 2013, p. 30). In this bountiful place we experience an opening of mind, heart, and will, and surrender to what is wanting to emerge. Leaving familiar ground behind, we open to the essence of who we are and our work as part of the whole. At the bottom of our U process, participants sense that, *"We all have a variety of fears and creativity"* and that, *"It is a deep way to meet life and its conversation."*

Participants leave the retreat with refreshed intention and expanded capacity to embody the new in the ecosystem, to see and act from the whole—and to co-evolve in an invisible web of collaboration with peers who also place leadership at the center of their lives, even when they may not be in direct contact with one another when they return to their day to day lives, *"I carry with me two very strong images: the call for leaders to be pilgrims and the call to embody leadership so that it really flows."*

Conclusion

There is a huge force field that opens when intention focuses and directs itself toward transformation. – John O'Donohue, *To Bless The Space Between Us*, 2007

We have seen the BELR become a powerfully transformative experience and an enduring support to leaders in their global systems change work because of the planned and emergent interweaving of U with other processes and practices which, over the four-day retreat, liberates them from limiting constraints so that they leave the retreat in a state of potentiality, poised to bring the fullest expression of their leadership back to their places of influence.

The journey of each participant up to, during, and beyond the gathering is both an individual and a shared one. Our view is that as participants continue to encounter ambiguity, uncertainty, and daunting choices, they will benefit from having reclaimed their centre of gravity and re-framed the intention they hold for leading into the future that is in need of them. To return to their sphere of influence held in a peer web of belonging and invisible collaboration will sustain their capacity to be present to what is the emerging. Having discovered their next horizon, their task becomes to perceive future horizons from where they stand (Omer, 2017). The direction each leader needs to face, and the step to take, will be unique to context, place, purpose, and work in the world.

As facilitators and designers, we hold a profound trust in the existing experience and capacity of participants, in what each person brings, in being and doing, to the collective – and in what will unfold after we all leave the BELR for another year. The paths to be walked are many. We carry the multiple connections interwoven during our time together in the Burren, into an emerging future.

We hope that the chapter has offered practitioners a valuable glimpse inside the BELR container, and the ways in which we interweave the U process with CDAI, the Power of Place, Creative Process, and Generative Facilitation to support leaders in coming into closer relationship with their authentic work and to expand their capacity to presence the future that is in need of the leadership they can bring.

We would like to acknowledge our partners in global systems change and Retreat co-founders at the Burren College of Art.

References

Bateson, N. (2017). *Liminal leadership*. Retrieved from https://www.kosmosjournal.org/article/liminal-leadership/

Beck, R. (2017). Circling and presencing videoconference [video file]. Retrieved from https://www.thewespacesummit.com/circling-presencing/

Bird, K. (2018). *Generative scribing*. Cambridge, MA: PI Press.

Blanton, S. (2014). Thin Places and the transforming presence of beauty. Retrieved from https://onbeing.org/blog/thin-places-and-the-transforming-presence-of-beauty/

Bushe, G. R. (2010). Being the container in Dialogic OD. *Practicing Social Change, 2*. Retrieved from http://www.gervasebushe.ca/container.pdf

Condren, M. (2010). *Brigid, matron of poetry, healing, smithwork, and mercy: Female divinity in a European wisdom tradition.* Journal of the European Society of Women in Theological Research,*18*, 5-30.

Corrigan, C. (2015). Hosting and holding containers. In G. R. Bushe & R. J. Marshak (Eds.), *Dialogic organization development: The theory and practice of transformational change* (291-304). San Francisco: Berrett-Koehler.

Cranton, P. (1994). *Transformative learning*. San Francisco: Jossey-Bass.

Gomes, P. J. (1996). *Reading the Bible with the mind and heart*. San Francisco: HarperCollins.

Gunnlaugson, O., Baron, C., & Cayer, M. (Eds). (2013) *Perspectives on Theory U: Insights from the field*. Philadelphia: Business Science Reference.

Guttenstein, S., Lindsay, K. & Baron, C. (2013). Aligning with the Emergent Future. In O. Gunnlaugson, C. Baron, & M. Cayer (Eds.), *Perspectives on Theory U: Insights from the field* (161-180). Philadelphia: Business Science Reference.

Hare, S. Z., & LeBoutillier, M. (2017). *Thin places: Seeking courage to live in a divided world*. Pawleys Island, SC: Prose Press.

Hawes, M. (2108). Retrieved from www.burrenleadership.org.

Hayashi, A. (n.d.). *Feminine principle and Theory U: Character based leadership*. Retrieved from http://www.oxfordleadership.com/wp-content/uploads/2016/08/oxford-leadership-article-femine-principle-and-theroy-u.pdf

Hebron, S. (2014). John Keats and 'negative capability'. Retrieved from https://www.bl.uk/romantics-and-victorians/articles/john-keats-and-negative-capability

Heaney, S. (1998). *Postscript*. Retrieved from https://www.poets.org/poet-sorg/poem/postscript-0

Hirshfield, J. (2015). *Ten windows: How great poems transform the world*. New York: Alfred A. Knopf.

Hougaard, R. (2016). *One second ahead: Enhance your performance at work with mindfulness*. New York: Palgrave-Macmillan.

Joiner, W., & Josephs, S. (2007). *Leadership agility: Five levels of mastery for anticipating and initiating Change*. San Francisco: Jossey Bass.

Jones, M. (2006). *Artful leadership: Awakening the commons of the imagination*. Orillia: Pianoscapes.

Jones, M. (2014). *The soul of place: Re-imagining leadership through nature, art and community*. Vancouver: FriesenPress.

Kegan, R. (1982). *The evolving self: Problem and process in human development*. Cambridge, MA: Harvard University Press.

Kegan, R. (1994). *In over our heads: The mental demands of modern life*. Cambridge, MA: Harvard University Press.

Leitch, J., Rooke, D., & Wilson, R (2015). *The hidden talent: Ten ways to identify and retain transformational leaders*. Retrieved from http://harth-ill.co.uk/harthill-resources/articles-and-papers/

Livesay, V. (2015). One step back, two steps forward: Fallback in human and leadership development. *Journal of Leadership, Accountability, and Ethics*, *12*(4), 173-189.

Machado, A. (2003). *There is no road*. Buffalo, NY: White Pine Press.

Mezirow, J. (1981). A critical theory of adult learning in education. *Adult Education*, *32*(1), 3-24.

Mezirow, J. (2000). *Learning as Transformation: Critical perspectives on a theory in progress*. San Francisco: Jossey-Bass.

Nicolaides, A., & McCallum, D. (2013). Accessing the blind spot: The U process as seen through the lens of developmental action inquiry. In O. Gunnlaugson, C. Baron, & M. Cayer (Eds.), *Perspectives on Theory U: Insights from the field* (48-60). Philadelphia: Business Science Reference.

National Intelligence Council. (2017, January). *Global trends: Paradox of progress*. Retrieved from https://www.dni.gov/files/documents/nic/GT-Full-Report.pdf

Omer, A. (2017, July 18). Imagination, emergence, and the role of transformative learning in complexity leadership. Retrieved from http://www.enliveningedge.org/features/imagination-emergence-role-transformative-learning-complexity-leadership/

Owen, H. (2008). *Open Space technology: A user's guide*. San Francisco:

Berrett-Koehler.

Rooke, D., & Torbert, W. R. (2005, April). Seven transformations of leadership. *Harvard Business Review*. Retrieved from https://hbr.org/2005/04/seven-transformations-of-leadership

Rushdie, S. (2013, April 27). Whither moral courage? *New York Times*. Retrieved from https://www.nytimes.com/2013/04/28/opinion/sunday/whither-moral-courage.html

Scharmer, C.O. (2009). *Theory U: Leading from the future as it emerges.* San Francisco: Berrett-Koehler Publishers.

Scharmer, C. O. (2013) Presencing Theory U: An interview with Otto Scharmer. In O. Gunnlaugson, C. Baron, & M. Cayer (Eds.), *Perspectives on Theory U: Insights from the field* (244-250). Philadelphia: Business Science Reference.

Scharmer, C. O. (2016). *Theory U: Leading from the future as it emerges* (2nd ed.). San Francisco: Berrett-Koehler.

Schein, E. (2013). *Humble inquiry: The gentle art of asking rather than telling.* San Francisco: Berrett-Koehler.

Stacey, M. (1998). *Constructivist learning environments for developing leadership capacity.* Unpublished master's thesis, Royal Roads University School of Leadership, Victoria, B.C.

Stacey, M. (2011). *Growing bigger minds: Action inquiry as a transformational leadership practice.* Retrieved from http://www.contextconsulting.com/wp-content/uploads/2015/03/GROWING-BIGGER-MINDS_F.pdf

Starr, A., & Torbert, W. R. (2005). Timely and transforming leadership inquiry and action: Toward triple-loop awareness. *Integral Review, 1*, 85-97.

Taylor, S. (2012). *Leadership craft, leadership art: Insights into the theory and practice of leadership development.* New York: Palgrave MacMillan.

Torbert, W. R. (1978). Educating toward shared purpose, self-direction and quality work: The theory and practice of liberating structure. *The Journal of Higher Education, 49*(2), 109.

Torbert, W. R. (2013). Listening into the dark: An essay testing the validity and efficacy of collaborative developmental action inquiry for describing and encouraging transformations of self, society, and scientific inquiry. *Integral Review, 9*(2), 264-299.

Torbert, W. R. (2017). The pragmatic impact on leaders and organizations of interventions based in the collaborative developmental action inquiry approach. *Integral Leadership Review, August-November*. Retrieved from http://integralleadershippreview.

com/15836-collaborative-developmental-action-inquiry/

Torbert, W. R., & Associates (2004). *Action inquiry: The secret of timely and transforming leadership.* Berrett-Koehler Publishers: San Francisco.

Torbert, W. R., Livne-Tarandach, R., McCallum, D., Nicolaides, A., & Herdman-Barker, E. (2010). Developmental action inquiry: A distinct integral theory that actually integrates developmental theory, practice, and research. In S. Esbjörn-Hargens (Ed.), *Integral theory in action: Applied, theoretical, and constructive perspectives on the AQAL model.* Albany: State University of New York Press.

Weiner, E. (2012, March 9). Where heaven and earth come closer. *New York Times.* https://www.nytimes.com/2012/03/11/travel/thin-places-where-we-are-jolted-out-of-old-ways-of-seeing-the-world.html

Whyte, D. (2003). *Everything is waiting for you.* Langley, Washington: Many Rivers Press.

Whyte, D. (2006). *River Flow: New and selected poems, 1984-2007.* Langley, Washington: Many Rivers Press.

Wickremasinghe, N. (2018). *Beyond threat.* Axminster, England: Triarchy Press.

Yeyinmen, K.C., & Stacey, M. (2018). *Team coaching at scale: Creating the conditions for the emergence of adaptive leadership cultures.* Manuscript submitted for publication.

CHAPTER 7

Leading System Transformation from the Emerging Future

Michael Schratz & Wilfried Schley

Introduction

Nowadays, schools and educational leaders are often confronted with disruptive processes caused by incoherent policy measures and government requirements, which pass on the pressures to perform in the "tyranny of conformity" (Prochaska, 2012) to counteract such pressures. *Presencing* can help educational leaders gain more ownership in dealing with the needs and expectations of their work context. We are demonstrating how Scharmer's (2007) "Theory U" can support system transformation in moving a highly bureaucratic, strongly regulated education system towards more mutual understanding and professionalization of leadership and learning by prioritizing a nation-wide leadership network. The chapter tells the story of a nation-wide transformation process initiated and supported by a Minister of Education who was interested in transforming the school system from an Ego-System towards an Eco-System. The authors show how they, as system change facilitators, have used Scharmer's "Theory U" as a viable social technology for whole system change in order to counteract the flaws of traditional implementation strategies in educational reform.

The chapter begins with the story of how the former Austrian Minister of Education, Claudia Schmied, first invited Otto Scharmer to reflect with her senior staff on key issues of the education system with a view towards whole system change. Next, it outlines the nation-wide dialogue in the nine provinces that connected key innovators from all levels of the education system. In her nation-wide dialogues, the minister inspired and opened the minds of the audience to new perspectives, and gave a clear view of her vision for the future of the Austrian schools. The third part of this chapter will present the needs and expectations of a nation-wide approach that engages educational leaders from all types of schools and all levels of the system during their year-long participation with the whole system in mind. Through these three sections, which include the personal accounts of two educational leaders, the authors explore the change process through the lens of Theory U as a way to validate, contribute to and challenge our understanding of Presencing.

Seeing the System: Suspending Dysfunctional Political Discourse

One of the first times I (Otto) met the Austrian minister of education and culture, Claudia Schmied, and her ministry team, was during a half-day workshop. We were sitting at a long rectangular table. The minister and her dynamic young assistants sat opposite me at the head of the table. Next to them, on one long side, were all her department heads, people who had spent most of their careers inside the ministry; across from them, on the other long side, was a group of school innovators from Germany and Austria. As I looked at the school innovators and the department heads facing each other, it felt as if the twenty-first century were meeting the nineteenth, with the minister and her team in between. The minister was full of energy and inspiration. She came to her job from a business and organizational change background – not a typical party career. (Scharmer & Kaufer, 2013, p. 210)

This was the starting point for an exciting journey with the minister who had requested that one of the authors (Michael Schratz) brings Otto Scharmer to this meeting at the ministry, where he would ask everybody to reflect on three aspects of the educational system: the changing learner-teacher relationship, the school as a learning organization and the countrywide system as a whole.

> It took the local innovators only an hour or two to establish that they all agreed on 80 or 90 percent of the changes the system needed, but none of these changes were reflected in the political discourse in the country. There was a complete disconnect between the education innovators at the school level and the national political discourse. (Scharmer & Kaufer, 2013, p. 210)

What was the reason for this disconnect? By tradition, Austria's education system has been highly bureaucratic, strongly regulated in details, hierarchically organized and scant in its focus on output. There are too many actors, numerous parallel structures and there is too little congruence in task-orientation and assumptions of responsibility. The system is characterized by a strong influence of social partnership structures, partisan politics, the (teacher) union and the teacher representatives, whereas parents, students, researchers and other less formally organized actors have relatively little voice (Schmid, Hafner, & Pirolt, 2007). As this policy context makes it very difficult to introduce coherent approaches to developing the school system, the minister's mission was to use Theory U to counteract the conventional managerial models which build on command and control and try to implement reform policies by means of prescriptive strategies rather than by capacity building.

This was a challenging starting point for a minister who comes from an organizational change background and is full of energy and inspiration. She was interested in moving the school system from an Ego-System towards Eco-System transformation. Since the Austrian school system still has many System 1.0 elements, including a culture of centralized regulation and control, the authorities were supposed to fix the problems with elements of System 2.0, and already developed elements of System 3.0. The minister's goal was to use *Theory U* and *Presencing* to realize the qualities and mental models of System 4.0. It was evident by her reflections:

> If we succeed, all school partners will focus on creating a successful school; teachers will see themselves as 'Zubin Metas', as conductors and orchestrators of the highest creativity in their students; students will experience co-shaping the system. The foundation of System 4.0 is the common will. This means moving the relational dimension to center stage. This is what matters most. It's about what our schools of the future will be able to perform in order to serve the individual and communal well-being. (Scharmer & Kaufer, 2013, p. 212)

To initiate system-wide change toward System 4.0, new reform initiatives have to counteract the flaws of traditional implementation strategies in school reform. Scharmer's *Theory U* (2007) as a field theory has proved a viable social technology to develop an approach for whole system change. His layered model (figure 1) builds on four critical fields referring to thinking (micro), languaging (meso), institutionalizing (macro) and global governing (mundo), which can reach four layers of depth of experience with "Presencing" at the bottom of a U-shaped process (Theory U). For Scharmer, through presencing the future emerges.

Moving from Field 1 to Field 2 requires *opening up* to the data of the exterior world and *suspending* ingrained and habitual (and often dysfunctional) patterns of action and thought (*open mind*). Moving from Field 2 to Field 3 entails taking *a deep dive* into relevant contexts and *redirecting* one's attention such that perception begins to "happen from the field" (*open heart*). Moving from Field 3 to Field 4 requires *letting go* of old identities and intentions and *letting come* new identities and intentions that are more directly connected with one's deepest sources of individual and collective action and energy (*open will*). (Scharmer, 2007, p. 241)

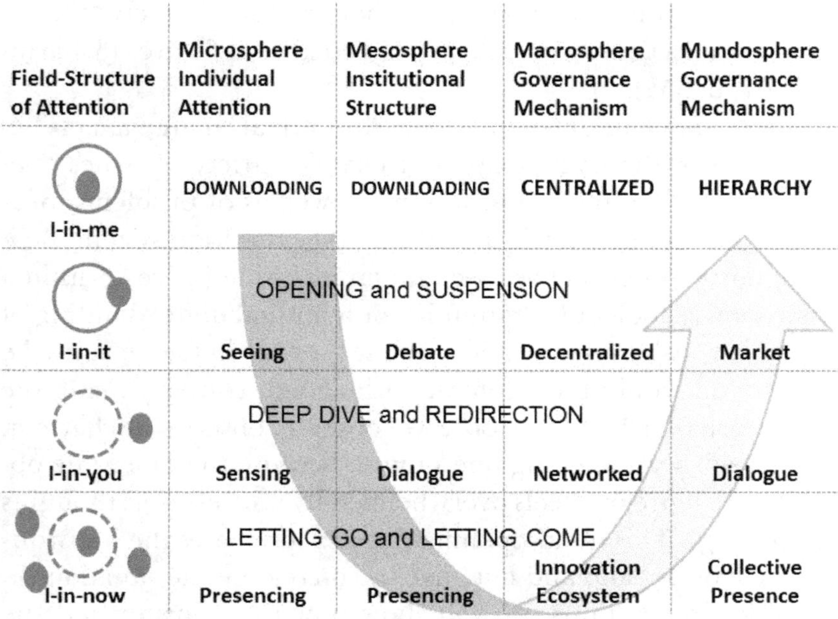

Field-Structure of Attention	Microsphere Individual Attention	Mesosphere Institutional Structure	Macrosphere Governance Mechanism	Mundosphere Governance Mechanism
I-in-me	DOWNLOADING	DOWNLOADING	CENTRALIZED	HIERARCHY
I-in-it	OPENING and SUSPENSION			
	Seeing	Debate	Decentralized	Market
I-in-you	DEEP DIVE and REDIRECTION			
	Sensing	Dialogue	Networked	Dialogue
I-in-now	LETTING GO and LETTING COME			
	Presencing	Presencing	Innovation Ecosystem	Collective Presence

Figure 1: Layers of the social field (Scharmer, 2007, p. 241)

For Scharmer, the greater a system's hyper-complexity, the more critical it is to build the capacity to operate from the deeper fields of social emergence. As he states, educational systems and institutions

> face three types of complexities: *dynamic complexity* defined by cause and effect being distant in space and time; *social complexity* defined by conflicting interests, cultures, and world-views among diverse stakeholders; and *emerging complexity* defined by disruptive patterns of innovation and change in situations in which the future cannot be predicted and is addressed by the patterns of the past (Scharmer, 2007, p. 352).

Taking these complexities into consideration, the minister was looking for a systems approach which would allow different stakeholders to see and act from the emerging whole and link it with leadership as a leveraging factor. Such a holistic perspective has been missing in the Austrian school culture, namely "the capacity to collectively sense, shape, and create our future" (Scharmer, 2007, p. 352).

Professional understanding of educational change means being aware of the complexity and chaotic variety of issues, elements, aspects, dimensions, factors, as well as of problems, programs and intentions, which make up the education system. Be it a diagnostic process of assessment, an inclusion process within a classroom, school and community, or a mutual understanding of challenges, achievement and qualities, every initiative must be understood within their complex whole and context. Using the framework of Theory U, "observe, observe, observe" (Scharmer, 2007) helps with opening one's mind, because the more one observes, the more one feels overwhelmed by impressions, thoughts and feelings. This mind-opening process stimulates the individual to take ownership and initiative by co-creating the situation. In the following sections, we will show how the minister and the authors have used Theory U working with various actors from the Austrian educational context towards system-wide change.

Sensing the Field: in Dialogue with the Minister

As a starting point of a system-wide change process, the minister wanted to connect innovative people from different system levels and different domains with a view to opening up perspectives and generating a flow of creativity among "system thinkers in action" (Fullan, 2005). To do so, she invited various stakeholders throughout the country to take part in a dialogue connecting the vertical (hierarchy) and horizontal (networks) forces of the system. All in all, 2,200 people from all over Austria were invited and, within three days, more than 1,100 agreed to take part. On this basis, network meetings were planned in each of the nine provinces to stage an open dialogue that would connect the hierarchy (ministry) with the innovators scattered all over the system. In creating these networks, the minister wanted to create a "culture space" for valuing differences and opening thinking, which:

- Strives to remove barriers to allow for the expression of individual differences without getting locked into habitual patterns or unexamined assumptions.
- Anticipates that change is inevitable and shows considerable elasticity without always "jumping on bandwagons".
- Acknowledges the role the external conditions play in making change easy or difficult for people.
- Is usually displayed in good listening skills, a non-judgmental approach to life, tolerance of differences and a lack of closed-mindedness. (Beck & Cowan, 2003, p. 78)

The social architecture of the nine meetings through the provinces entitled "In Dialogue with the Minister" (one day each) built on the following components: 1) The minister would begin with a short dialogue to inspire the audience and open minds for new perspectives and give the innovative practitioners a clear view of her vision for the future of the Austrian schools. 2) As her ministry also comprises culture and the arts, a short video clip on excellence in symphony music featuring a world-famous Austrian conductor, Nikolaus Harnoncourt, was shown to create a deeper "understanding of the primary field conditions that structure these patterns of emergence" (Scharmer, 2007, p. 293). 3) By comparing and contrasting professionalism in different segments of society, the participants in the dialogue events were then invited to discover and discuss what the stages from "open mind" to "open heart" to "open will" could mean to them. 4) Student performances from the fields of theater and music complemented the power of a cultural approach to education.

Fundamental to the event program was storytelling. Three leaders of educational initiatives which had had an impact on student learning were asked to tell stories of their adventures in changing mindsets, attitudes, interactions and systems, all directed at open and personalized learning, participation and activity, innovation and creativity. The meeting organizers highlighted the concept of the "positive change core," which was embedded in each innovator's story from "Appreciative Inquiry":

Co-operative search for the best in people, their organizations, and the world around them. It involves systematic
discovery of what gives a system 'life', when it is most effective and capable in economic, ecological and human terms
(Cooperrider & Whitney, 1999, p. 10).

Appreciative Inquiry was also used to structure the afternoon
by involving "the art and practice of asking questions that
strengthen a system's capacity to heighten positive potential"
(Cooperrider & Whitney, 1999, p. 10). The meeting used its key
design principles to create a rich context and a hospitable space,
explore questions that matter, encourage contributions from all
participants, connect diverse perspectives, listen together for patterns and insights and share collective discoveries. In the meeting, innovators were asked to mix with other innovators and ask
each other about their success stories in an endeavor to change
attitudes and mindsets so as to bring about change. By listening
to each other's stories, they began to "pay increasing attention to
what is coming in through the 'back door' of one's mind. It is at
this stage, that groups begin to function as an instrument for an
emerging future" (Scharmer, 2007, p. 293). By deepening their
mutual understanding, they started "crystallizing" core themes,
patterns and puzzles, a process that Scharmer characterizes as the
shift from network to ecosystem (figure 1).
    Of course, this shift was not visible as an immediate result,
however people who had participated in one of the events reported "It felt different" when the minister invited participants to
build their future work on trust. While preparing the dialogue
tour, she referred to her personal objectives:

- building trust
- conveying appreciation
- sensing reality
- awakening emotions
- strengthening agency
- reassuring courage

The minister emphasized that we should all hold the space to "observe, observe, observe" to allow enough time for mutual understanding. The intensive exchanges among the professionals led to a high level of energy, created an open space with a shared mindset and mutual understanding of how they could shape the future of learning and create inspiring schools for the next generation to be educated in.

Whenever the minister entered one of the auditoriums, one could sense an open atmosphere right from the beginning, which felt somehow different from conventional gatherings. She introduced herself by telling and sharing her latest dialogues with students at innovative schools or from having a breakfast session with heads of the regional school board reflecting on collaboration. Building on Scharmer's work, the minister had prepared the following four questions which she asked everybody to answer for themselves first and then share amongst each other:

1. What inspires you in your professional life?
2. What are the hard truths and conflicts that you have to face?
3. What is ending? What is dying? What wants to come into the world?
4. What is the essence? What is the core?

In that moment she was part of the community. By expressing her challenging experiences in politics and decision-making situations she became part of the community. Referring to the professionals in the room, she shared the stories of how she made change happen in certain situations that made a difference and were meaningful. Openly, she expressed her understanding of the larger paradigm shifts that are needed in education. By sharing her ambitions for the system, it became clear why she was gaining support by educators throughout the country. Then the minister took a seat at the round tables like all the other innovators and listened to the participants' success stories and their initiatives, before she asked inspiring questions herself. In sharing her impressions, her empathy and identification with teachers, school members, principals and regional heads impressed almost everybody, and thus she was able to suspend her hierarchical and official function. She established a natural atmosphere of interest and sharing of thoughts, insights and resonances.

The process of capacity building with more than 1,000 educational innovators throughout the country met the needs and desires of many people in networks and regional institutions. Also the minister herself experienced a learning curve with regard to issues, innovative ideas and a shared sense of purpose and principles. She showed her awareness by seeing, sensing and reflecting along with the audience. Her impressions were emotional and inspiring. Being so close to the members of the networks shifted the level of trust and created mutual understanding. The specific constellation of diverse players collectively formed what Scharmer (2007) would call "a vehicle for seeing current possibilities and sensing emerging opportunities" (p. 293). In each of the nine events, depending on the location, between 80 and 200 members met at 10 to 25 round tables to discuss the minister's questions and moved around in flexible arrangements.

The moments in Vienna and the capital cities of the other provinces allowed for the deepening and broadening of impact across regions and their respective school systems. Leaders, educators and policy makers need spaces that allow them to both share their valuable insights with other educators and find new inspiration and support in creating the necessary learning environments. Through storytelling and sharing personal accounts, members of various networks along with rectors of the university colleges of education, political heads of regional administration and specialists started shifting from debate to dialogue in a dynamic interaction practicing the movements between the layers of the social field. When some teachers asked the minister to acknowledge their presence at the event by noting her initials in their official in-service report books, the minister started a discussion about the culture of trust: "Is it a matter of presence or presencing?" For the first time the participants experienced a generative flow in a mutual space of trust. One teacher felt so empowered that she reported after the event "I actually wanted to quit my teaching job, but this dialogue has motivated me to continue with new impetus." We count remarks like that as indicators of a deeper understanding of professional awareness. For her, like others, it was a first step from transactional to transformational communication.

What is dying? What is emerging?

What was mentioned most often answering the question "What is coming to an end? What is dying?" were eclectic government interventions, disconnected policies, hierarchical decision-making causing confusion between the different levels within the school system (regional, district, local levels). This in turn has led to de-energizing and fragmentation that create leadership dilemmas and pull school managers in different directions between *sollen* (duty) and *wollen* (desire) (Schratz, 2003, pp. 409-410). Despite a shift towards more school-based innovation and more decentralization and deregulation in Austria (Schratz & Hartmann, 2009), local school governance and leadership are primarily characterized by a flat hierarchical structure whereby school heads are confronted with restricted autonomy (finance, curriculum, personnel) that makes it difficult for them to empower their faculty for collective action.

Nationally, school leaders are an important link in the synchronization of top-down and bottom-up processes (Fullan, 2005) and are the key actors in promoting quality processes in schools (Firestone & Riehl, 2005; Hall & Hord, 1987). Pont, Nusche and Moorman (2008) also refer to the decisive role of school leadership in school reform: "It bridges educational policy and practice" (p. 19). If central reform initiatives are to be coherently integrated into the life of schools and classrooms (Stoll, Bolam, & Collarbone, 2002), a new approach to capacity building for professional school leadership has to be developed as a prerequisite to system-wide change.

To support system-wide change, the authors had been commissioned by a previous minister of education to develop a national leadership initiative to counteract the flaws of conventional implementation strategies in school reform, such as the introduction of a testing culture, a new segregating structure of secondary education, and a centralized school leaving exam. In order to learn from previous reform initiatives in Austria and the research findings on innovation and change, the need for a new approach was framed around the following questions:

- How can the complex decision-making structure be disentangled and the different demands of central and federal interests be brought into balance?
- How is it possible to coordinate communication and actions both of policy and practice among the different levels of the system?
- How can a learning context be created which aims at influencing the pattern of how professionals go about changing their organizations?
- How can the system be energized by more individual and organizational empowerment?
- How can leadership be more closely connected with learning by creating better conditions for student achievement?
- How can professional development create system-wide culture change and be linked with the improvement capacity of the actors on the different horizontal and vertical levels?

In addressing these questions, we looked for a model that allows enough flexibility for forms of learning on both the individual and system levels. Consequently, the Austrian Leadership Academy (LEA) was established and is organized as a network organization. Its networking character aims at creating a new mentality of leadership, which relies on trust and authenticity rather than on power through position. Its ultimate goal lies in sustainably improving the preconditions and processes of young people's learning in all educational institutions. Networking serves the capacity building, professionalisation and empowerment of leaders in the Austrian educational system. Leaders are motivated to strategically target complex development tasks through priority setting, focusing on solutions, developing individual projects and creating organization profiles. In collaboration, the participants learn to translate challenges into innovative development processes and entice and empower staff in their work environment to achieve top performances. Networking requires a new understanding of theory and practice, one that transforms the educational system by taking the quality of leadership as the starting point for systemic innovation.

Opening Mind, Heart, Will, Future: A Systems Approach to Educational Reform

Systemic innovation succeeds best when it includes as many people as possible and engages them fully in the change process (Holman, Devane, & Cady, 2008). Considering these findings, the Austrian Leadership Academy is organized in cohorts of up to 250 participants from across the whole education system. Its goal is to make use of the manifold expertise of educational leaders enabling them to identify with and the overall goal of systemic innovation and become agents of reform.

Each *cohort* is composed of participants from all provinces and school types as well as the ministry, regional education authorities (including the inspectorate) and teacher education institutions. This ensures right from the outset that a systemic impact on change and transformation is possible and that the "whole system" is involved in a joint learning process. The role of the LEA is in congruence with the principles of a learning organization and cooperates closely with responsible decision makers in the ministry. Moreover, the joint efforts of the large number of representatives from different sectors of the education system generate the productive energy necessary for an inspiring and inclusive vision as a basis for profound change (Bruch & Vogel, 2005). As a part-time program, the LEA consists of four forums that take place over one year, in which all participants within a cohort meet for three days each (figure 2).

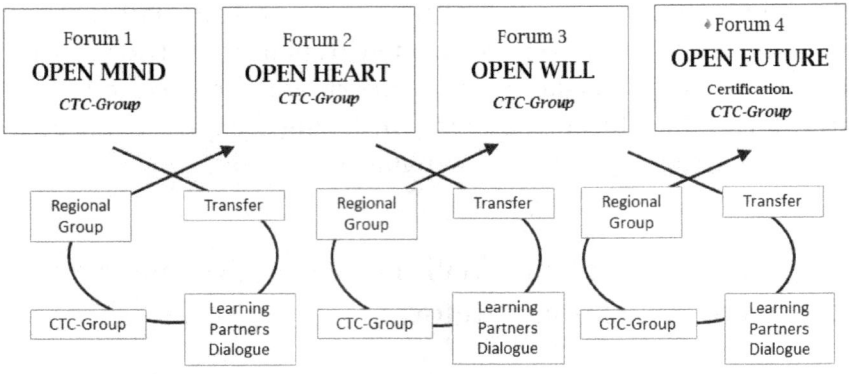

Figure 2: Phases of a cohort's one year journey through the Austrian Leadership Academy

The forums are built along Scharmer's (2007) phases and move through the different levels of the social field (figure 1). *Forum 1*, titled "Open Mind", helps the participants to open and suspend judgement by stopping the process of downloading the patterns of past practices. Its goal is to open participants to a new way of looking at their daily routines and educational practices in their work context. The kick-off takes place in the *first forum*, which is designed to orient participants on the philosophy, organization, structure and underlying processes of the LEA. They are introduced to setting their own goals and choosing their personal professional projects, which lie at the heart of their individual professional development. The creation of trust in the network takes center stage, as well as the forming of *learning partnerships* and *collegial team coaching groups* (*CTCs*) (Schley & Schley, 2010) and the elaboration of possible innovation themes. In the LEA, the social technology of CTC is used to practice system thinking in action. Each CTC team consists of a heterogeneous mix of groups of six participants who work within a strict structure. This fosters a culture of trustworthy support, which is essential in the process of Presencing. In each collegial team coaching session, one participant represents the "actor" and is guided and encouraged by the team to move towards "letting go". The collaboration in the CTC helps to utilize a team's intellectual, creative and emotional potential in the phase of "seeing the seeing" and "seeing from the whole" (Scharmer, 2007). CTC is used for each participant in every forum and back home between the forums as a continuous learning and development process *of* colleagues *by* colleagues. It is practiced so that it becomes an integral part of an organization's culture and a significant strategy for building a learning organization which respects, and reflects, the complexity of the work, especially its leadership and management.

Between forums the learning partners meet regionally or locally. They reflect on the reactions of their stakeholder groups in their schools, education authorities and inspectoral systems or teacher education institutions with reference to their individual development projects. These processes develop through cycles of anticipation, action and reflection. The principle of ownership and responsibility is combined with a goal and result, which demands respect, openness and flexibility from everybody involved. When the educational leaders return to *forum 2* with the title "Open Heart", they are expected to bring back new experiences seen with "fresh eyes" (Scharmer, 2007, p. 40). This "seeing with fresh eyes" should help them to achieve a deeper, more resonating and less judgmental understanding of their realities so that they become aware of the blind spots, and the system begins to see itself (Scharmer, 2007, p. 39). In the *second forum* the individual development projects of the participants are defined, developed and outlined, using project management methods and tools. In this phase, the CTCs offer space for collaborative reflection on individual development processes with a view to challenge established patterns of thinking and time worn "solutions".

In *forum 3*, which is dedicated to Scharmer's "Open Will", participants reach the phase of Presencing by "connecting to the deepest source, from which the field of the future begins to arise" (2007, p. 39). In their development projects the educational leaders are expected to become aware of new ways of identifying and working toward an emerging future. This usually happens when they reflect on their mutual experiences in their educational settings when they realize that their previous interventions do not work anymore. This is the creative space where skepticism, resistance, conflicts and tensions come to the fore just as much as agreement, motivation and enthusiasm. Different workshops on communication, motivation, conflict resolution and decision-making are offered as a support for individual learning and capacity building. Art workshops, dance or survival camp techniques support the holistic learning approach.

Forum 4 is called "Open Future", the final meeting, which is dedicated to mutual feedback on their work celebrating new achievements. It is also *certification forum,* where participants present their professional learning processes and their results – first in the privacy of their CTCs before deciding collaboratively on one project of their CTC to be presented to the others in a final phase of parallel sessions. For successful certification each participant of the LEA has to submit a portfolio on their individual personal and professional development process for review.

Presencing: Making Educational Leaders Agents of Reform

School systems are usually organized along the hierarchical structure of the political system with the Ministry on top and the schools at the bottom. As school reform does not work along "detailed deliverology" (Hargreaves & Shirley, 2009, p. 110) the LEA invites educational leaders from all levels of the hierarchy (schools, local administration, inspectorate, ministry, teacher education institutions) and takes them into a stimulating setting outside the (hierarchical) system (see figure 3). Specifically, the LEA has its venue at the renowned campus of the Alpbach Conference Centre, where politicians and decision-makers from all over Europe discuss and brainstorm new ideas and solutions to the world problems. Locating the LEA there highlights the importance given to educational leaders and their transformation of the educational system.

For Hargreaves and Shirley (2009) the hardest part of educational change is not to start it, but how to make it last and spread, which calls for coherence in the nature of activities, which bridge policy and practice.

> The challenge of coherence is not to clone or align everything so it looks the same in all schools ... The challenge, rather, is how to bring diverse people together to work skillfully and effectively for a common cause that lifts them up and has them moving in the same direction with an impact on learning, achievement, and results (Hargreaves & Shirley, 2009, pp. 94-95).

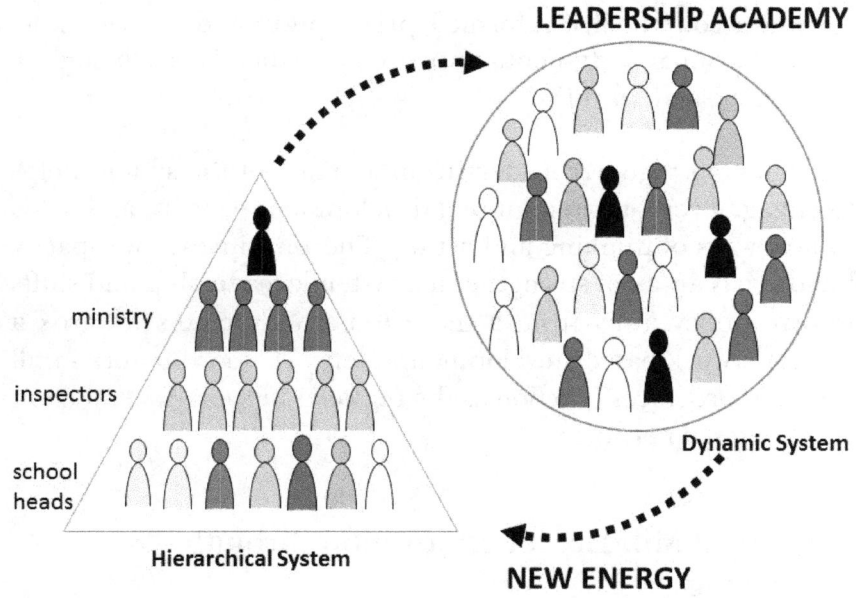

Figure 3: Connect horizontal and vertical system levels

They suggest the following four catalysts that create this coherence: sustainable leadership, integrating networks, responsibility before accountability as well as differentiation and diversity. The bringing together of key actors from all levels in the system in the LEA is an attempt to pay attention to these four catalysts with a view to greater coherence in systems development. Through the dynamic work arrangements in various settings (large groups, small groups, coaching groups, critical friendship, regional networks), new energy for change processes is created, which can then be taken back into their traditional work places, helping to contribute to overall system coherence.

With regard to making educational leaders agents of reform, the LEA is organized as a network organization and is not built as a physical environment in order to avoid dysfunctional routines. As Fullan (2005) argues,

> We need a radically new mind-set for reconciling the seemingly intractable dilemmas fundamental for sustainable reform: top-down versus bottom-up, local and central accountability, informed prescription and informed professional judgment, improvement that keeps being replenished (p. 11).

Bringing together leaders from all parts of the system helps to engage everyone in a mutual development process, and leads to new ways of thinking and acting. The LEA invests in capacity building as a way of strengthening systemic leadership and shifts reform policy away from a mere top-down process towards a more network-based development. Network coordinators in all Austrian provinces function as the regional support system to ensure regional networking.

Creating a Mindset for Innovation through Presencing

In many ways, knowledge and excellence based on experiences have lost their validity as a portent for future success. What we learned about management and processes and what has worked for us up until now does not necessarily provide the answers to the diverse problems of today and even less so for tomorrow. Very often education systems have reacted to pressure in an attempt to improve achievement within the existing framework of functionality. This "more of the same", however, often leads to little improvement, since a typical learning curve reaches the upper limit of further out-reach. Old patterns bump up against the limitations of the potential solutions. Sometimes, special arrangements are made (e.g. through incentives) to attain best practice status, which, however, are difficult to implement because of their special status (e.g. model schools). Von Hentig (1993) therefore argues that it is not enough to renew or improve schools; he calls for re-imagining school, demanding a new mindset as to how we envisage school. In research, theoretical and methodological discussions have taken place in the process of reframing the "classical approach" to changing patterns of schooling at large, and teaching and learning in particular (e.g. see Vosniadou, 2008). We see this reframing process as a shift of pattern from *best* practice to *next* practice (see figure 4).

For new patterns to emerge, critical incidents or interventions are necessary to open up new perspectives for next practice (Kruse, 2004). However, leaving the trodden path initially causes insecurity and instability; the old patterns of mind do not function any more, and new ones have not yet gained stability. The experience is similar to an incubation phase for the emergence of the new, which conjoins with the old or even questions it. Creating a mindset of sustainable change is a key concept, which runs through all the phases. To do so, the LEA establishes networking activities for sharing impressions, thoughts and perspectives which will help shift the level of consciousness on the following three layers: 1st: seeing and leading yourself; 2nd: seeing and leading people; 3rd: leading systems.

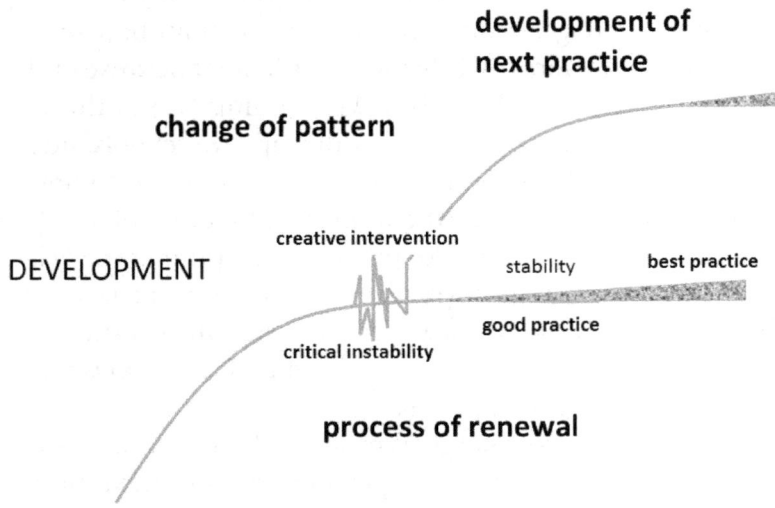

Figure 4: Pattern change through creative intervention

To illustrate this process, let us take the example of Nina's professional project, who is the principal of a high school in Vienna. She wants to transform the learning culture at her school by initiating a mindset shift from teaching to learning throughout her system. This challenge is defined by a high level of social complexity, which means to change the roles, the learning design and the methodologies. In order to develop the teachers' competencies and experiences, Nina offered workshops, teamwork and feedback sessions. The practice of teaching turned into an enabling mode with mentorship, tutorial work and coaching. The crucial message that she got from her CTC group was to "focus on seeing your own patterns and assumptions", which helped her to see and lead herself before others. Furthermore, seeing the needs and expectations of her teachers helped her to lead the system at large.

During Nina's CTC session, her colleagues challenged her to activate the essence of system thinking, which inspires a system sensing and seeing itself. Nina described her purpose and initiative, and the collegial team coaches responded in a way that mirrored the situation of the staff members and students at her school. Through this process, Nina could sense the ambivalence and skepticism of her colleagues. The CTC team of the LEA acted as a sensitive and resonance based instrument, like a violin in a chapel. In this moment, Nina was able to realize that she stressed her system when she regarded it as an organism. She took the opportunity to turn the social complexity by inviting the skeptic members of her system to engage and become part of the process. The CTC group's resonance helped her to find a slow-down mode in order to eventually speed up the transformation process. They became very much engaged in brainstorming and creating solutions which enabled her to see the opportunities by participation and transparency. Through this process, Nina was able to see herself within her system and her system as such at the same time, which increased her capacity to lead her school's transformation process onto a new level of understanding and awareness.

Creating a mindset of change cannot be imposed or enacted; it is rather about a human being's innate capacity to create new knowledge. Otherwise, as Scharmer (2007, p. 119) argues, we are "downloading" patterns of the past, patterns that prevent us from creating a new future. In his "Theory U; Leading from the Future as It Emerges" he develops a systemic theory of leadership which centers on "Presencing", a term which he co-constructs from "presence" and "sensing". For him the essence of leadership builds on the capacity to feel in the here and now those future possibilities, which are most salient rather than "downloading the patterns of the past."

Nina lived through such transformative experience of Presencing in her CTC group when her colleagues confronted her with the resonance she had created in telling the story of her change process at school. For Scharmer (2007), leadership "in its essence is the capacity to shift the inner place from which we operate" and he thinks leaders need to understand "how they can build the capacity of their systems to operate differently and release themselves from the exterior determination" (p. 373). As he states, this leads eventually to a "shift from sensing exterior causation to sensing something collective that is emerging from within" (p. 373). Using Theory U as a social technology in the

LEA helps to challenge participants' traditional views on leadership. It takes them on a very intimate journey of personal and professional learning about one's understanding of the world and organizations. It also highlights that learning for both the individual as well as the system is an interwoven and essential dialogue. This becomes evident through Brigitte's journey of the emerging future in school renewal in the following section.

Brigitte's Journey of the Emerging Future in School Transformation

Brigitte is a principal at an inner-city middle school in the Tyrol and experiences the drawbacks of early segregation in the national school system: The school has to educate children who feel downgraded when perceived as "just average" or "below average" and not allowed to transfer into the academic branch of the school system after four joint primary school years with their schoolmates. A high percentage of children with a family background originating in other countries and the high number of refugee students add to the complex dynamics. Parents and legal guardians more and more transfer general educational measures to teachers and schools, which intensifies the burden for the staff to meet the high demands of creating a place where children feel accepted and perceive school as a social space for cultivating interaction and friendships beyond conventional school life and tasks.

As a LEA participant, Brigitte was initiated into Theory U as a social technology during the second forum, where we provide the participants with a template of the U shape, which they fill in individually. From the CTC group she got the reassurance to start a learning journey through the individual phases with her school staff by clarifying the shared intentions: "We want a different school, we want to be different, *it can't go on as it is*." (See figure 5.)

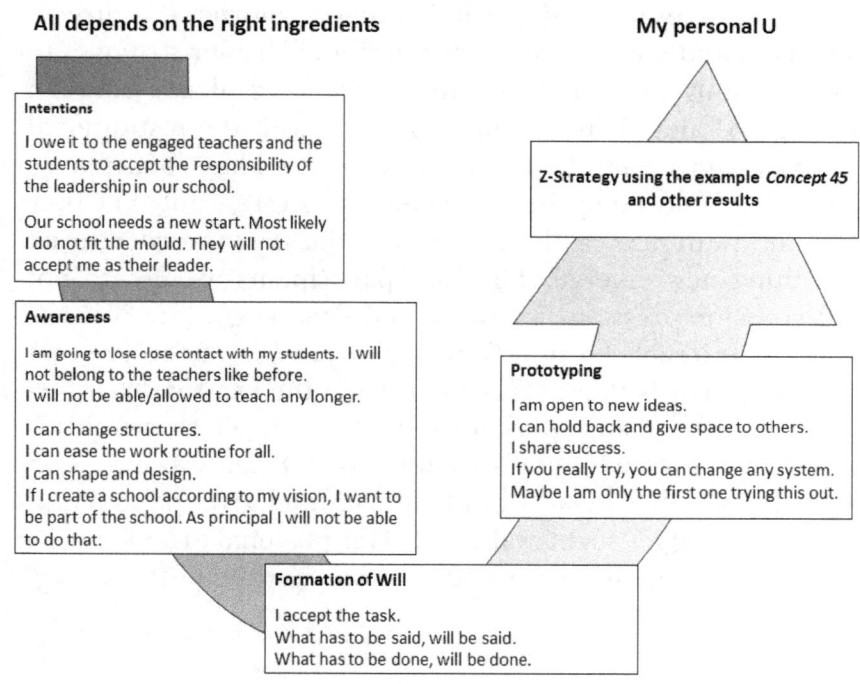

Figure 5: Brigitte's personal U journey

If we follow Brigitte's personal U journey we can trace her ambivalence in taking responsibility as a principal and becoming aware of the consequences: what she will lose and what she will gain. We usually find it very difficult to introduce the concept of Theory U and try to create an awareness for the 250 educational leaders present in the room by means of modelling the process for and with them. Creating a mindset of change cannot be imposed or enacted; it is rather about a human being's innate capacity to create new knowledge. To do so, we introduce the participants to the structure of the social technology from Scharmer's work and create a space so each participant can work on their own in a trusting environment, supported by the critical friendship of their collegial coaching group. Figure 6 presents additional compositions of how the participating educational leaders presented their pathways along the phases of Theory U during the LEA.

The compositions of the individual U journeys (figure 6) help us to understand how each educational leader struggles to cope not only with their personal Presencing phases between "letting go" and "letting come", but also with the institutional constraints given by the particular context. They soon realize that there is no blueprint for change processes, but that they need an awareness of the patterns of the past in order to let something new emerge. The LEA participants usually do not find verbal expressions for the actual *Presencing*, since it is not visible or traceable ex post facto – they just become aware that something new is there. This stems from the fact that transformative learning is an experience of its own (Meyer-Drawe, 2017; Schratz, Schwarz & Westfall-Greiter, 2014). Brigitte's confession "I am open to new ideas. I can hold back and give space to others" acknowledges such awakening. Her personal process is also mirrored in Brigitte's organizational journey along the U (figure 7).

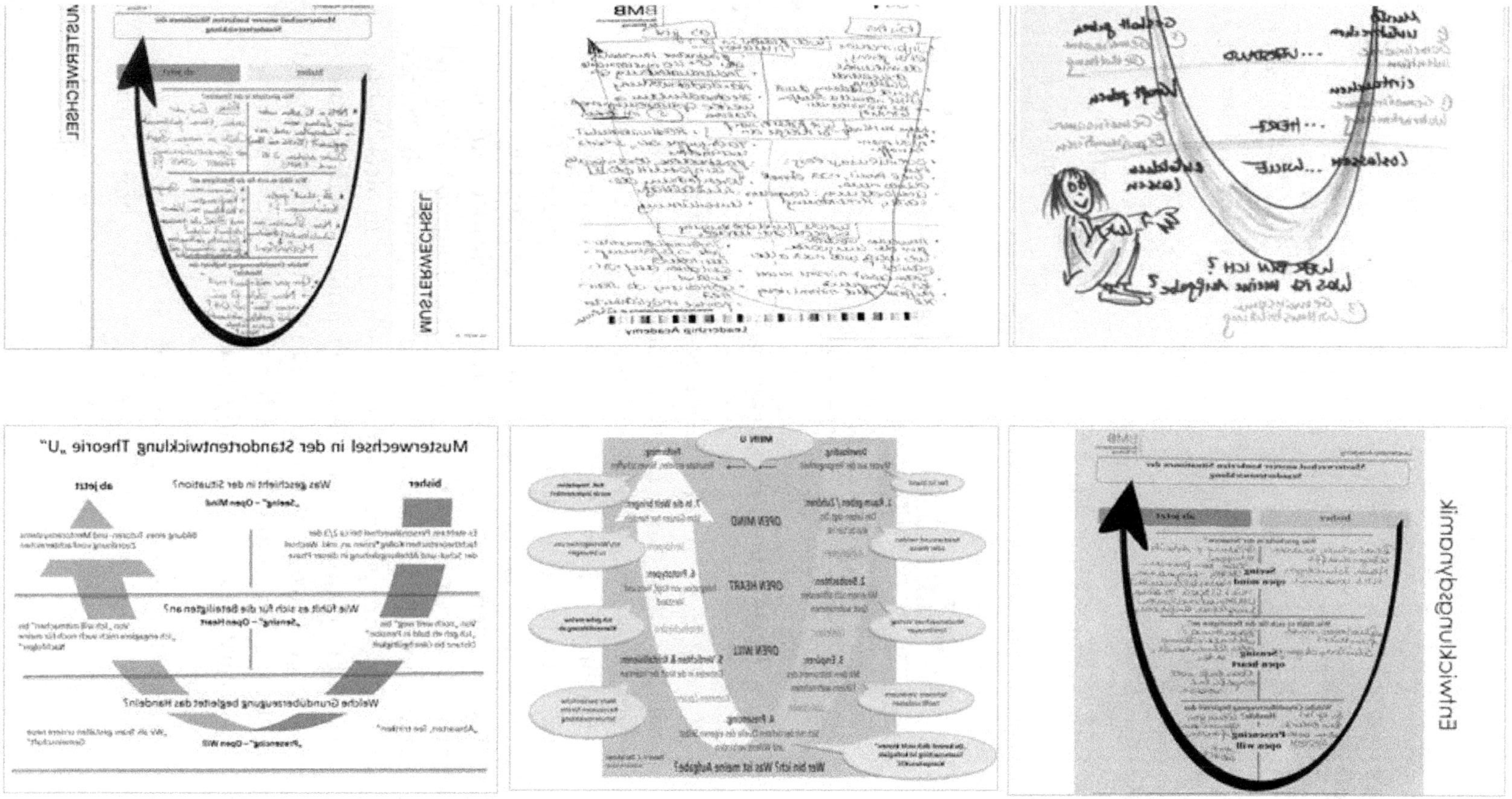

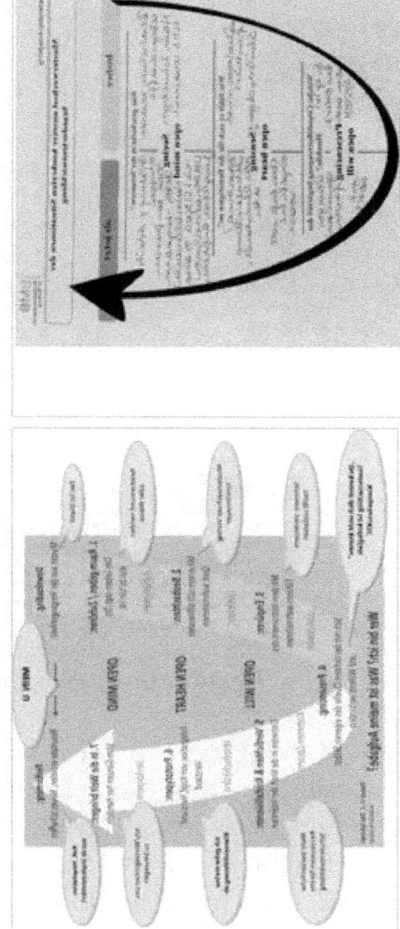

Figure 6: Examples of educational leaders' compositions of their personal U journeys

All depends on the right ingredients   **Sharing the U among staff**

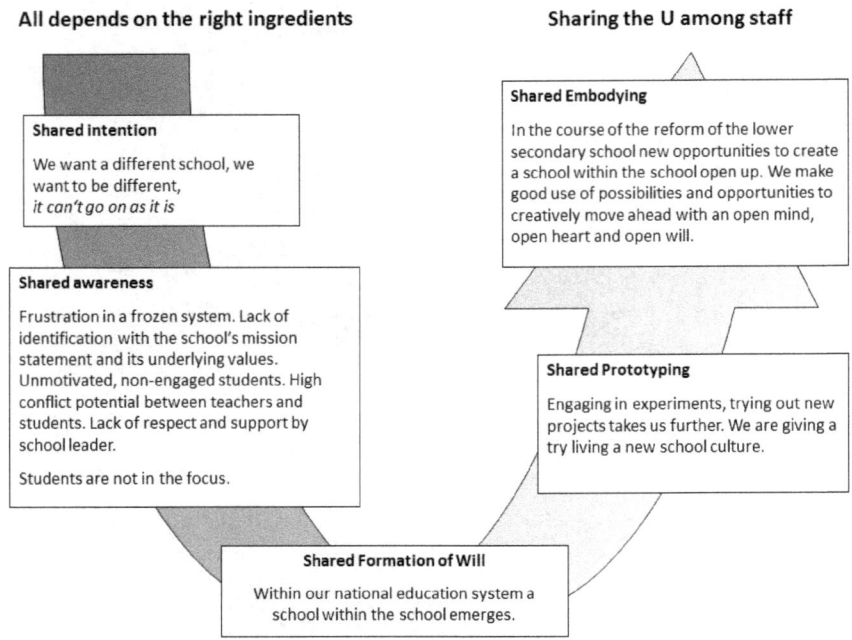

Shared intention

We want a different school, we want to be different, *it can't go on as it is*

Shared Embodying

In the course of the reform of the lower secondary school new opportunities to create a school within the school open up. We make good use of possibilities and opportunities to creatively move ahead with an open mind, open heart and open will.

Shared awareness

Frustration in a frozen system. Lack of identification with the school's mission statement and its underlying values. Unmotivated, non-engaged students. High conflict potential between teachers and students. Lack of respect and support by school leader.

Students are not in the focus.

Shared Prototyping

Engaging in experiments, trying out new projects takes us further. We are giving a try living a new school culture.

Shared Formation of Will

Within our national education system a school within the school emerges.

Figure 7: Brigitte's organizational U journey

When Brigitte shares her vision with her staff, the collective awareness about the frustration within a frozen system becomes eminent. There is no real identification with the school's mission statement and the underlying values. Teachers experience their students as de-motivated and disengaged. Conflicts are manifold and ready to explode between teachers as well as teachers and students. The students are not their focus any more. At the same time, teachers experience a lack of support from and appreciation by the school principal. In the process of "Open will" a new positioning takes root, which Brigitte depicts "Within our National Education System a school within the school emerges." As a consequence, new things are tried out and prototyped, teachers engage in new and unfamiliar methods and approaches, new projects are created and slowly, over time, a new school culture comes into life.

Through CTC the principal is supported in her opening up to new ideas (e.g. "Concept 45") and is ready to give her staff more space and is able to share her success with them. The concept of the school within the school is carried by a mission and put into practice by a design that leaves teachers with more time in the classroom that they can use more freely and according to their immediate needs. The result becomes visible in a multilayer mix of "ingredients", as Brigitte calls them, leading towards a new structure of hours of instruction as well as to new priorities. Project phases and sports activities allow for new possibilities of learning. The school building was re-designed, for example, a "relief zone" was introduced, where students can find a retreat space if needed. Further measures to foster resilience and aspects of a healthy school support, the enactment of a new school culture and responsibility is distributed and shared. Democracy emerges as the encompassing principle, and is lived in the classroom councils, in the culture of asking questions, the school rules and regulations and the staff meetings and work ethics.

Outlook

Fourteen generations of graduates of the LEA (over 3,000 out of 6,000 school leaders in Austria) have joined the network of "system thinkers in action" (Fullan, 2005) and have begun collectively to sense, shape and create a new future for Austrian schools, which is already a critical mass using leadership as a leveraging factor for systems development. Looking back on our journey at this point, we still think of the meeting in the ministry, which we referred to at the beginning. There, Otto Scharmer initiated an ongoing process with civil servants but also contributed to the transformational journey by visiting our Leadership Academy. There he asked the participants of the LEA:

- Where they saw a world that was dying and where they experienced a world wanting to be born. What was dying, they said, was 'the teacher who transfers knowledge, who acts as a single player …' What was being born was 'the teacher as coach and team player.'
- 'What is dying is a pedagogy that revolves around techniques and recipes. What is being born is a pedagogy that

revolves around sensing and actualizing the best potential in students.'

- 'What we need to let go of,' added others, is 'thinking of school in terms of lessons or periods' and 'a culture of regulation and control. What we need to develop is a new form of equal collaboration among parents, teachers, and students.'

- A third cluster of statements focused on evaluation. 'There are many good things in the system, but the focus on standards and outputs is killing the new; the old standards of evaluation impose their stamp on the new.'

- And a fourth cluster focused on the system as a whole: 'We are constantly tinkering with rebuilding the school; we are replacing a window here and another door there – but what we really need is a *new foundation for the entire house.* (Scharmer & Kaufer, 2013, p. 211)

Building a new foundation for the entire system has been an ongoing challenge throughout this "bold and ambitious initiative". This was confirmed by an OECD team (Stoll, Moorman, & Rahm, 2008, p. 246) looking out for prototypes for upscaling leadership competences throughout Europe. Making educational leaders agents of nation-wide school reform in the case of LEA has helped bring people from all levels of the education and government system to work together towards proactive, problem-solving, collaborative and system-wide education demanding "a world wanting to be born". We have learnt that leadership in social contexts with a systems perspective demands orientation towards the emerging future within the given context (from crisis management to future action).

This requires participation, shared responsibilities and dialogue. To strengthen systems in their dynamics and responsibility for goals, quality and processes a transformational concept of leadership is required. Therefore, educational leaders need a notion of leadership as the enfolding of resources and potential on both school and system levels with an orientation towards the future with emerging strategies and concepts. This proves most successful when stakeholders become agents of their contexts, as it fosters identification with the development. To sustain change dynamics, it is vital to build up a powerful network structure that connects people in all sectors, regions, hierarchy levels and functions of the education system. Empowering these change agents leads to a culture of mutual understanding and creates a high level of energy directed towards the demanding goals and development tasks. Engaging with a nationwide ecosystem of people sharing the same goals and personalizing the vision, requires also stewardship for sustainable change: building small units of people working together in professional learning communities (PLCs) with the aim of enhancing the system's capacity for learning and student progress. Establishing a professional network of stakeholders in regional school management has helped to build centers of excellence as a supportive link in capacity building. The fourth field of action relates to a strategy which connects students, parents, teachers and other stakeholders in the different units of the educational system to a higher level of motivation and commitment.

In this chapter, Theory U and Presencing were outlined as a tool to be used in large group interventions that help educational leaders gain ownership in dealing with the needs and expectations of their work context in spite of a lack of autonomy offered by the system at large. The experience of Presencing was applied in the LEA to increase educational leader knowledge and skills in their nascent stage of development. Using Theory U as a social technology in a nation-wide initiative challenges deeply rooted cultural mindsets of thinking and behaving. These traditional actions have made it difficult for educational leaders to easily overcome the patterns of the past, especially when they return to their home settings such as schools, local or regional school boards, ministries or teacher education institutions. The individual actors need the support of the network so that they feel part of a larger movement. They also need to be sensitive to context, which means they must be willing to: live the change, foster participation and co-creation for all, prioritize by condensing and evaluating their actions, stimulate sustainable change, orchestrate diverse voices, and accomplish all stakeholders' commitments.

The experience working with fourteen cohorts of more than

200 educational leaders each has proven that Theory U is a powerful technology that can guide participants along the path of personal transformation, but it also needs accompanying measures to support issues of complexity, diversity, ambiguity, ambivalence and uncertainty. Successful leaders need to be able to make use of their knowledge and skills in their nascent stage of development. As we have discussed, the minister played an important role as a model for LEA and she was essential as a politically potent change agent for system-wide change on the macro level. On the micro level it was the CTC collegial teams that supported each individual participant on their journeys along the U procedure, and having a learning partner act as critical friend and support as they returned to their work places. A growing network of LEA alumni has helped upscale a paradigm shift on the meso level. By presenting two participants' personal journeys through the phases of Theory U, we show that there is no direct way to break from past routines without including the challenging task of gaining the commitment by colleagues and staff. Clearly, as outlined in the Austrian experience, school reform cannot be implemented by top-down deliveries, but needs Presencing experiences in order to have transformative effects.

References

Beck, D. E., & Cowan, C. C. (2003). *Spiral dynamics: Mastering values, leadership, and change; exploring the new science of memetics* (Reprint.). *Developmental Management.* Malden MA: Blackwell.

Bruch, H., & Vogel, B. (2005). *Organisationale Energie: Wie Sie das Potenzial Ihres Unternehmens ausschöpfen.* Wiesbaden: Gabler.

Cooperrider, D. L., & Whitney, D. (1999). *Appreciative Inquiry.* San Francisco: Berrett-Koehler.

Firestone, W. A., & Riehl, C. (Eds.). (2005). *A new agenda for research in educational leadership. Critical issues in educational leadership series.* New York: Teachers College Press.

Fullan, M. (2005). *Leadership & sustainability: System thinkers in action.* Thousand Oaks Calif.: Corwin Press.

Hall, G. E., & Hord, S. M. (Eds.). (1987). *Change in schools: Facilitating the process. SUNY series in educational leadership.* Albany N.Y.: State University of New York Press.

Hargreaves, A., & Shirley, D. (2009). *The fourth way: The inspiring future for educational change*. Thousand Oaks Calif.: Corwin Press.

Hentig, H. v. (1993). *Die Schule neu denken: Eine Übung in praktischer Vernunft; eine zornige, aber nicht eifernde, eine radikale, aber nicht utopische Antwort auf Hoyerswerda und Mölln, Rostock und Solingen*. München: Hanser.

Holman, P., Devane, T., & Cady, S. (Eds.). (2008). *The change handbook: The definitive resource on today's best methods for engaging whole systems* (2nd ed. rev. and expanded.). San Francisco: Berrett-Koehler.

Kruse, P. (2004). *Next practice - erfolgreiches Management von Instabilität: Veränderung durch Vernetzung*. Offenbach: Gabal.

Meyer-Drawe, K. (2017). Phenomenology as a Philosophy of Experience - Implications for Pedagogy. In M. Ammann, T. Westfall-Greiter & M. Schratz (Eds.), *Erfahrungsorientierte Bildungsforschung: Vol. 3. Erfahrungen deuten - Deutungen erfahren: Vignettes and Anecdotes as Research, Evaluation and Mentoring Tool* (pp. 13–21). Innsbruck: Studien Verlag.

Pont, B., Nusche, D., & Moorman, H. (2008). *School Leadership Development: Policy and Practice. Improving school leadership: Vol. 1*. Paris: OECD.

Prochaska, F. (2012). John Stuart Mill: The Tyrrany of Uniformity. In F. Prochaska (Ed.), *Eminent Victorians on American Democracy* (pp. 23–46). Oxford University Press.

Scharmer, C. O. (2007). *Theory U: Leading from the future as it emerges: the social technology of presencing*. Cambridge Mass.: Society for Organizational Learning.

Scharmer, C.O., & Kaufer, K. (2013). *Leading from the emerging future: From ego-system to eco-system economies*. San Francisco: Berrett-Koehler Publishers.

Schley, V., & Schley, W. (2010). *Handbuch Kollegiales Team-Coaching*. Innsbruck: Studien Verlag.

Schmid, K., Hafner, H., & Pirolt, R. (2007). *Reform von Schulgovernance-Systemen: Vergleichende Analyse der Reformprozesse Österreich und bei einigen PISA-Teilnehmerländern. IBW-Forschungsbericht: Vol. 135*. Wien: IBW.

Schratz, M. (2003). From Administering to Leading a School: challenges in German-speaking countries. *Cambridge Journal of Education, 33*(3), 395–416.

Schratz, M., & Hartmann, M. (2009). Schulautonomie in Österreich: Bilanz und Perspektiven für eine eigenverantwortliche Schule. In

W. Specht (Ed.), *Nationaler Bildungsbericht Österreich* (Vol. 2, pp. 323–340). Graz.

Schratz, M., Schwarz, J. F., & Westfall-Greiter, T. (2014). Beyond the Reach of Teaching and Measurement: Methodology and Initial Findings of the Innsbruck Vignette Research. Pensamiento Educativo. *Revista de Investigación Educacional Latinoamericana*, 51(1), 123–134. Retrieved from http://pensamientoeducativo.uc.cl/index.php/pel/article/view/573/1297/article/view/573/1296

Stoll, L., Bolam, R., & Collarbone, P. (2002). Leading for Change: Building capacity for learning. In K. A. Leithwood & P. Hallinger (Eds.), *Second international handbook of educational leadership and administration* (pp. 41–73). Dordrecht, Boston: Kluwer Academic.

Stoll, L., Moorman, H., & Rahm, S. (2008). Building leadership capacity for system improvement in Austria. In B. Pont, D. Nusche, & D. Hopkins (Eds.), *Improving school leadership: Vol. 2. Improving School Leadership: Case studies on system leadership* (pp. 215–252). Paris: OECD.

Vosniadou, S. (Ed.). (2008). *International handbook of research on conceptual change*. New York: Routledge.

CHAPTER 8

The role of the shift from I-to-We and Theory-U in overcoming 21st century illiteracies

Markus F. Peschl, Katharina Roetzer, Gloria Bottaro, Martina Hartner-Tiefenthaler

Introduction

Innovation has received new attention over the last decade(s) (e.g., OECD 2005, 2015, 2017; European Commission, 2008, 2015) due to the world's current challenges related to rapid and disruptive societal and technological changes (e.g., climate change and environmental/energy issues, financial crisis, migration, disruption in education and the future of work, etc.). However, it has turned out that classic approaches to innovation and creativity (e.g., Dodgson & Gann, 2010; Amabile, 1996; Peschl, Fundneider, & Kulick, 2015; Witt, 2009) have reached their limits as the challenges we are confronted with in today's world go far beyond "problem solving", ill-structured or wicked problems (Dorst, 2006), incremental innovation (Ettlie, Bridges, & O´Keefe 1984, 1984), or bounded rationality (Felin, Kauffman, Koppl, & Longo, 2014; Simon, 1996). Today, we have to face an almost unknowable and highly uncertain future (Sarasvathy, Dew, Velamuri, & Venkataraman, 2003) and are becoming aware of these circumstances. Hence, change and innovation have become essential answers to these challenges in today's economy, organizations, and society. However, it seems that we are not properly prepared for these new challenges; as we will show this is in part due to what we refer to as *illiteracies of the 21st century*.

In this chapter we will go beyond classic perspectives of innovation theory (e.g., Baregheh, Rowley, & Sambrook, 2009; Tidd & Bessant, 2009) and apply an approach that is based on the concept of *learning from the future as it emerges*, or *presencing* (Scharmer, 2007, p. 52). We will address the following questions: What is meaningful change/innovation? How do we bring about change and innovation that is sustainable, flourishing, and significant? How do we have to design didactic processes, educational eco-systems, and curricula to enable students and employees to innovate in a meaningful way? How do these educational systems translate into organizational/corporate contexts in order to make them future-ready? These are the areas in which we need to begin thinking about new approaches to innovation and knowledge creation. Sustainable innovations require future-oriented approaches that are not primarily driven by past experiences, i.e., innovating by extrapolating the past into the future; compare also Scharmer's (2007, p. 244) "reenacting patterns from the past". As is shown by Scharmer (2007a/2007b) it is sometimes necessary to develop completely new mindsets, attitudes, as well as (cognitive) skills for such a future-driven approach to innovation and knowledge creation. Future-driven organizations have to deal with the challenge of constant change. Adapting to changes does not suffice, but we have to anticipate them and create new niches in a proactive manner. As a consequence, it is necessary to educate people how to drive these changes. Currently, such change- and future-related skills and mindsets are almost completely absent from our curricula and educational systems (both in academic and corporate contexts). Thus, we suggest an *educational* perspective, and will subsequently translate our insights from educational contexts to the organizational/business context.

The contribution of this chapter is to illustrate how Scharmer's (2007) Theory-U serves as a means to overcome the above mentioned 21ˢᵗ century *illiteracies* to develop future-oriented innovation strategies. Using empirical examples of Theory-U processes and presencing from the higher education context, we will show how the *shift from I-to-We* can act as key ingredient for a successful process of presencing, and how this shift and specific *attitudes* relate to *collective knowledge creation* or a *collectivization of presencing* experiences and ideas. Subsequently, we will discuss how these insights may be employed to overcome these 21ˢᵗ century illiteracies.

The remainder of the paper is structured as follows: First, we will briefly introduce the illiteracies of the 21ˢᵗ century and show how *Emergent Innovation* (Peschl & Fundneider, 2017) that is based on Theory-U (Scharmer, 2007, 2016) may overcome these forms of illiteracies. Second, we describe a concrete educational setting and illustrate how such a presencing-based form of innovation can be taught in an academic setting and discuss the importance of the role of the facilitator in this process. Finally, we derive implications for practical use in organizational contexts.

21ˢᵗ century illiteracies

According to classic definitions (e.g., Cambridge Dictionary), *illiteracy* encompasses being unable to read and write, including a lack of numeracy skills or knowledge about a particular subject. We suggest to take a broader perspective on illiteracies (see also UNESCO, 2005; OECD, Guerriero, 2017), and to include the following incapabilities into our understanding of illiteracies: the lack of critical thinking (e.g., Pithers & Soden, 2000; Halpern, 2014), not being able to use and cope with new technologies, not being able to access knowledge/information, or a lack of social capabilities, such as empathy, leadership, or collaboration skills (e.g., dealing with conflicts, communication strategies, group decision making, agile group roles, self-reflection, etc.). These skills are necessary to master the current societal and technological challenges mentioned in the introduction.

Above, we have identified skills and literacies that are key for driving future-oriented innovation (see, for instance, Miller, 2015). However, they seem to be largely absent both in the educational field and in organizational contexts. This leads to what we refer to as three key illiteracies of the 21st century:

1. Inability to "see" and change our perspective: Innovation is about perception and cognition; what are the patterns through which we perceive and think about the world, what are our blind spots, and how or by which patterns and semantic frameworks do we understand and make sense of the world? These patterns prevent us from seeing novelty (Grisold & Peschl, 2017). Only if we become aware and start "seeing" our own patterns of perception and thinking (e.g., through reflection or dialogue, Bohm, 1996; Isaacs, 1999), we will be able to change them. Only then unexpected and novel structures can be perceived as a result of a changed perspective. Changing the perspective has a second dimension as well: in the *social* realm it means to be capable of changing from one's own perspective to another person's perspective; which is particularly important in interdisciplinary cooperation when designing collective knowledge creation processes.

2. Inability to deal with a future that unfolds in complexity, uncertainty, and exponential dynamics: Looking at the world from the perspective of systems science/thinking (e.g., Weinberg, 2011; Kauffman, 2000; Kim, 1999; Senge, 1990) our reality unfolds over time by following the dynamics of a network of complex (socio-technological) systems. As Weinberg (2011) states, we have to admit that our cognitive system is overwhelmed by the complexity (and speed) of events, especially in our modern technology-driven world. Even when we try to look behind the "raw" appearances and observations to identify underlying patterns, it is evident that we have only access to partial information, and that it is almost impossible to make sense of the world in a way that we can "understand" or explain, let alone predict it. This is due to the fact that socio-technological systems do not follow simplified mechanistic dynamics any more (Longo, Montevil, & Kauffman, 2012;

Kauffman, 2000). "Many real-world problems appear intractable and are difficult to resolve. Part of the difficulty arises when only single causes are sought, when such problems arise from the interaction of multiple, underlying, interrelated causes" (Mitleton-Kelly, 2007, p. 112). We have to deal with increasingly complex systems that exceed our human cognitive abilities and cannot be "deciphered" by simply relating cause and effect in a linear manner. Instead, we are confronted with a complex network of nested feedback-loops and interacting (eco-)systems leading to emergent, exponential, and/or quasi-chaotic behaviors and phenomena with a high level of complexity, uncertainty, and unpredictability (e.g., Kauffman 1993, 2000; Sarasvathy, Dew, Velamuri, &Venkataraman, 2003). Hence, what we are confronted with is a form of "future that is not only unknown, but also unknowable" (Sarasvathy et al., 2003, p. 144) and we lack the (cognitive) capacity to deal with such an uncertainty and a systems thinking perspective.

3. Inability to anticipate and "see" novelty even though it is not here yet: This third form of illiteracy is about our inability to "make use" of the future: "A better understanding of the nature and purpose of different anticipatory systems is important...because it significantly enhances effectiveness and efficiency, when attempting to identify both systemic assumptions and the distinctive attributes of continuity and emergence in the present." (Miller, 2015, p. 4). In other words, this illiteracy is about future potentials and concerns the context of sensing, identifying, and creating opportunities or new niches that are not here yet. The dynamics of the world can be understood as an evolutionary and open-ended (creative) process unfolding over time: "future is not predetermined, merely waiting to be revealed, but it is continuously originated by the pattern and sequence of human choice.... Future parts of a market simply do not exist; they are, by definition, not present. There are, at any point in time, many potential futures imaginable, based on more or less informed reflections." (Buchanan & Vanberg, 1991, p. 179 & 176). This form of illiteracy is connected with the previous one and concerns our inability to create something new in the future space of uncertainty; something that is not here yet, but that "wants" to emerge out of a potential that is already present in a latent and hidden manner (Poli, 2006). We lack an ability to "learn from the future as it emerges" (Scharmer, 2007) and a future-oriented way of thinking going beyond pure predictions that are mainly driven by past experiences (Peschl, Fundneider, and Kulick, 2015).

If innovations aim at creating novelty that is sustainable and leads to a thriving future, just "being creative" or "out-of-the-box-thinking" (e.g., Kelley, 2004) does not suffice to overcome this form of illiteracy. A completely new set of (epistemic) skills, attitudes, and mindsets (e.g., openness, deep observation, "sense for potentials", being able to deeply immerse into reality, etc.) is necessary. Miller (2015), for instance, introduces the importance of "not doing": "*Not doing* takes agency in a different direction, not passivity, but patience and attentiveness that facilitates taking advantage of changes in the conditions of change." (p. 4) As we will see in the context of discussing Theory-U, this form of "active patience" and being able to wait plays an important role in developing innovations that are resulting from a process of learning from the future as it emerges.

The three forms of illiteracy are inherently connected to each other. They concern our cognitive abilities to perceive and to make sense of the world and its possible future states. Scharmer´s (2007) Theory-U approach provides a valuable framework to overcome these illiteracies, but also serves as conceptual foundation for giving rise to future-oriented innovations.

The role of Theory-U in overcoming 21st century illiteracies

The three forms of illiteracy are heavily influenced by a phenomenon that is well known from contemporary cognitive/neuro-science, namely *predictive coding*, which is also referred to as the predictive mind framework/hypothesis (e.g., Clark, 2013, 2016; Hohwy, 2013). It proposes that the main task of the human brain consists in applying generative (mental) hierarchical models that predict what will be happening in the environment. These mental models are based on past experiences and existing hypotheses/knowledge about the world. More specifically, the framework claims that the brain uses past experiences for making sense of new ones. In other words, it is trying to test and make sense of whatever happens by "projecting" past experiences into the world. As Clark (2013) underlines, our brain is "in the business of active, ongoing, input prediction" (p. 187). Or, as Hohwy (2013) asserts, "[w]e try to make sense of the world given of what we know." (p. 149).

These predictions are realized as hierarchical top-down neural pathways in our brain leading to (behavioral) dynamics that aim at reducing prediction errors rather than being open to novelty and surprise that might occur in the environment. Clark summarizes this mechanism by citing the cyberneticist Ross Ashby, who claims: "The whole function of the brain is summed up in: error reduction" (Clark, 2013, p. 181). Looking back at our three forms of illiteracy, one can see that the dynamics of predictive coding (i.e., predicting the future by using/projecting past experiences and trying to minimize prediction errors) seem to be one of the main causes for all three forms of illiteracies. Predictive coding prevents us from changing our perspective (unless one explicitly applies techniques of reflection). It is intrinsically cognitive conservative (Clark, 2017), and thus—if it is not overridden—an inadequate strategy for dealing with an unpredictable and uncertain future. Consequently, predictive coding is not concerned with creating emergent new futures, but with trying to sustain already existing structures.

If we are interested in creating futures that are novel and follow alternative dynamics or that question existing structures, systems of meaning, and processes, we have to ask ourselves how our cognitive limitations can be overcome. New skills and mindsets are necessary for shaping future organizations, social and education systems, and innovations. Techniques such as reflection (e.g., Bohm, 1996; Rodgers, 2002), creativity (e.g., Kelley, 2004; Runco, 2014), innovation (e.g., Dodgson & Gann, 2010), unlearning (e.g., Grisold & Peschl 2017), design thinking (e.g.,

Brown 2008, 2009), or critical thinking (e.g., Pithers & Soden 2000), are a first step toward addressing these limitations. Nonetheless, these techniques are still limited with respect to profound novelty, as they are mostly determined by and concerned with past experiences. Future-oriented and meaningful innovation affords completely different approaches. Scharmer´s, 2007, 2016. *Theory-U/presencing* approach is a powerful framework for enabling profound change and innovation that includes a process of learning from the future as it emerges. It can be applied both on the individual and on the collective, or organizational level.

The process of Theory-U is a "journey" that starts with suspending and questioning existing solutions, knowledge, habits, and premises, followed by changing and redirecting one's standpoint through reflecting on patterns of perception and thinking. It continues by sensing and leaving behind (i.e., letting-go) already existing knowledge and entering the (open or "empty") space of presencing. The turning point is the change into a mode of learning from the future as it emerges (the "bottom of the U"). From there, one gains (fragile) insights about future potentials that are in a state of emergence. These insights have to be enacted in a process of crystallizing and prototyping. Finally, the resulting knowledge and prototypes are embodied and brought into a state of operational performance.

This process is sophisticated and demanding on various levels: cognitively and epistemologically (e.g., being able to deeply reflect on one's knowledge, habits, and behaviors), emotionally (e.g., being able to deal with uncertainty, anxiety), socially (e.g., trust, collaboration in a space of the unknown), and even existentially (being able to leave behind one's well established and beloved thinking patterns and trying out new ones in a process of a potentially personal transformation).

Despite its high relevance for society and economy, we argue that our educational systems mostly fail to teach these skills and mindsets in a systematic manner. Therefore, professionals are challenged to develop adequate knowledge, tools, skills, and mindsets for bringing about meaningful change and innovation in their organizations. That is why we want to introduce an educational format to describe how these skills and mindsets can be facilitated, and discuss practical implications for organizations based on these insights.

Theory-U in practice: course design

To understand Theory-U and being prepared to the changed demands for the future workforce one has to *experience* this process. We designed and implemented a university course based on Theory-U and let student teams experience the whole innovation process. We applied a radical constructivist approach (Glasersfeld, 1989, 1995b) as an underlying epistemological foundation and followed the Emergent Innovation process (Peschl & Fund¬neider, 2008, 2013, 2017). Opposed to conventional drill-and-practice approach based on learning facts (which is commonly pursued in Higher Education), the constructivist epistemology (e.g., Glasersfeld, 1974, 1989, 1995b; Peschl, 2006) views knowledge as an interplay of subjective construction and inter-subjective negotiation and validation processes and, therefore, as being highly versatile. Knowledge is not understood as an object, but rather as a dynamic process of sense-making and creating meaning. Rather than being a "justified true belief" (Steup, 2012), knowledge is the outcome of a subjective process of construction and knowledge creation, resulting in knowledge that functionally fits the environment (Glasersfeld, 1995a). In most cases the construction of knowledge includes an aspect of novelty: it takes some kind of creative act to construct knowledge that is capable of producing (new) behavioral patterns (i.e., "innovations" in the most general sense). Metaphorically speaking, it is the creative act of designing a key that is capable of unlocking the dynamics of a given environment by entering into a (novel) pattern of successful interaction with it (cf., Gibson´s (1986) concept of affordances).

With this constructivist approach in mind, we adapted the Theory-U approach. Our university course lasted approximately 4 months and students worked in interdisciplinary teams of 3-6 people, and collaboratively engaged in an innovation project, aiming to, ultimately, create novel knowledge by realizing a prototype. The process had a strong focus on reflecting and challenging one's patterns of perception and thinking, in-depth observation, going through the presencing and crystallizing phase, and, finally, realizing a prototype.

The process encompasses several phases and was organized as a sequence of several workshops and class events, which are interlinked, and recursive in nature. Between face-to-face events and workshops, coaching sessions were offered for the teams as a place for receiving feedback, asking questions more deeply, discussing social issues in the group, etc. with the team of instructors. For reasons of brevity, below we describe only the most important phases (i.e., questions that really matter, observing and creating collective sense organs, and presencing and crystallizing) that have to be dealt with great care from the instructor's/facilitators' perspective. For more details see Peschl, Bottaro, Hartner-Tiefenthaler, and Rötzer (2014) and Figure 1.

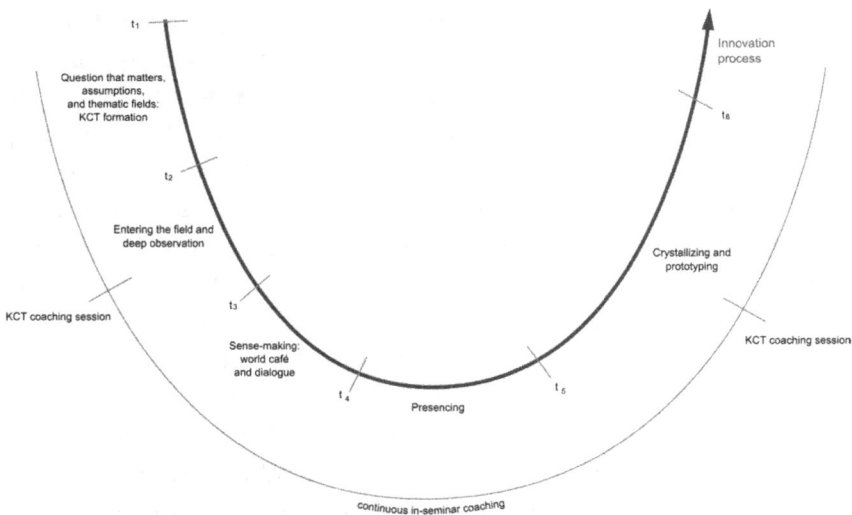

Figure 1: Course design following Scharmer's (2007, 2016) Theory-U approach and indicating time points of data collection

Using "questions that really matter" to prepare the ground

Foerster (1972) points out that every knowledge construction process is based on the individual's pre-existing world constructions. Contrary to classical educational approaches, students are not seen as white canvas. Rather, they enter the educational setting with their individual mindsets, experiences/knowledge, their subjective worldviews and, specific (personal) interests. Taking this into account, the implemented process is based on "questions that really matter" which students have to prepare and bring to class. These questions function as a point of departure for the remaining innovation process. This ensures that students work on projects that are really relevant to them and that they identify with, and, as a consequence, deeply engage in. These questions are only a starting point and they change considerably in the course of the following phases. In class, students critically reflect their questions and explore the (hidden) assumptions they are based on. As a result, topics are formed based on these assumptions. Finally, students assign themselves to one of the topics that have emerged in order to use the potential of the group (we refer to these groups as *knowledge creation teams*, abbr. *KCTs*) in the next phases.

Observing and creating collective sense organs to "enable seeing"

The KCTs are asked to deep-dive into their chosen topics by conducting in-depth observations in the respective fields. At this point, students start to deal with the first illiteracy: enabling *to* "*see*". They are invited to apply qualitative participant and first-person based observation methods (e.g., Spradley, 1980; Kawulich, 2005; Petitmengin, 2006; Senge & Scharmer, 2001; Scharmer, 2007b). After this phase of intensive and deep observation, the participants present their insights to their fellow KCTs. This phase aims at the creation of "collective sense organs" (Scharmer, 2007, p. 398) in a process of collective sense making.

"Because of the situatedness of the separate knowledges each with its particular terminology and semantic field, it is critical that educators are able to integrate their knowledge with the concept of the whole." (Peterson, 2013, p. 880).

To achieve a collective understanding of the observations, instructors have to encourage the exchange and moderate it with methods such as world café (e.g., Brown & Isaacs, 2005) or dialogue (Bohm, 1996; Isaacs, 1999). This allows students to reflect on the assumptions "behind" the observations and insights. Thus, students do not only deepen their understanding of the chosen topic and field of interest, but also discover their observation biases, their patterns of perception, thereby widening the scope of the original issue/topic. Questioning current patterns of perception and thinking redirects their standpoints on an individual level. On a collective/group level, this leads to a broader and deeper collective understanding of the observed domain(s). Furthermore, by sharing and challenging their insights, participants engage in changing respective perspectives. They start to tap into the complexity and the uncertainties of the observed phenomena which refers to the second illiteracy, i.e., the inability to deal with uncertainty and complexity.

Presencing and crystallizing to encounter future potentials

The presencing phase of Theory-U is key to overcome the third form of illiteracy, the *inability to anticipate novelty*. This phase is the central part of the innovation process in our course design. It is the crucial point, where students have to liberate themselves from the past ("letting-go") and listen to "what wants to emerge from the future" (Scharmer, 2007). The students' goals in this course setting is not to produce incremental innovations (Ettlie et al., 1984), or adaptations of existing concepts, services, or products, but to create something radically new that may shape the future by creating new sustainable niches (Kauffman 1993, 2014; Koppl, Kauffman, Felin, & Longo, 2014). As Foerster reminds us, the (final) cause lies in the future: "At any moment we are free to act toward the future we desire." (Foerster, 1972, p. 38).

In this spirit and in an (intellectually) stimulating environment outside the university buildings (in our case, a setting in nature where participants spend half a day in the woods), each student enters an "empty space" of listening. In this state, students suspend their own ideas and switch into a mode of "listening to what wants to emerge" (Scharmer, 2007; Scharmer & Kaeufer, 2010; Senge, Scharmer, Jaworski, & Flowers, 2004). Starting with a mode of silence, "contemplation", and "active waiting", students entered a state of high awareness, openness, and leaving the ground of certainties in order to "listen" to emerging potentials. In this process of presencing both radically new and at the same time organically "grown" insights emerge out of a "left-behind" profound understanding of the thematic fields (Peschl & Fundneider, 2008).

While still fragile, the outcomes and insights gained during the individual phase of presencing are then discussed within the KCTs to achieve a common understanding. Ideas start to *crystallize* in this phase; that is, first intuitions and (concrete) ideas regarding the projects that might lead to an innovation artifact/prototype are incubated and cultivated. In these conversations, participants encounter a high level of uncertainty (corresponding to the second form of illiteracies) since the insights are still highly intuitive and fragile. Due to an already established atmosphere of trust within their KCTs, most students open up and accept their vulnerability and uncertainty. Novelty may only emerge in such a state when students engage into joint co-creation of emerging potentials and leave behind their certainties. In an iterative process this leads to crystallizing a concrete idea for an innovation project. Besides its novel character we made the interesting observation that a kind of reframing has taken place although the resulting ideas of the innovation projects are still somehow connected to the core of their original topics or questions that matter. But now—due to having gone through the process of presencing—these ideas shed a completely new light on the topics and develop a new and sustainable perspective opening up new niches and possibilities that have not been previously present in the original topics or observations (corresponding to our third illiteracy).

In the following prototyping phase, the concrete innovation artifacts are brought into the (material) world. Prototyping (e.g., Brown, 2009; Moggridge, Fulton, Suri, & Bray; Houde & Hill, 1997; Kelley, 2004) as knowledge creation technique allows for fast cycle learning through immediate realization and adaptation (details can be found in Peschl, et al., 2014).

Sample description, data collection, and data analysis

The results presented below are based on 12 Theory-U processes in the years 2013, 2014 and 2015 (six KCTs in 2013, and three in 2014 and 2015 each, consisting of four to seven students) in the context of three university courses. Students had to create novel knowledge in teams following Scharmer's (2007, 2016) Theory-U process (see Figure 1).

All three courses were attended by students ($n=61$; 31 males, 30 females; mean of age is 27.61 and median is 26.50; $SD = 4.90$, range = 21 to 44 years) enrolled in bachelor's, master's, or PhD programs from two Austrian universities. Students varied greatly in terms of their disciplinary backgrounds, including economics, management, mathematics, engineering, informatics, psychology, philosophy, cognitive science, cultural anthropology, sociology, linguistics, architecture, and arts. Students worked in heterogeneous teams along the Theory-U-inspired process described above and had to present an innovative prototype at the end of the course. The prototypes were rated by the four course instructors—who also formed the research team—along the dimensions of originality, level of implementation, and feasibility on a 7-point Likert scale. At six points in time during the process (indicated by t_1 to t_6 in Figure 1), students were asked to reflect on their learning and group processes in so-called learning journals (a diary-method to investigate individual reflections of the students, cf., Ohly, Sonnentag, Niessen, & Zapf, 2010). In addition, socio-demographical data (age, gender, academic background discipline, etc.) was collected. Data was only used and considered in our analysis with students' informed consent right from the beginning of the course.

Furthermore, the instructors/researchers applied participatory and exploratory observation methods during the seminars, which were systematically discussed and documented within the research team in an action research setting (Argyris, Putnam, & McLain Smith, 1985; Reason & Bradbury, 2001).

Data analysis was based on Charmaz' (2006) grounded theory approach, which is well-suited for a qualitative, theory-generating analysis of elicited texts, such as diary entries. Grounded theory is a qualitative method of data analysis and synthesis that aims to construct and conceptualize theories that are "grounded" solely in the data, based on several phases of coding and a repeated comparison with data on different levels of analysis (Charmaz, 2006). Using the software ATLAS.ti (version 7), we coded the journal entries in three coding phases: firstly, initial coding without categories or leading questions, using data of the university course from 2013. Secondly, focused coding with categories that emerged from initial coding in two steps: focused coding considering data from 2013 in the first step, and in a second step, extended focused coding of the data from 2014 and 2015. Thirdly, theoretical coding of the entire data material based on themes/concepts derived from focused coding, until theoretical saturation (cf. Charmaz, 2006) was achieved. During the coding process, the researchers wrote memos to reflect on their data analysis, and regularly discussed their memos within the research team.

In a last step of informed synthesis and integration, additional data (demographical data, prototype ratings, observation notes) was critically and systematically considered to contextualize the grounded theory analysis. In the following, the findings from these analyses will be presented. More details about the process of data collection and data analysis can be found in Hartner-Tiefenthaler, Roetzer, Bottaro, & Peschl, 2018 which partly consists of the data used here (year 2013).

Findings

The findings presented in this section are structured as follows. First, we describe the core phenomenon of interest that guided our further analysis, namely the emergent phenomenon of *collective knowledge creation*. In our context, collective knowledge creation describes the process of collectivization after the individual presencing experiences, i.e., a collectivization of experiences and individually identified future potentials. Second, we describe a development that our analysis revealed to be related to this collectivization: a perceptual shift from an "I" to a "We"-perspective within the student teams. We provide a detailed description of the gradual development and dimensions of this *shift from I-to-We*. Third, we present our findings on *attitudes* we found when further investigating this shift, and describe which attitudes appear to support a shift from I-to-We and collective knowledge creation. Finally, we report our findings regarding the *role of instructors*, environments, and didactics in this process.

The shift from I-to-We supports the presencing process and collective knowledge creation

Analyzing journal reports from students of 12 KCTs, we argue that the collective experience within the KCTs (after the individual experience of the presencing phase) is essential for creating a prototype with high innovation potential. The KCTs that did not experience such collective processes created a less innovative prototype. The emergent phenomenon of *collective knowledge creation* was described as sudden experiences of joint understanding; an enlightened moment with sudden clarity perceived as a joint feeling within the whole group. Students described it as an immediate, surprising, and unexpected event, in which no one knew where the initial idea or cause came from afterwards (loss of idea-ownership), as well as feelings such as being relieved, happy, and excited after these moments of emergent collective knowledge creation occurred. One student summarized this in the following way "I wonder a little bit where the actual idea for the prototype came from - suddenly it was there, and all group members simultaneously [sic!] had the feeling that this is it. Quite surprising, though..." [51:9][1]

Collective knowledge creation occurred in most teams after the individual presencing phase, i.e., during crystallizing, but not in all teams. The teams that experienced collective knowledge creation received the highest instructor ratings, i.e., their prototypes were rated to have the highest innovation potential. Furthermore, the data reveals that only those KCTs who entirely experienced the *shift from I-to-We* prior to the collective emergent knowledge creation were able to create a prototype of high potential. Some KCTs experienced a shift from I-to-We *after* the presencing phase, but this might have been too late in the process as the prototypes were "only" rated to be mediocre.

Our data suggests that the shift from I-to-We developed gradually from an *"egocentric" I-perspective* (focusing on personal ideas, motives, or goals and lacking reference to the KCT), to a *"relational" I-perspective* (reflections of the self in relation to the group, considering group goals and ideas and how oneself could contribute), leading to a rather sudden semantic shift to an *"explicit" We-perspective* (made explicit by using the plural-first-person form "we" in the journals and reporting all processes from a group-perspective), to a *"latent" or "implicit" We-perspective*. When this final latent or implicit We-perspective was reached, students no longer differentiated between the self and the group with regard to the project idea, idea ownerships, and the process in general. Furthermore, all group members consistently reported similar perceptions of their group and idea processes.

Our analysis further indicates that the shift from I-to-We took place on multiple dimensions, such as on the cognitive and semantic dimension, the emotional and social dimension, and the existential and transformational dimension.

The cognitive and semantic shift. Occurrences in the data (i.e., the students' journal entries) encompass a *cognitive and semantic shift* when students describe their knowledge and group processes: from an individual (e.g., "I think....", "For me...", "In

---

1 The number in the brackets define [case number: paragraph]

my opinion...") to a more group-related perspective. Students started expressing their thoughts in a plural first-person perspective (e.g., "We think...", "We feel...", "In our mind...", or even without a differentiation between self and group), and reported coherent perceptions within their KCT. This shift was often preceded by explicit descriptions on the individual role with regard to the group. Students reflected their role, position, and contribution in and for the group in a relational perspective directed toward the KCT. At this point, individual cognitive processes (i.e., thinking, assuming, or decision making) become externalized and extended to the group level and semantics shift from I-descriptions to We-descriptions.

The emotional and social shift. The shift from I-to-We was also described on an emotional and social level. Participants seemed to appreciate the safety and guidance provided by their group and emphasized their common understanding regarding the team and its work as the following quote illustrates "[. . . none of this would have been possible without my group. Whenever I was stuck some group member came up with a new idea and that kept us going. It was fascinating to see how different the inputs from all the group members are since we're all working on the same topic. [...]" [43:5]

Students have started to reflect the emotional and social aspects of their group processes rather than describing the actual content of the projects in their journals. After experiencing this emotional and social shift, students emphasized the importance of a common ground and joint understanding within the groups in their journals.

The existential and transformational shift. Students seem to collectively immerse in the process, and "suffer" to let go of their pre-existing, known, and dear beliefs and patterns of thinking. They open up to question themselves and being questioned by others, thus becoming "vulnerable" in regard to their beliefs. They report struggles, but at the same time describe overcoming them as a positive experience on a deeply personal level. The following quote is an example of letting go and positively re-framing (potential) conflicts or challenges within the team:

The process then in which we tried to find a common sentence or agreement because of time pressure was a rather painful process. I really felt very frustrated, because the work was not focused and there was no readiness to come to a common agreement. So we had to postpone the meeting. The time we had then after Lobau [referring to the outdoor setting] and before the subsequent meeting was I think necessary and good because it helped to reflect the day, all we said and shared, get down from the emotional involvement, and also to order and structure the ideas, and gave a bit more time for them to concretize [sic!]."[17:63ff]

Attitudes experienced in collective knowledge creation processes

The appearance of sudden emergent moments of collective knowledge creation and the preceding perceptual shift from I-to-We seem to be associated with certain attitudes that are shared within the KCT. Shared attitudes determine the way how group members handle upcoming ideas, as well as how knowledge is expected to be created in general, including how work and tasks are organized within a KCT. It seems that being able to change perspective and experience the shift from I-to-We requires a certain mindset or work mode, instigated by shared attitudes. We analyzed which sets of attitudes shared within a KCT support or hinder the collectivization of individual experiences and ideas stemming from presencing, i.e., collective knowledge creation, as well as their relation to the shift from I-to-We.

Supporting attitudes	Inverse and hindering (grey) attitudes
Being open/openness	Being focus-driven/not open
Being appreciative/appreciation	Lacking appreciation
Being willing/willingness	Being unwilling

179

Being engaged/engagement	Being disengaged
Being confident or believing/confidence	Lacking confidence
Identifying/"togetherness"	Being individualistic/lacking sense of "togetherness"
Integration	Lacking integration/focusing on ownership
–	Being persuasive
–	Pursuing leadership/taking on a leader role

Table 1: Overview of supporting and hindering attitudes

Attitudes supporting the process

The most prevalent attitudes supporting collective knowledge creation were found in relation to being open and appreciating others. *An attitude of openness* encompasses being open toward others in the group, but also being open toward oneself (e.g., emotions, personal experiences, etc.), and the process of knowledge creation in general. Here, students reported that they were able to openly express and share whatever comes to their mind, without the fear of being (negatively) judged. This seems to be associated with appreciating others. Student teams sharing an *appreciative attitude* reported that every single member, each idea, expressed feeling and thought, etc., were valued. The contributions and ideas of each member were perceived as crucial for the process. Even conflicts or challenges were described as something positive that needs to be appreciated, as they allow students to progress with their ideas, and help them to grow together as a team. Both attitudes directly influence how the team members communicate and interact with each other as the following quote illustrates: "I experience that our group work happens in an open atmosphere of authenticity and integrity and that even in disagreement regarding the work or work process a mutual appreciation and respect stands at first place" [17:154]

A pre-requisite for success in any group endeavor seems to be group members' willingness and engagement. We identified attitude descriptions of *willingness* in relation to the organization of work, contribution, and fairness. Being willing means that every team member is willing to contribute to the team, and is motivated to overcome conflicts that arise within the team - even if this touches a deeply personal level.

Engagement was emphasized by the students with regard to an exceptional high involvement within the group observed by all group members. Such an *attitude of being engaged* results in being deeply immersed in the process, which is necessary to create future-oriented innovation. The following quote illustrates this further: "Most of us participated and in the whole process actively and helped the rest of the group as much as she/he could. We had very ordered timing and schedule and used the whole potential" [26:125]

Furthermore, overcoming difficulties made KCTs believe in themselves. Student teams seemed to share a *confidence attitude*, i.e., they finally had confidence about the projects' success and believed that issues or challenges lying ahead can be resolved together as a group: "Of course this prototype should neither be some sort of sect-like manipulating thing, nor something which aims to replace psychiatric treatment. How to accomplish this will be a tough task, but somehow I am a little bit more optimistic now" [1:105]

Overcoming critical moments in the group and developing a sense of confidence that difficulties ahead can be coped with also encourages the identification process with the KCT or the project. Groups that had developed a sense of *"togetherness", identification*, or a social identity perceived themselves as a team, and were standing united behind their project and ideas. They were taking responsibility for their work as a team, even if this was not in line with instructor feedback or course requirements.

The last attitude we identified in our data that supports future-oriented innovations relates to integration. Having an *integrative attitude* touches the existential level of every team member and at the same time highlights the importance of the group.

Students described how they built upon each other's ideas and how they integrated the personal aims and ideas of each group member. When sharing an integrative attitude, students reported that every group member has to be heard, and her personal interests should be met, so that in the end, every single member would be satisfied with the prototype and could relate to it on a personal level.

To conclude, our data suggests that the attitudes are contingent upon each another. Their appearance in the data is chronologically aligned with the process of Theory-U, passing the cognitive, emotional and social, and, finally, the existential dimension. Our data further suggests that only the KCTs that established an integrative attitude within the team experienced a complete shift from I-to-We and emergent collective knowledge creation and achieved high prototype ratings.

Inverse and hindering attitudes

We found descriptions about attitudes that are inversely related to the attitudes described above and represent the lack of the supporting attitudes (e.g., a lack of openness or appreciation, lacking confidence or being unwilling, etc., for an overview see Table 1). In addition to that, we discovered being persuasive and pursuing leadership as two attitudes that we consider as detrimental for a successful knowledge creation process. These two attitudes only occurred in KCTs that neither experienced a shift from I-to-We, nor collective knowledge creation. These KCTs also received the lowest prototype ratings.

Being persuasive means the effort to convince others in the KCT about one's own ideas in a manipulative manner while concealing one's personal agenda. In this attitude, members did not value or consider ideas from others when they were not in line with their personal ideas or goals. The attitude to *pursue leadership or to take on a leadership role* was manifested within teams that had some dominant members, who were only focused on realizing their own ideas. Instances of this attitude further described attempts of trying to overrule others and making critical decisions without consulting the team members.

Intensity of attitudes seems to matter

Interestingly, the occurrence of supportive attitudes was observed in all KCTs. But the teams with the highest prototype ratings described more instances in their journals than the other teams and the respective attitudes were mentioned by more or all team members. However, two attitudes were only found in KCTs that were rated highly: integration and identifying/"togetherness". This may indicate that future-oriented innovations are collectively created when the individual experiences and ideas from the presencing phase can be cultivated on a collective level through a feeling of "togetherness" and an integrative attitude within the team. Furthermore, the absence of inverse attitudes seems to be crucial. Although inverse attitudes were found in all teams, the intensity seems to differ in relation to the innovation outcome: We postulate that the lower the occurrence of inverse attitudes is within a team, the better the outcome (i.e., the prototype) will be in the end. Since the two inverse attitudes were only prevalent in weak KCTs, we assume that the existence of supportive attitudes is not enough. Nonetheless, the absence of inverse attitudes that hin¬der the collective creation of knowledge is of high relevance during the Theory-U process, especially during crystallizing and prototyping.

The role of the instructor in the Theory-U process

To derive practical knowledge on managing a Theory-U process, we systematically analyzed the role of instructors and how they can positively intervene in the process. We identified the following four key elements: moderated sessions to foster supportive attitudes, coaching sessions to reflect on existing mental models, the facilitator as a "role model", and the role of the physical environment.

Moderated knowledge (creation) processes

Students indicated that they benefited from being encouraged to reflect on their personal interest and assumptions before forming a group (i.e., "question that really matters" from the first session), as this helped them to create awareness regarding their own points of view and differences concerning the opinions of others. After group formation, a dialogue setting (Bohm, 1996; Isaacs, 1999) as well as the world café method (Brown & Isaacs, 2005) was used for collective sense-making. These moderated sessions aimed to give students guidelines how they could interact within their teams.

Students confirmed the benefit of the dialogue method to aid their group communication processes as they have described struggling to communicate with each other due to their differing disciplinary backgrounds. This didactic method may be crucial for developing a We-perspective, given that the ability to reflect the own point of view in relation to the perspective of the group and/or other team-members oftentimes preceded the explicit shift from I-to-We, and thus should be fostered.

The world café setting supports students' common understanding by exchanging ideas and thoughts across KCTs to gain a group-external perspective. Additionally, KCTs have reported to benefit from this setting on a socio-emotional level, as they have realized that other groups are facing similar issues or concerns within their groups. Furthermore, the possibility of not only working on projects on a theoretical basis, but having a "hands-on" experience during the deep observation, and primarily during prototyping, as well as multiple possibilities for directly cooperating with other KCT-members or across groups, was reported as inspiring and rewarding, and helped participants to gain novel insights.

Coaching sessions

The importance of the coaching sessions during the observation and prototyping phase, as well as the dialogue method and the presencing phase (see Figure 1) itself have been described by the students as positive and supportive experiences. They help students to reflect on their projects, to "detangle" thoughts and ideas and reflect on their mental models as well as to make relevant decisions. Our data suggests that it is important for instructors to only coach the KCTs with respect to their general process following Theory-U, but not directly on a content-level. Instructors should mainly support participants in critically reflecting and questioning their ideas and assumptions to uncover latent concepts and themes regarding their topic and provide constructive feedback for improvements. If instructors intervene on a content-level directly, this is reported as a negative experience, especially when they appear to be "judging" the idea based on personal taste, or when omitting personal opinions and their reasons for this "judgment". Furthermore, instructors should address the whole group when coaching, as interactions with only one individual from the group without consolidating the KCT (e.g., interacting with mainly one individual although the whole KCT is present, or coaching only one individual of the group) too are reported as negative, creating "barriers" within the KCT.

The instructors as "role models"

The continuous interaction between students and instructors, as well as students' observing the interactions within the instructor team, implicitly influences them. For example, in the beginning of the course, some students have reported that they try to convince, impress, or even "flatter" the instructors to convey their ideas. However, students stopped this behavior after the first phases and started to view the instructors as "process guides" who provide valuable feedback. Students indicated that they are highly involved in the project out of personal interest and no longer just work to obtain ECTS-credits or a good grade, but aim to do something meaningful that is relevant to them personally. Thus, we have observed that the way instructors act and approach students and their projects during seminar and coaching sessions enables students to "take charge" of their projects, which results in a deep immersion on a personal and sometimes even existential level. It appears that instructors act as "role models" for establishing supporting attitudes within the KCTs, and that their behavior (including usage of didactical means) provides a safe environment for students to explore and nurture their ideas.

The role of the physical environment (during the presencing phase)

Apart from the didactical setting and methods employed, students also emphasized the effect of the physical environments. While not explicitly mentioning the physical setting in the "typical" classes held within a university seminar room, the outdoor setting in the presencing session was repeatedly cited as a positive experience. In general, participants reported mixed perceptions regarding the presencing itself. Some individuals experienced it to be an unnecessary pause within their projects, and some reported that nothing significant happened to them during presencing. But most students described it as an interesting and important experience that allowed them to "take a step back", and, at the very least, relax a bit or "take a break".

Being in nature and confronting oneself with the project appears to enable students to gain a new perspective of their topic. Reported experiences that facilitated presencing was that students were in the nature surrounded by woods, left their usual environment, were all by themselves, not using technological devices, as well as not having to pay attention to time passing and suspending decisions for a while. The start of the crystallizing phase took place in the same nature environment, directly after the individual presencing. The KCTs shared their presencing experiences and were asked to reflect on them within their KCT. Not changing the environment and being "forced" to instantly consolidate within the team was reported as a catalyst for idea development. In most cases, this setting helped the KCTs to uncover and understand novel connections and themes within their project topic.

Discussion: Overcoming the three forms of 21st century illiteracies with Theory-U

Illiteracy 1: Overcoming the inability to see

Overcoming the illiteracy of not being able to see involves changing cognitive and perceptual patterns as well as semantic frameworks (Bohm, 1996; Schein, 1993). We have fostered this within our course design by starting the Theory-U process with a reflection on the "question that really matters" for the students. Further, students had to persistently question their patterns of thinking and beliefs. This had cautiously enabled them to uncover implicit assumptions, concepts and themes and had turned out to be highly relevant for the progress of the KCTs projects. Thus, we postulate that learning to "see" (corresponding to the first form of illiteracies), can be achieved by immersing deeply into observation situations and by consistently and critically (self-)reflecting on (personal) assumptions and observing behaviors of others, considering their perspectives, motivations, as well as their personal assumptions and beliefs.

Participants underwent a gradual development from an egocentric I-perspective to a relational I-perspective. This entails an awareness of the own role in relation to the group: one shifts perspectives and starts to "see" oneself in the group. It is situated in the cognitive and semantic dimension of the shift and represents the necessary point of departure for developing a We-perspective in the next step.

Illiteracy 2: Overcoming the inability to deal with uncertainty

Uncertainties and challenges to deal with multiple, complex possibilities automatically arise - not only because our world is hard to predict, but also when framing Theory-U as an open-ended learning process with an outcome that cannot be known in advance (neither by the students, nor by the course instructors). Within our course design, we intend to address this illiteracy by means of collective sense organs (e.g., Scharmer 2007, p. 398) and the dialogue (or similar modes or methods of communication), which assist participants with understanding and reflecting their perspectives and insights thus far, as well as recognizing the challenges ahead. Based on our findings, we suggest that challenges should be faced and mastered on a team level, and that the whole group needs to show a readiness or willingness to take on these challenges, viewing them as a potential to grow. The group experience, its perspective, and its development are crucial for the ability to deal with uncertainty, and should be explicitly supported by continuous coaching with external facilitators.

According to our findings, the method of creating collective sense organs (see, for instance, Scharmer, 2007, p. 398), as well as dialogical communication foster a shift from I-to-We on an emotional and social dimension: the development of We-perspectives (explicit and implicit). This coincides with loosing individuality (in terms of an isolated and egocentric I-perspective) and leads to a joint understanding within the KCT.

The inability to deal with complexity seems to be related to a general (oftentimes implicit) belief in right-or-wrong dichotomies, which can also result in a persuasive communication style. This has its roots in uncertainty, based on an egocentric I-perspective, which isolates the individual cognitively, but also emotionally and socially (similar to an ego-system, in Scharmer, 2007, p. 218). To overcome this isolation, it is crucial to connect with others in an *appreciative* and *trustful* manner. Regarding attitudes established within the team, willingness and confidence attitudes as well as feelings of togetherness become important at this point. They entail a future-oriented belief in a positive outcome, and the ability to face and resolve challenges, uncertainties, and conflicts within and for the team. Thus, it provides a necessary framing that allows the team to operate. Interactions and coaching sessions should help the innovation team to address conflicts and to not shy away from them, but to understand conflicts as necessary and relevant for "growth".

We propose that these frameworks and methods allow for developing fundamental skills for dealing with complexity and uncertainty. This includes social skills (communication, conflict solving, decision making, ect.), taking (calculated) risks, and collaborating in a space of the unknown. These skills are fundamental for dealing with complexity and uncertainty and lead to behavioral patterns and approaches supporting innovation, like trusting in team and process, commitment, playfulness, and taking responsibility.

Illiteracy 3: Overcoming the inability to anticipate novelty

With our course design we intend to address the illiteracy of not being able to anticipate novelty although it is already emerging (in potentials). Our data suggests that this can be influenced positively from the very beginning by allowing participants to engage within projects on a personal level ("question that matters"). Furthermore, the didactics tackles this illiteracy indirectly throughout the entire process of Theory-U- namely, by changing (learning) settings and environments (e.g., individual tasks and group settings, autonomous project work and explicit coaching sessions, in-class environments, and non-university environments outside in an urban or nature environment). The need to enable overcoming the anticipate novelty illiteracy peaks in the solitude experience of presencing, and needs to be triggered (on multiple occasions) before this point.

It is important here for the Theory-U process, that it is not "merely" about an abstract innovation process, but about *personal change*, thus, touching individuals on a personal, or even an existential level (Peschl & Fundneider, 2017; Roth, Socha, & Tenenberg, 2016; Ingold, 2013). As demonstrated, a prerequisite for this is a personal involvement and engagement that is provided by the initial "question that matters". Furthermore, the previously mentioned ability to see, and the ability to deal with uncertainty, as well as the related attitudes and shifts, act as an important basis for developing the skills relevant for "recognizing" emergent novelty. These skills include re-framing, re-directing, and potential-oriented sensing the future. When entering the presencing phase equipped with the mindsets, attitudes, and skills described above, individuals manage to "deep-dive" the U and sense what is not "here" yet, but what "wants" to emerge from the future.

Implications for the organizational context

Although stemming from an educational setting, we believe that our findings contain valuable insights for Theory-U and presencing in general and for the organizational context in particular. They are potentially beneficial for everyone orchestrating or directly working with teams in the context of innovation and Theory-U. This may include practitioners or educators alike, as well as team leaders, or managers working in human resources or organization development. We present the implications in a chronological fashion, along the Theory-U process.

The "way down" the U: Overcoming Illiteracies

Although situated in an education setting, our course design is based on "real-life" frameworks of economic or social innovations stemming from organizational projects we (the team of instructors/research team) have been conducting over the past years. The students do not "just" theoretically learn about innovation, but actually go both through an innovation and personal transformation process, and produce an innovative prototype. Some of the projects were eventually realized and still exist, some of the participants got inspired and became entrepreneurs afterwards and founded start-ups.

One of the crucial aspects in this process is the appointment of a facilitator (or better, a team of facilitators), explicitly taking on this role. The decision, who is taking this role, has to be well-considered – especially in the organizational context. Should it be a person from inside the organization or an external person? Someone who is part of the innovation team or an employee who is not involved on a team level? These considerations are very important, as it is the task of the facilitator to frame the innovation or change process and guide the team through the Theory-U process as an open learning experience. This is a learning process that has a not-yet-known outcome. It contains elements of open-endedness, complexity, change, transformation, co-creation, as well as uncertainty (e.g., Grisold & Peschl, 2016; Sanders & Stappers, 2008). Facilitators must be aware of their role in such uncertain situations, and provide stability and a positive stance toward uncertain developments or futures; framing it as a potential, rather than an obstacle or risk. At the same time, facilitators need to assist in reflecting, challenging, and questioning assumptions and beliefs, supporting the team to open up and immerse in the innovation process on a deeply personal and existential level, which, in turn, may create uncertainty. Fostering a trusting and open atmosphere is a prerequisite to make this process happen successfully.

We observed that participants show a high readiness to deal with these circumstances and to commit to the process if they are able to involve themselves on a personal level. Thus, the framing of the innovation process as a point of departure should be relevant, comprehensible, as well as significant to the participants on a personal level. This seems to be one of the core principles in order to foster engagement. Of course, Theory-U is a future-oriented, transformational process of change in the sense that the initial ideas may fundamentally change and develop throughout the process, which demands radical open-endedness and the readiness to commit to the process, including its complexity. Thus, the process of Theory-U touches upon cognitive, emotional and social, as well as existential levels. Facilitators need to prepare and support the innovators undergoing this process to cope with the challenges coming along with operating on these levels, or even to embrace them.

We identified two key issues concerning the facilitation of the Theory-U process. Firstly, a *perceptual shift to a We-perspective* within the team, followed by the transition from an individual to a collective presencing process, i.e., the collectivization of presencing experiences. This collectivization appears to lead to higher quality in innovation outcomes. But how should the transition be realized, and how and when may facilitators intervene to support it? Secondly, we identified specific *attitudes* that help to cultivate individual presencing experiences within the teams. Here, the

191

question arises of how these attitudes may be fostered by a facilitator. This might be even more challenging in an organization than in the education context since hierarchical interdependencies between innovators are likely. In the following, we will discuss overcoming the illiteracies of the 21st century from an organizational perspective and reflect on the facilitator's role.

Enabling to see in organizations

Mapping Theory-U to an organizational context, it is important to offer space and time to *not* work primarily on topics relevant to the organization (only), but on an issue that is at the same time personally interesting and significant for the innovators. Engagement and (personal) involvement cannot be mandated externally, but have to evolve and grow intrinsically in a sphere of personal interest, relatedness, and relevance. Facilitators who know the company very well may bring in a "question that really matters" that establishes a close link between the participants' (personal) interests and the organization's goals or issues. This can be achieved in a participatory fashion aligning these two lines of interest.

In a next step, it is crucial to uncover the underlying assumptions of the "questions that matter" in order to become aware of and challenge related cognitive frameworks and cognitive patterns — from an individual to a team level. Ultimately, this change of perspective can have the power to transform the organization as a whole (see also Grisold & Peschl, 2017a, 2017b). To achieve this, it is necessary to guide innovation teams through continuous reflection, via explicit coaching, as well as persistently accompanying the innovation process in a guiding and coaching manner.

On a process level, the observation phase is crucial to develop the *ability to "see"*. This is, however, completely different from "just doing another" market or trend research. In the observation phase, innovation teams should literally get the possibility to experience new ways of seeing and learn to immerse into the object/phenomenon of observation. To design this phase as fruitful as possible, innovation teams should be "liberated" from organizational structures. They should have the possibility to become "explorers" who are leaving the organizational environment and context to make their observations. However, the goal of this observation phase is neither about finding and proving "objective truths" in the world "out there", nor is it about testing existing hypotheses; it rather aims at deeply and openly immersing into the world and, by that, gaining a profound understanding concerning the innovation object and its ecosystem. This may be achieved by employing qualitative methods such as biographic interviews, action research, user journeys, shadowing, ethnographic methods, first and second person methods, etc. (e.g., Laurel, 2003; Kawulich, 2005; Spradley, 1980; Scharmer, 2007b). These are methods inspired from qualitative social research, but are applied in an exploratory and practical manner.

A further crucial element in this knowledge creation process concerns the team composition. Building a diverse team (based on socio-demographics, ethnicity, disciplinary knowhow, levels of creativity, expertise, etc.) is necessary to stimulate the innovators' change of perspective. People in diverse teams are forced to constantly challenge their subjective world perceptions and need to find a way to communicate and understand each other. Transferring this idea to organizational contexts, people from different departments with a variety of different backgrounds, differing in age, sex, hierarchy and level of expertise, should form an innovation team. To sum up, following this strategy allows for experiential learning and understanding the necessities to overcome the first form of illiteracy (i.e., inability to see).

Enabling to deal with uncertainty in organizations

After having gone through the observation phase, consolidating within the innovation team and sharing the observations early on is important. To support this, dialogical communication methods (e.g., Bohm, 1996; Isaacs, 1999) proved to be useful. Such ways of conversing are often quite unfamiliar to most people. Therefore, it is essential to explicitly train and cultivate them before collective sense making takes place.

Furthermore, it is of immense importance to gain insights from a group-external perspective. But these insights and perspectives have to stem from peers. It can be organized by interacting and discussing with either other innovation teams, or, if there is only one innovation team operating within the organization at this moment, exchange with peers from other departments within the organization. This is necessary in order to question collective norms and perspectives developed in the group. Similarly the facilitator should not involve him/herself in the collective sense organs process on a content-level, neither should individuals from higher management or in leading positions get involved (unless they are members of the innovation team), as they tend to approach them with a judging attitude, and may create a hierarchical imbalance which could negatively affect the innovation team and its development. The underlying rationale is that "collective sensing mechanisms use the power of shared seeing and dialogue to tap an unused resource of collective sense making and thinking together." (Scharmer, 2007, p. 398).

Collective sense making can be supported by workshop formats such as world cafe (Brown & Isaacs, 2005) or similar methods. Such settings draw their strength from informal organizational peer structures and enable the innovation team to interact and communicate with peers in a critical, but appreciative and open fashion. This exchange with peers re-situates the observations in the context of the organization and is crucial for bonding and developing a common understanding among innovation team members. Furthermore, it is a way to reassure the innovation team not only on the content, but also on a socio-emotional level to cope with the inherently prevalent uncertainty and overcome the second form of illiteracy (i.e., inability to deal with uncertainty).

The "bottom" of the U: Presencing

Presencing is a highly sophisticated and fragile process of sensing the future and getting in resonance with wants to emerge (Scharmer, 2007, 2016) and, by that, it is about starting to "see" what is not here yet (compare also Bloch, 1986; Kellner & O´Hara, 1976). It is a fragile and non-specific process and requires exposing oneself to the uncertainty of an unknown and unfolding future by being sensitive to what "wants" to emerge. Thus, it helps to overcome the third form of illiteracy (i.e., inability to anticipate novelty).

Enabling to anticipate novelty in organizations. The Theory-U process "peaks" in the bottom of the U: in the presencing. Before entering the silent solitude of the presencing phase, the facilitator should once again frame the right mindset, reminding participants of the core principles of Theory-U. It is relevant for the innovation process to once more let the teams consolidate explicitly on their current status and understanding of their insights and ideas before their individual presencing experiences. Innovators should not try to have a clear idea about their innovation projects at this state, but have a profound understanding of the *scope* (it can also be seen as a "semantic container") in which such a project might emerge. Having this in mind for the emergent field, the individual presencing almost "automatically" contributes to the team's project idea afterwards. Furthermore, presencing should take place in an outdoor natural and/or quiet environment with a low level of artificial stimuli and distractions. Ideally, this takes place in physical and structural (enough time, being alone) distance to the organization. It is important that the innovators do not experience time pressure or the pressure to perform (individually). The natural setting supports the process of letting go and immersing in the presencing. Only if participants are exposed to as few as possible distracting stimuli, they will open up and get into resonance with an emerging future. Entering this "empty space" and leaving behind expectations and projections from the past enables and makes room for the emergence of novelty.

Collectivization of (the individual) presencing

The innovators have to deal with loosing and willingly letting go of ownership of own thoughts and ideas. It is important to leave behind and let go of one's own patterns of thoughts and beliefs in order to open up for other forms of perception (sensing). Thus, presencing is connected to the existential and transformative dimension of the shift from I-to-We. We postulate that only when *all illiteracies have been overcome* and the shift from I-to-We was successfully accomplished before the presencing, the individual presencing experiences will lead to collective and emergent knowledge.

Therefore, it is important that the members of the innovation team immediately share their presencing experiences after they return from their individual "journeys". This will then initiate the process of crystallizing. Fellow team members' ideas must not be seen as rivaling or competing. If so, it would be necessary to stop working on the content level, but address group dynamics and ensure to create an integrative, respectful, and listening attitude. Only then, the continuance with presencing is fruitful. Coaching and intervention will be necessary, until the team develops a coherent We-perspective. Following this loop might be even easier in the organizational than in the educational context, as organizations normally follow a common purpose. It is important to consider that even in case of serious group conflicts the team should not split or exclude team members. Overcoming group conflicts creates a motivating and positive energy for the process and excluding team members would only encourage the establishment of hindering attitudes.

The "way up" the U: Collective emergent knowledge creation

After the presencing phase the role of the facilitator will change as the teams start to emancipate themselves from the facilitator. The importance and the frequency of facilitator interventions are decreasing as the facilitator is not in charge anymore to guide the process, but can be addressed for support anytime. Thus, on "the way up" the U, teams can be encouraged to foster their supporting attitudes, but they need to already have established the right mindset on "the way down" in order to be able to collectively experience emergent knowledge creation after presencing. The innovation teams mostly work autonomously and have established their own network of support and feedback within and outside the organization.

Conclusions

Our grounded theory analysis based on journal entries from 61 students (six journal entries per student) in 12 Theory-U processes, revealed three major issues (i.e., the timing of the shift from I-to-We, sharing supportive attitudes, and the importance of coaching sessions) that have to be kept in mind when facilitating knowledge creation processes. These conclusions are generally valuable for Theory-U-based settings that benefit from the collectivization of presencing experiences and ideas, and are relevant to both the field of education and organizational contexts.

The timing of the shift from I-to-We matters

We found that the timing of the shift from I-to-We is critical for achieving a promising outcome. Teams that experienced emergent moments of collective knowledge creation all show a shift from I-to-We *before* the individual presencing. Conversely, groups that did not experience the shift prior to this point did not report instances of collective knowledge creation and their prototypes were rated lower than the prototypes of the groups that did already experience collective knowledge creation. Sharing a We-perspective *before* presencing enables the KCTs to collectively converge the individual ideas irrespective of idea ownership. When the KCTs have not established a We-perspective at this point, their individual ideas are treated as competing or rivaling concepts. Thus, we postulate that *the perceptual shift from I-to-We has to occur before the presencing.*

To support the shift form I-to-We, facilitators should encourage the development of supporting attitudes within the teams and encourage the suppression of hindering attitudes as early on as possible. The shift from I-to-We does not manifest suddenly, but appears to be a *gradual* development. We identified four stages of the shift within the most successful teams. First, participants started off with an egocentric I-perspective, marked by students' focus on reflections about their personal interests, gains, and motivation, without considering their groups at all (yet). The second stage (i.e., the relational I-perspective) was made visible through a change in students' perspective as they oriented their reflections in reference to their groups. Participants' reflections addressed their role and contributions in and for their KCT. This initiated the following stage, which encompassed an established We-perspective indicated by a plural-first-person perspective in the journal entries. Finally, the fourth and last stage refers to an implicit We-perspective. Here, coherent reports of group processes from all members without explicit differentiation between self and groups were found, in particular during crystallizing and prototyping.

Facilitators may support this shift from I-to-We by constantly initiating reflection and feedback loops and fostering supportive attitudes. Since facilitators act as role models, it is important that they also develop supportive attitudes within their own team before starting the knowledge creation process. Furthermore, group coachings at all critical stages (for an overview see Figure 1 or Peschl et al., 2014) to explicitly support group dynamics are seen as vital means to encourage the shift from I-to-We.

Sharing supportive attitudes

All KCTs reported instances of both supporting and hindering attitudes at certain times during the innovation process. A distinguishing feature between teams that were rated as more successful than others was that supporting attitudes were shared among all team members. In the beginning of the process, an appreciative and open attitude seems to be most essential, followed by the relevancy for being willing and having confidence in the project during the phases of deep observation and collective sense making. In the subsequent phase (presencing) the importance for shared engagement understanding is critical as this also encourages team members' sense of "togetherness" as well as integration. In relation to establishing a We-perspective, an integrative attitude allows team members to collectively create (novel) knowledge by converging their presencing experiences and insights, instead of treating them as rivaling ideas that have to be "fought over". However, once the successful teams had developed a joint idea, their openness toward new ideas faded as they started to focus and prototype their idea in an integrative fashion. This clear process (high openness in the beginning with fading openness after presencing, accompanied by a focused, but integrative attitude, see Figure 2) distinguishes successful teams from less successful teams.

Almost all teams reported either task-related or relationship-related conflicts at some point during the knowledge creation process. We experienced that seemingly unsolvable group problems and differences can be solved with enough patience and the right attitudes (openness, appreciation, willingness, respectfulness, and confidence/belief). Different to other teams, the most successful teams did not develop hindering attitudes, such as being persuasive or pursuing leadership. Developing supporting attitudes can overcome the negative effect of hindering or inverse attitudes. To be willing and confident in the project, for example, lead to a positive re-framing of uncomfortable dynamics and encouraged team members to perceive the challenges as an opportunity to grow and explore. Establishing an attitude of being open and appreciating very early on in the process prepares the ground for coping with the sometimes challenging experiences throughout the process (see Figure 2 for an overview). Nonetheless, the most crucial attitude (which is certainly closely interlinked with the other attitudes) seems to be the idea that all team members need to be represented within the project (i.e., integration). This "fundamental rule" might sometimes require uncomfortable discussions, but the teams then also report enjoying working on their projects and identify with their teams and their projects on both a personal and content level. Furthermore, it leads to highly committed team members who take responsibility for their ideas and the decisions made. Consequently, the developed innovative prototypes bear a high potential for realization in these groups. A team lacking sufficient supporting attitudes can develop them over time and it does positively affect the team if the facilitators explicitly believe in and support the team's ability to do so. The facilitator, however, must not let him-/herself be discouraged by the group members' struggles or fears of failing to create novelty. We are convinced that with enough time and emphasis, every group can be coached to a level of good performance.

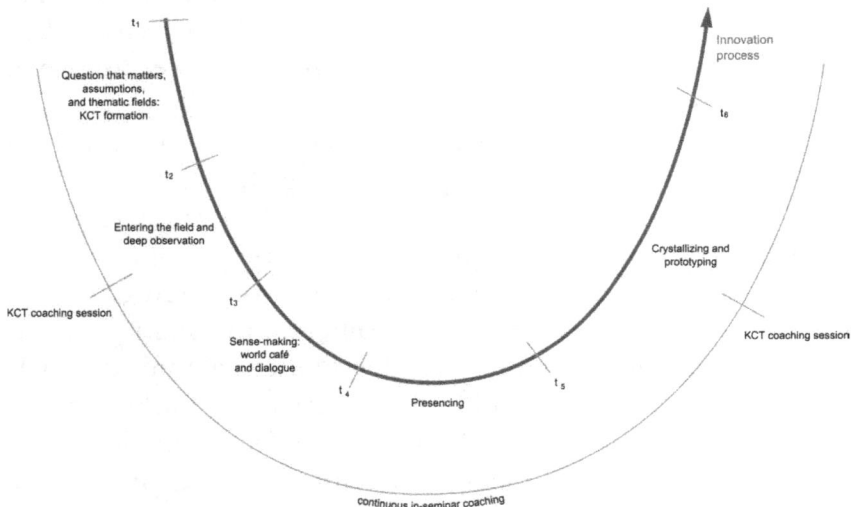

Figure 2: Occurrences and associations of supporting attitudes in relation to the shift from an I-to-We and collective knowledge creation in high-performing teams

Coaching sessions with the teams

As described above, there are moments in the process that have been experienced to be challenging for the team members. In order to support coping with that, instructors offered coaching sessions for the KCTs. These coaching sessions aimed to provide critical reflection in an appreciating atmosphere. Instructors provided guidance regarding the innovation process in general and were reported to positively influence KCTs' idea development.

An appreciative and sensitive coaching in a Socratic manner helps the teams to create convergence and a feeling of joint understanding of the novelty within their project, which has yet to "come forth" in the future of their process. Team building support benefits the development of a We-perspective within the teams, and should take place before the presencing. Support for knowledge creation should encourage KCTs' engagement and (personal) involvement in the project. However, a balance between facilitating social and knowledge creation processes has to be found. As the facilitators' involvement should fade after the presencing, it is crucial for the coach to *not* get involved on a content-level, but merely to help the team to uncover the implicit and latent connections, concepts, and themes arising within their project (Poli 2011). This requires an integrative and "listening" stance aimed at converging individual presencing experiences at a collective level, rather than treating them as competing concepts. Thus, instructors themselves must not be involved in the idea creation since it is important that they do not judge ideas as good or bad, but approach the topic in a reflective manner (e.g., by asking profound questions). Furthermore, to foster an integrative attitude, it is important that they coach the whole KCT and do not engage in individual coaching. Otherwise, these kinds of behaviors would be in conflict with the perceived role of instructors as "process guides" who provide valuable insight and feedback in an appreciative, but critical and reflective fashion.

Facilitators were found to act as role models who transpire certain values and modes of working into the KCTs. They need to be aware of this role in order to foster supporting attitudes within the KCTs by displaying these sets of attitudes (within the team of facilitators) when interacting with the KCTs. We propose that facilitators work in a team. Firstly, a facilitator team can mirror and demonstrate attitudes in more concrete and relational terms. Interactions within the facilitator team serve to role-model mindsets and attitudes. Secondly, more than one facilitator can cover a wider range of needs of the KCTs in terms of information, expertise, perspectives, and competences. Thirdly, working in a team makes it possible to share work and responsibility (didactical, organizational, and methodological) and to support each other cognitively and emotionally, as the facilitators too follow the U.

If hindering or inverse attitudes appear, coaching should deal with that without judging the team for showing them—and stress the positive effects of adopting beneficial attitudes on the Theory-U process in general. In addition to coaching on the level of group dynamics, concrete methods to facilitate beneficial instead of hindering attitudes can be offered to the teams. The dialogue method proved to be very useful, and the collective sense organs turned out to be beneficial too.

Limitations and directions for future research

It should be noted that our results originate from a qualitative action research setting applying grounded theory. Thus, we may generalize our insights in a conceptual manner, but cannot claim normative or "objective" results in terms of a "quantifiable" generalization to populations.

Whilst our findings stem from an educational setting, we do belief that practitioners in both educational as well as organizational contexts may benefit from our insights. An issue that does require further research is that the findings stem from team members that had not experienced the Theory-U process previously. We cannot make predictions whether the positive effects may "flatten", or what kind of challenges may arise when continuously employing Theory-U to create innovations within a team. Neither can we make claims with regard to the facilitator interventions that may be required in such cases. Future research may take this issue into account. Investigations in the organizational contexts could prove to be a promising research setting for this attempt (e.g., by accompanying an innovation team throughout the course of several projects). Furthermore, small interventions and actions of facilitators (e.g., providing food or concrete bodily arrangements within a physical setting) which may often be overseen but might have considerable impact also require further research.

Although we belief that our research identified crucial developments and aspects that foster high performance in innovation processes, facilitators cannot force groups to evolve to that point. They can only prepare the grounds. It seems as if high performance in innovation processes involves a certain amount of what the ancient Greeks called "Kairos" (the right moment). We cannot produce Kairos deliberately or impose it artificially. But by setting the right framework, intervening at crucial points, and transpiring mindsets, attitudes, and skills, we can prepare innovation teams for this moment, enable them to anticipate and identify it, and encourage them to take advantage of it (in the sense of an Enabling Space; Peschl & Fundneider, 2014).

References

Adolf, M., & Stehr, N. (2014). *Knowledge*. Abingdon, Oxon: Routledge.

Amabile, T. (1996). *Creativity in context*. Boulder: Westview Press.

Argyris, C., Putnam, R., & McLain Smith, D. (1985). *Action Science. Concepts, methods, and skills for research and intervention*. San Francisco, CA: Jossey-Bass Inc. Publishers.

Baregheh, A., Rowley, J., & Sambrook, S. (2009). Towards a multidisciplinary definition of innovation. *Management Decision, 47*(8), 1323–1339.

Bloch, E. (1986). *The principle of hope* (3 Volumes). Cambridge, MA: MIT Press.

Bohm, D. (1996). *On dialogue*. London; New York: Routledge.

Brown, T. (2008). Design hinking. *Harvard Business Review, 86*(6), 84–93.

Brown, T. (2009). *Change by design. How design thinking transforms organizations and inspires innovation*. New York, NY: Harper Collins.

Brown, J., & Isaacs, D. (2005). *The world cafe. Shaping our futures through conversations that matter*. San Francisco, CA: Berrett-Koehler.

Buchanan, J. M., & Vanberg, V. J. (1991). The market as a creative process. *Economics and Philosophy, 7*(2), 167–186.

Charmaz, K. (2006). *Constructing Grounded Theory. A practical guide through qualitative analysis*. SAGE Publications Ltd.

Clark, A., & D. Chalmers, D. (1998). The extended mind. *Analysis, 58*(1), 7–19.

Clark, A. (2008). *Supersizing the mind. Embodiment, action, and cognitive extension*. Oxford, New York: Oxford University Press.

Clark, A. (2013). Whatever next? Predictive brains, situated agents, and the future of cognitive science. *Behavioral and Brain Sciences, 36*(3), 1–73.

Clark, A. (2016). *Surfing uncertainty. Prediction, action, and the embodied mind*. Oxford, New York: Oxford University Press.

Clark, A. (2017). A nice surprise? Predictive processing and the active pursuit of novelty. *Phenomenology and the Cognitive Sciences 2017*, 1–14.

Dodgson, M., & D. Gann, D. (2010). *Innovation. A very short introduction*. Oxford: Oxford University Press.

Dorst, K. (2006). Design problems and design paradoxes. *Design Issues, 22*(3), 4–17.

Enna, N. (2014, May). 10 Skills the workforce of the future will need. *Huffington Post Impact x*.

Ettlie, J. E., Bridges, W.P., & O´Keefe, R. D. (1984). Organisational strategic and structural differences for radical vs. incremental innovation. *Management Science, 30*(6), 682–695.

European Commission (2008). Decision No 1350/2008/EC of the European parliament and of the council of 16 December 2008 concerning the European Year of Creativity and Innovation (2009). *Official Journal of the European Union L 348*, 115–117.

European Commission (2015). State of the innovation union 2015. Brussels: Directorate-General for Research and Innovation.

Fagerberg, J. (2006). Innovation. A guide to the literature. In J. Fagerberg, D. C. Mowery, & R. R. Nelson (Eds.), *The Oxford handbook of innovation* (pp. 1–26). Oxford: Oxford University Press.

Fagerberg, J., & Verspagen, B. (2009). Innovation studies. The emerging structure of a new scientific field. *Research Policy, 38*(2), 218–233.

Felin, T., Kauffman, S., Koppl, R., & Longo, G. (2014). Economic opportunity and evolution: beyond landscapes and bounded rationality. *Strategic Entrepreneurship Journal, 8*(4), 269–282.

Foerster, H.v. (1972). Perception of the future and the future of perception. *Instructional Science, 1*, 31–43.

Frey, C. B., & Osborne, M. A. (2013). *The future of employment: How susceptible are jobs to computerisation*. Oxford: Oxford University.

Froese, T., & Di Paolo, E. A. (2011). The enactive approach. Theoretical sketches from cell to society. *Pragmatics & Cognition, 19*(1), 1–36.

Gibson, J. J. (1986). *The ecological approach to visual perception* (new ed.). New York: Psychology Press. Taylor and Francis Group.

Glasersfeld, E.v. (1974). Piaget and the radical constructivist epistemology. In C.D. Smock and E.v. Glasersfeld (Eds.), *Epistemology and education* (pp. 1–24). Athens, GA: Follow Through Publications.

Glasersfeld, E.v. (1989). Cognition, construction of knowledge, and teaching. *Synthese, 80*(1), 121–141.

Glasersfeld, E.v. (1995a). A constructivist approach to teaching. In L. P. Steffe & J. Gale (Eds.), *Constructivism in education* (pp. 3–16). Hillsdale, N.J.: Lawrence Erlbaum Associates.

Glasersfeld, E.v. (1995b). *Radical constructivism: a way of knowing and learning*. London: Falmer Press.

Grisold, T., & Peschl, M. F. (2016). Facilitating radical innovation by double loop learning. Introducing a strategic framework and toolbox. In E. Tome (Ed.), *Proceedings of the International Conference Theory and Application in the Knowledge Economy, TAKE 2016* (pp. 440–451).

Grisold, T, & Peschl, M. F. (2017a). Change from the inside out. Towards a culture of unlearning by overcoming Organizational Predictive Mind. In N. Tomaschek & D. Unterdorfer (Eds.), *Veränderung. Der Wandel als Konstante unserer Zeit* (pp. 45–63). Münster, New York: Waxmann.

Grisold, T., & Peschl, M. F. (2017b). Why a systems thinking perspective on cognition matters for innovation and knowledge creation. A framework towards leaving behind our projections from the past for creating new futures. *Systems Research and Behavioral Science, 34*(3), 335–353.

Guerriero, S. (Ed.) (2017). *Pedagogical knowledge and the changing nature of the teaching profession*. Paris: OECD Publishing.

Halpern, D. F. (2014). *Thought and knowledge: an introduction to critical thinking* (5th ed.). New York: Psychology Press. Taylor and Francis Group.

Hohwy, J. (2013). *The Predictive Mind*. Oxford: Oxford University Press.

Houde, S., & Hill, C. (1997). What do prototypes prototype? (2nd ed.). In M. Helander, T. Landauer, & P. Prabhu (Eds.), *Handbook of human-computer interaction* (pp. 367–381). Amsterdam: Elsevier.

Ingold, T. (2013). *Making. Anthropology, archaeology, art and architecture.* Abingdon, Oxon; New York, NY: Routledge.

Isaacs, W. N. (1999). *Dialogue and the art of thinking together: A pioneering approach to communicating in business and life.* New York: Doubleday Currency.

Kauffman, S. A. (1993). *The origins of order: Self-organisation and selection in evolution.* Oxford: Oxford University Press.

Kauffman, S. A. (2000). *Investigations.* New York: Oxford University Press.

Kauffman, S. A. (2014). Prolegomenon to patterns in evolution. *BioSystems, 123*(2014), 3–8.

Kawulich, B. B. (2005). Participant observation as a data collection method. *Forum: Qualitative Social Research, 6*(2), Art. 43.

Kelley, T. (2004). *The art of innovation. Lessons in creativity from IDEO, America's leading design firm.* London: Profile Books.

Kellner, D., & O´Hara, H. (1976). Utopia and Marxism in Ernst Bloch. *New German Critique, Autumn 1976*(9), 11–34.

Kim, D.H. (1999). *Introduction to systems thinking* (Vol. 16). Waltham, MA: Pegasus Communications.

Koppl, R., Kauffman, S., Felin, T., & Longo, G. (2014). Economics for a creative world. *Journal of Institutional Economics, 2014,* 1–31.

Krippendorff, K. (1989). On the essential contexts of artifacts or on the proposition that "Design is making sense (of things)". *Design Issues, 5*(2), 9–39.

Laurel, B. (Ed.) (2003). *Design research. Methods and perspectives.* Cambridge, MA: MIT Press.

Longo, G., Montevil, M., & Kauffman, S. (2012). No entailing laws, but enablement in the evolution of the biosphere. In (Ed.), *Proceedings of the Fourteenth International Conference on Genetic and Evolutionary Computation* (pp. 1379–1392).

Malone, T. W. (2004). *The future of work. How the new order of business will shape your organization, your management style, and your life.* Boston: Harvard Business School Press.

Menary, R. (Ed.) (2010). *The extended mind.* Cambridge, MA: MIT Press.

Miller, R. (2015). *Making Experimentalist Leadership practical. The theory and practice of futures literacy.* Victoria: Centre for Strategic Education. Seminar Series Paper (24).

Mitleton-Kelly, E. (2007). The emergence of final cause. In M. Aaltonen (Ed.), *The third lens. Multi-ontology sense-making and strategic decision-*

making (pp. 111–124). Adlershot: Ashgate Publishing.

Moggridge, B., Suri, J. F., & Bray, D. (2007). *People and prototypes*. In B. Moggridge (Ed.), *Designing interactions* (pp. 641–735). Cambridge, MA: MIT Press.

OECD/Eurostat (2005). *Oslo Manual: Guidelines for collecting and interpreting innovation data*. Paris: OECD Publishing. (3rd Ed.).

OECD (2015). Frascati Manual 2015: *Guidelines for collecting and reporting data on research and experimental development*. Paris: OECD Publishing.

OECD (2017). *OECD Digital Economy Outlook 2017*. Paris: OECD Publishing.

Ohly S., Sonnentag S., Niessen C., & Zapf D. (2010). Diary studies in organizational research: An Introduction and some practical recommendations. *J. Pers. Psychol., 9*, 79–93.

Peschl, M. F. (2006). Modes of knowing and modes of coming to know. Knowledge creation and knowledge co-construction as socio-epistemological engineering in educational processes. *Constructivist Foundations, 1*(3), 111–123.

Peschl, M. F., & Fundneider, T. (2008). Emergent Innovation and Sustainable Knowledge Co-creation. A Socio-Epistemological Approach to "Innovation from within". In M.D. Lytras, J. M. Carroll, E. Damiani et al. (Eds.), *The Open Knowledge Society: A Computer Science and Information Systems Manifesto* (pp. 101–108). New York, Berlin, Heidelberg: Springer (CCIS 19).

Peschl, M. F., & Fundneider, T. (2013). Theory-U and Emergent Innovation. Presencing as a method of bringing forth profoundly new knowledge and realities. In O. Gunnlaugson, C. Baron, & M. Cayer (Eds.), *Perspectives on Theory U: Insights from the field* (pp. 207–233). Hershey, PA: Business Science Reference/IGI Global.

Peschl, M. F., Bottaro, G., Hartner-Tiefenthaler, M., & Rötzer, K. (2014). Learning how to innovate as a socio-epistemological process of co-creation. Towards a constructivist teaching strategy for innovation. *Constructivist Foundations, 9*(3), 421–433.

Peschl, M. F., & Fundneider, T. (2014). Designing and enabling interfaces for collaborative knowledge creation and innovation. From managing to enabling innovation as socio-epistemological technology. *Computers and Human Behavior, 37*, 346–359.

Peschl, M. F., Fundneider, T., & Kulick, A. (2015). On the limitations of classical approaches to innovation. From predicting the future to enabling "thinking from the future as it emerges". In Austrian Council for Research and Technology Development (Ed.), *Designing the Future: Economic, Societal and Political Dimensions of Innovation* (pp.

454–475). Vienna, Austria: Echomedia.

Peschl, M. F., & Fundneider, T. (2017). Future-oriented innovation. How affordances and potentials can teach us how to learn from the future as it emerges. In W. Hofkirchner & M. Burgin (Eds.), *The future information society. Social and technological problems* (pp. 223–240). Singapore: World Scientific Publishing.

Peterson, E. P. (2013): Constructivist Pedagogy and Symbolism: Vico, Cassirer, Piaget, Bateson. *Educational Philosophy and Theory, 44*(8), 878-891.

Petitmengin, C. (2006). Describing one's subjective experience in the second person: An interview method for the science of consciousness. *Phenomenology and the Cognitive Sciences, 5*, 229–269.

Poli, R. (2006). The ontology of what is not there. In J. Malinowski & A. Pietruszczak (Eds.), *Essays in Logic and Ontology. Poznan Studies in the Philosophy of the Sciences and the Humanities: Vol. 91.* (pp. 73–80). Amsterdam/New York: Rodopi.

Poli, R. (2011). Ontological categories, latents and the irrational. In J. Cumpa & E. Tegtmeier (Eds.), *Ontological categories* (pp. 153–163). Heusenstamm: Ontos Verlag.

Pithers, R. T., & Soden, R. (2000). Critical thinking in education: a review. *Educational Research, 42*(3), 237–249.

Reason, P., & Bradbury, H. (Eds.) (2001). *Handbook of action research. Participative inquiry and practice.* Thousand Oaks, CA: SAGE.

Rodgers, C. (2002). Defining reflection: another look at John Dewey and reflective thinking. *Teachers College Record, 104*(4), 842–866.

Roth, W. M., Socha, D., & Tenenberg, J. (2016). Becoming-design in corresponding: re/theorising the co- in codesigning. *CoDesign, 12*(1).

Runco, M. A. (2014). *Creativity. Theories and themes: Research, development, and practice* (2nd ed.). London: Elsevier.

Sanders, E. B.-N., & Stappers, P. J. (2008). Co-creation and the new landscapes of design. *CoDesign, 4*(1), 5–18.

Sarasvathy, S. D., Dew, N., Velamuri, S. R., & Venkataraman, S. (2003). Three views of entrepreneurial opportunity. In Z. D. Acs & D. B. Audretsch (Eds.), *Handbook of entrepreneurship research* (pp. 141–160). Dordrecht, NL: Kluwer Academic Publishers.

Scharmer, C. O. (2007). *Theory U. Leading from the future as it emerges. The social technology of presencing.* Cambridge, MA: Society for Organizational Learning.

Scharmer, C. O. (2007b). *Toolbook 1.0 — The Presencing Institute*. Cambridge, MA: The Presencing Institute.

Scharmer, C. O. (2016). *Theory U. Leading from the future as it emerges. The social technology of presencing* (2nd ed.). San Francisco, CA: Berrett-Koehler Publishers.

Scharmer, C. O., & Kaeufer, K. (2010). In front of the blank canvas. Sensing emerging futures. *Journal of Business Strategy, 31*(4), 21–29.

Schein, E. H. (1993). On dialogue, culture and organizational learning. *Organization Dynamics, 22*(2), 44–51.

Senge, P. M. (1990). *The fifth discipline. The art and practice of the learning organization*. New York: Doubleday.

Senge, P., & Scharmer, C. O. (2001). Community action research: Learning as a community of practitioners, consultants and researchers. In P. Reason and H. Bradbury (Eds.), *Handbook of action research: Participative inquiry and practice* (pp. 238–249). London: SAGE.

Senge, P., Scharmer, C. O., Jaworski, J., & Flowers, B. S. (2004). *Presence. Human purpose and the field of the future*. Cambridge, MA: Society for Organizational Learning.

Simon, H. A. (1996). *The sciences of the artificial* (3rd edition). Cambridge, MA: MIT Press.

Spradley, J. P. (1980). *Participant observation*. Fort Worth, Philadelphia: Harcourt Brace College Publishers.

Steup, M. (2012). Epistemology. In E. N. Zalta (Ed.), *The Stanford Encyclopedia of Philosophy*. Retrieved from http://plato.stanford.edu/entries/epistemology/.

Tidd, J., & Bessant, J. (2009). *Managing innovation. Integrating technological, market and organizational change (fourth)*. Chichester: John Wiley & Sons.

UNESCO (2005). *Towards knowledge societies*. Paris: United Nations Educational, Scientific and Cultural Organization (UNESCO World Report).

Weinberg, G. M. (2011). *An introduction to general systems thinking*. New York: Wiley & Sons.

Witt, U. (2009). Propositions about novelty. *Journal of Economic Behavior & Organization, 70*, 311–32

CHAPTER 9

Beyond the Prism:
What Ancient Wisdom Traditions offer Facilitators and Participants of the Presencing Process

William Brendel

Introduction

A Zen master once shared with his disciples that the greatest study of the self is to forget one's Self. Similarly, during workshops Otto Scharmer describes Presencing as a process of standing outside of the prism through which we make sense of our worlds. He often illustrates this shift in perspective as a small red dot representing awareness, moving from the center of a circle to its periphery and then beyond. Letting go of one's notion of self altogether in order to see what exists beyond one's egoic horizon is an act of surrender and liberation so profound that it is the basis for some of the world's greatest wisdom traditions, religions and philosophies. The study and practice of Presencing has much to gain by integrating perspectives and practices from Buddhist and Hindu traditions as well as the great Western Existential philosophies that borrow from them. This chapter begins by introducing some of the most salient perspectives shared by these canons. It then moves into some of the most critical features that allow for transformation and transcendence during Presencing practice. Finally, it culminates in a case study of a small religious community that deepened its faith paradoxically, by moving beyond its own borders.

The Veil

Presencing provides a practical framework for opening the door to universal world philosophies. A close inspection yields evidence of a surprising dialogue between Eastern and Western thought. A copy of the Upanishads for instance, was always present on the desk of Arthur Schopenhauer, who spoke frequently about the connection between the ancient Hindu Vedas and his own edicts concerning being (Easwaran, 2007). Leo Tolstoy was himself a pen pal with Mahatma Gandhi, sharing a deep respect for Ahimsa, the Hindu philosophy of non-violence (Dalton, 1996). In each of these cases, value is placed on observing and moving beyond the anxieties, attachments and assumptions with which we identify ourselves, as well as the many pernicious ways we attempt to distinguish ourselves from others. Shifting one's notion of self in this way, from one that is separate and distinct to one that is intimately connected with the world resembles Scharmer's expressed hope for the industrialized world, to move from an ego-system to eco-system mentality.

The circle that Scharmer draws for his students resembles the Hindu concept of Maya, a self-constructed veil that obscures the boundlessness of reality. The fabrics of this veil contain the roles and scripts we rehearse to become distinguishable and valuable in contrast to others. However helpful it may seem at first, the veil produces a breathtakingly narrow view of what is and what can be. Sensing into the future is nothing less than an act of lifting the veil. Scharmer's U Journaling Activity, which can be found in the Presencing Institute Toolkit (2019), examines these features by considering being and time, two dimensions that make meaning-making a practice in relativity. The journaling activity accomplishes this by inviting us to visit the young child we once were and the dying adult we will eventually be, to examine the length, width, and narrative patterns we have created throughout our-lives. This is similar to a Buddhist practice that takes place before dialogue with another person: the practitioner sees the other as the child and the dying adult. This fundamentally stretches one's view of the other, so that the dialogue may be led by empathy versus ego. In journaling, Scharmer also instructs participants to consider the distorting impact of inner voice, such as cynicism and judgment. Toward the close of this activity, participants are instructed, with eyes closed, to step into the future that yearns to be created, allowing sketches of what may be to reveal themselves. It is in this open space that an individual may allow unfettered insights through the veil. This journaling activity calls to mind an excerpt from the Buddhist Phenapindūpama Sutta (referenced in Huifeng, 2016), that demonstrates how transient our sense-making is at the crossroads of being and time:

> Suppose, monks, that a magician or a magician's apprentice would display a magical illusion at a crossroads. A man with good sight would inspect it, ponder, and carefully investigate it, and it would appear to him to be void, hollow, coreless. For what core could there be in a magical illusion? So too, monks, whatever kind of cognition there is, whether past, future, or present, internal or external, gross or subtle, inferior or superior, far or near: a monk inspects it, ponders it, and carefully investigates it, and it would appear to him to be void, hollow, coreless. For what core could there be in cognition?

In its first movement, the U Process resembles something of a brief death as participants become aware of, before ceasing, the habitual process of downloading, which is largely a modus operandi for ego. The final chapter of the Upanishads, titled Death as Teacher, points to ego as the source of selfish concerns and encourages us to die to them (Easwaran, 2007). Buddha suggested that suffering results from the delusion of self, and that by establishing a new relationship with our thoughts – having them versus being them – we can liberate ourselves from harmful habits of mind (Loy, 2018). All that remains is a centered form of being that allows us to experience the world as it presents itself -

including our thoughts and insights - moment by moment. The corpse pose is a meditation position that evokes a sense of stillness that one might experience at the bottom of the U. Much of the imagery in mindfulness practice, which is itself a gateway for Presencing, resembles a U shape. Consider how still and grounded water is at the bottom of a lake, unlike the choppy waters that may exist where the water meets the shore. Or how the U shape resembles a grave. In both cases, the movement is one in which we return home, as part of this world, rather than aside from it.

At the same time as this process is liberating and can lead to life changing insights, it can be experienced through a a profound sense anxiety. While anxiety indicates that we are in unfamiliar territory, it also indicates that an individual is on the precipice of liberation. In other words, freedom and anxiety are both sides of the same coin. The father of Existentialism, Soren Kierkegaard (1844) captured this concept well in his treatise, The Concept of Anxiety:

> Anxiety may be compared with dizziness. He whose eye happens to look down the yawning abyss becomes dizzy. But what is the reason for this? It is just as much in his own eye as in the abyss, for suppose he had not looked down. Hence, anxiety is the dizziness of freedom, which emerges when the spirit wants to posit the synthesis and freedom looks down into its own possibility, laying hold of finiteness to support itself. Freedom succumbs to dizziness. Further than this, psychology cannot and will not go. In that very moment everything is changed, and freedom, when it again rises, sees that it is guilty. Between these two moments lies the leap, which no science has explained and which no science can explain.

Scharmer refers to this process in his Journaling activity as a process of shedding the old skin, our habits of mind that obscure wisdom. Another Existentialist, Karl Jaspers (1932) said that existence is a philosophy, or a "way of thought by means of which man seeks to become himself; it makes use of expert knowledge while at the same time going beyond it. This way of thought does not cognize objects but elucidates and makes actual the being of the thinker" (Schilpp, 1957, p. 52).

Similarly, Heidegger poses that to exist "means to stand outside oneself, to be beyond oneself... Being, rather, is spread over a field or region which is the world of its care and concern" (Barret, 1958, p. 187). Heidegger's concept of Dasein, translates to mean something very much like Presencing or more simply put "being there." Just being indicates a process of no process, or a theoretical framework of no framework. Nothing to do, nowhere to go, and nothing to even think. Just being, or what the Soto school of Zen Buddhism refers to as Shikantaza, a process of silent illumination. It is during these moments of just being, that great insight arrives. Presencing practitioners often utilize mindfulness practice as a vehicle, but for the reasons stated above they must be careful not to make it too grand a spectacle, raise expectations, or boast about the benefits of meditation. In fact, practitioners might encourage participants to bury the term meditation altogether.

Many who participate in the Presencing process quickly come to realize that the self is a construct, and that an ego in motion is a performance in what Scharmer refers to as the Social Field, that we perpetuate for ourselves and others. When we cease to type-cast ourselves in our own starring roles, Buddhists believe that our true nature is revealed. In Presentation of Self in Everyday Life, Erving Goffman suggests that the ego is activated most fully in the performance,

> When an individual plays a part he implicitly requests his observers to take seriously the impression that is fostered before them. They are asked to believe that the character they see actually possesses the attributes he appears to possess, that the task he performs will have the consequences that are implicitly claimed for it, and that, in general, matters are what they appear to be (Goffman, 1959, p. 17).

What makes this phenomenon even more illusory is that the self we project changes depending on our audience. We are often one person for our boss, another for our colleagues, and yet another at home. In Either/Or, Kierkegaard (1843) challenges us to unveil ourselves before it is too late:

> Do you not know that there comes a midnight hour when everyone has to throw off his mask? Do you believe that life will always let itself be mocked? Do you think you can slip away a little before midnight in order to avoid this? Or are you not terrified by it? I have seen men in real life who so long deceived others that at last their true nature could not reveal itself; In every man there is something which to a certain degree prevents him from becoming perfectly transparent to himself; and this may be the case in so high a degree, he may be so inexplicably woven into relationships of life which extend far beyond himself that he almost cannot reveal himself.

The Everyday

Many Presencing practitioners facilitate the U process in workplaces or at conferences where colleagues are present. The additional benefit of Presencing in this context is a deeper under-standing of the unhelpful ways we define the self at work, or a work-self. For instance, outside of traditional working hours, adults are in large part bombarded, preoccupied, and in many cases overwhelmed by anxieties associated with work. An existen-tialist might ask "Is it the work itself that distracts us, or is our distraction something that stems from our ultimate association or identification with work?" In other words, are you your work? Does the thought of being terminated not evoke a sense of dread similar to the midnight hour in Kierkegaard's Either/Or? Exis-tential Psychologists such as Irvin Yalom and his mentor Rollo May have gone as far as to say that all anxieties ultimately stem from the deepest anxiety of all, ego annihilation. One's role at work is so central to ego that the absence of it often yields despair.

Many of us also attempt to hold two selves apart from one another, such as having a home life and work life. Despite our best efforts, the lines we draw between work and home tend to fade faster than we can establish them. The vacations we plan, the lunches we pack, the dinners we schedule to truly let our hair down all rely on the mindset that work life and truly living – only accomplishable at home - are separate and require balance. Out-of-office replies only provide a false sense of protection. Even though the intention stems from the heart, the lines we draw are as wisdom traditions would suggest, illusions. Work-life balance is a veil.

Nonetheless a persistent dread haunts us, that our deepest yearnings to live authentically will be insufficient or go unfulfilled in our lifetime. To compensate we do the opposite of Presencing, or what Scharmer refers to as Absencing: striving harder than our health allows, reacting in harmful ways, and being violent to ourselves. When it comes to the context in which many of us facilitate the U Process, we must hope that both facilitators and participants begin asking fundamental questions. How does our internalization of a work-life balance paradigm support or undermine our presence?Has drawing this line been the least bit conducive to breathing deeper meaning into our working hours? Making this shift requires letting go of these lines and establish a new way of being that embraces work and life as one.

This draws us into a more central inquiry: What can we do for ourselves and for others to establish and sustain Presencing as a way of being in the workplace? An advanced developmental frameworkis needed: one that draws our attention to life in the here and now regardless of location, unveils the anxieties, narratives, and assumptions that trap us in our own expectations and intellect, and helps us to knock down the finite walls that limit our sense-of-self and deeper relationships with others and understanding of the emerging future. This is precisely what Presencing does. Presencing, by nature, is not something that comes easily to a distracted workforce, but it is required in the most ordinary of contexts. It is unabashedly existential in nature, but it is also something we do. Some find it brazen in its effect, particularly during a time when many employees crouch in emotional bunkers, shielding themselves from their very own doomsday scenarios: pink-slips, slander, demotion, scapegoating, exclusion, and anything else the fearful mind can conjure. At the same time, by opening up to what Kierkegaard and other existentialists refer to as the infinite, Presencing not only provides a way to see a horizon beyond these harmful narratives, but it also creates a space to receive healthy insights regarding our condition.

Mindfulness

At large, it is fair to say that the conventional expression of what we commonly know and understand modern society to be is woefully though often unintentionally alienated from the present moment. Greater freedom in living cannot be fully accessed without a greater sense of wakefulness and presence and yet we bind ourselves to various forms of unconscious habits that undermine these precious conditions. Through mindfulness practice we begin to become aware of how quickly we are swept away by worries about the future, the fetters of the everyday, or anxieties that arise from our past. To identify and recognize these thought-patterns we might simply take a moment to close our eyes and concentrate on the primary inhale and exhale of our breath. How quickly do we move away from the present moment to our secondary stream of arising assumptions, anxieties, and attachments?

Breathing life back into the present moment can be done by paying attention to breathing itself, which anchors us to the body and sensate awareness. In breathing meditation, we drop into a sense of being in which we no longer identify with our thoughts, but take on the role of the observer of these thoughts. Presencing interventions, when executed successfully, lift the heads of those who are hardest at work so that they can see and receive the world as it is, grounded in real-time. Mindfulness practice requires a non-striving, non-judgmental attitude that continuously returns to the present moment, which Kabat-Zinn (2009) described as Beginners Mind:

Too often we let our thinking and our beliefs about what

we "know" prevent us from seeing things as they really are…An open, "beginner's" mind allows us to be receptive to new possibilities and prevents us from getting stuck in a rut of our expertise, which often thinks it knows more than it does (p. 35).

Regular mindfulness practice can help us recognize our habitual approach to both work and love, the narratives that uncritically support these outlooks, and the related institutional pressures that reinforce these habits of mind that are no longer healthy, functional, or effective. Through Presencing, employees may not only become aware of, but also let go of the many habits that comprise the more parochial features of their identity. Presencing helps participants recognize their burst-ready potential for being in an age of having. To meet the aims expressed above, Presencing might be seen less as an intervention, than as a continuous practice and ultimately a way of being. In Erich Fromm's To Have or to Be: The nature of Psyche (1976), he states:

Our conscious motivations, ideas, and beliefs are a blend of false information, biases, irrational passions, rationalizations, prejudices, in which morsels of truth swim around and give the reassurance albeit false, that the whole mixture is real and true. The thinking processes attempt to organize this whole cesspool of illusions according to the laws of plausibility. This level of consciousness is supposed to reflect reality; it is the map we use for organizing our life (p. 84).

Buddhists refer to a specific way of being called Dharma. It is difficult to translate but generally indicates a wisdom-in-action that includes the ability to know clearly versus thinking and acting narrow-mindedly. Dharma relies greatly upon the power of concentration, and manifests in ethical or what Buddhists refer to as "right" behavior. By regularly fostering greater levels of wakefulness, employees can practice seeing the reality they have essentially constructed and its connection with the suffering that results in one's self and in others. Ironically, it often takes solitude and introspection to bring this to light, as Miguel de Unamuno (1925) once suggested, "Only in solitude do we find ourselves..."

It seems that in every waking moment we may be operating in a way of being that establishes and continuously confirms a distinct and special "self" or what I refer to in workshops as a Super Self. We may also operate in a way that confirms Heidegger's concept of Dasein, turning our sense of being as a field of care and potential, which we might call a Supra Self. The Super and Supra contrast is offered merely to demonstrate an existential choice. We may choose to engage in the world as a finite caricature of ourselves so that the decisions we make and relationships we forge are inherently limited. Or we can let go of this habit of mind and emerge as a self that is one with the world, always emerging, and never quite definable.

Imagine what the latter looks and feels like. Imagine its implications for group dynamics, leadership, and organizational culture. Imagine the implications for dialogue, where an active relinquishing of ego makes our perspectives more permeable and habits of mind less rigid. Imagine the broader implications for society if we were to all, essentially, get out of our own way.

Presencing is in many ways a process of what you might call Supra Self Inquiry, a method that I facilitate in workshops on transformative learning, because it in part asks us to stand outside of ourselves before capturing and examining deep insights concerning our identity and sense of duty. Presencing facilitators might guide participants into recognizing how they privilege certain "I am..." narratives in day to day living. Those whose narratives portray greater value in being a hard worker for instance, might answer 'I am an accountant', when asked 'who are you?' Those whose narratives seek to imply greater value in family might answer 'I am a father or mother.' Supra Self inquiry does not place value on being any 'thing', but rather suggests how we are invaluable simply by being.

One activity that I frequently use as a form of Supra-Self inquiry is to ask employees or students the following question –

without any further instruction – 'What's your story?' This is a particularly disorienting challenge as it provides no scaffolding, yet it requires a narrative. The writer tends to assume that the purpose of such an activity is to make a clear, cohesive, and rational determination. The narrative, as western society has been deeply influenced by Aristotle's suggestion, has finite bounding with a clear beginning, middle, and end. In this way, the writer often feels compelled to bracket "who they are" by expressing evidence they have sought and amassed through periods of time, in order to be distinct from everyone else. By caging or bracketing the "who", we inherently limit the "who." The purpose of Supra-Self inquiry in this activity is to see the narrative as an infinite range of potential versus finite determination. Such a narrative explores the importance of insightful questions over the answers that follow.

Transformation

To capture the weight of our interpretation over experience, in Beyond Good and Evil, Nietzsche (1886) wrote, "Until the text has disappeared under the interpretation." To deconstruct and recognize the power and control we have relinquished through our finite interpretations, Presencing practitioners would do well to turn to the field of Transformative Learning Theory (Mezirow, 1990; Mezirow et. al, 2000; Taylor, 2005; Cranton, 2006). Transformative Learning Theory is both elegant and complex. In the scope of a chapter like this, an author can merely paint the contours of this process. Yet it should be enough to give the reader a helpful sense of direction with regards to Presencing. Scholars and practitioners dealing with adult learning generally agree that transformative learning occurs when an individual is faced with a disorienting event – one that is potentially life altering. It could be as monumental as winning the lottery, or as simple as seeing things a bit differently after watching a movie. In either case, the experience itself somehow does not comport well with an individual's existing narrative. They suddenly realize that their intellect has boxed them into a limited reality. In the context of workplace wellness, disorientation can range anywhere between developing an ulcer that requires hospitalization to noticing one's own passive aggressive behavior toward a colleague.

Since the nature of the mind is largely habit forming, our way of being at work and home are bound with our Habits of Mind, described as "a set of assumptions – broad, generalized, orienting predispositions that act as a filter for interpreting the meaning of experience" (Mezirow, 2000, p. 17). Therefore, it is not enough to recognize how our assumptions beget specific behavior, but also patterns in behavior. The result of examining these patterns can be a perspective transformation. This transformative practice is an essential step in the ongoing process of Supra-Self Inquiry. Perspective Transformation is described as:

> ... a deep shift in perspective, leading to more open, more permeable, and better-justified meaning perspectives (Mezirow, 1978) – but the ways of getting there can differ depending on the person or people and the context or situation (Taylor & Cranton, 2011, p. 3)

Transformation like this however, only reveals itself in observable fashion when a person's transformed habit of mind prompts concrete action, thus genuinely reflecting a change of heart. Sometimes the disorientation can be prompted by a simple question. You might ask a person 'why' they work for instance: Why are you here? Why are you really here? Why are you really, really here? Do they respond with a narrative that suggests they work to live, live to work, or perhaps live through a greater sense of meaning in the work? These questions are inherently personal, cannot be approached scientifically, and require a form of attention that often elicits some sense of existential yearning.

Transformative Learning is essentially a process of discovery fueled by disorientation and driven by appropriate supports and challenges for learning Unless a 'realization' concerning our existence shakes us to our core in some regard, a process of transformation is less likely to be authentic and take hold. A common subject of disorientation in Presencing pertains to a sudden awareness of the way our narratives alienate us from the connected nature of life and Self. For transformation to occur it is helpful that this type of disorientation is followed by:

1. Critical reflection concerning the anxieties, narratives, and attachments that comprise our narratives.
2. Robust dialogue with others, can result in a new way of being that breathes authenticity, creativity, self-renewal, and compassion for self and others into work.
3. Ideation of what this can look like in the hours, days and weeks to come.
4. Practicing this way of being across all contexts.

Critical reflection, reflective discourse, ideating and testing-out (i.e. trying on) new ways of being are competencies that require an advanced ability to practice awareness, openly experience a sense of urgency (the calling, yearning, and even dread related with living authentically at work), and let go of the assumptions, narratives, and attachments that limit our sense of Self.

Through Presencing interventions that utilize this framework, employees may take a leap of faith into a new way-of-being at work; one which wholly embraces the wider reality, unbounded beauty, freedom, and individual responsibility of the life they live each day. Through such a leap, an employee will most likely appear to others a "different person", not necessarily in the "doing" but through the "being." You might recall the looks on people's faces when greeted by Ebenezer Scrooge on Christmas day. Something as simple as a smile, or question can seem so outside of the ordinary that it not only indicates a fundamental change, but it reignites a hope for personal growth in all of us. In this way the personal transformation can have a profound impact on an entire eco-system, both within and surrounding an organization.

Transcendence

Our ongoing dialogue around selflessness can greatly benefit from an existential understanding of care (Heidegger, 1962).

Self-renewal is not merely an indulgence, but rather an existential responsibility in an age of having, when many employees find themselves consumed by what Heidegger calls "our many unfinished affairs" (Loy, 1996, p. 32). Yet there is a significant difference between striving to be "something" (i.e. a good employee or parent), rather than residing and living from the true, unadulterated, unbounded being which we already are. This already greater than concept is captured well by another Existentialist. In Being and Nothingness, Jean-Paul Sartre (1943) points out:

> Indeed, by the sole fact that I am conscious of the causes which inspire my action, these causes are already transcendent objects for my consciousness; they are outside. In vain shall I seek to catch hold of them; I escape them by my very existence. I am condemned to exist forever beyond my essence, beyond the causes and motives of my act. I am condemned to be free (p. 439).

To understand existentialism in practice, via Presencing, we must first understand how our way of beingranges between what Yalom (1980) calls the Everyday (i.e. How things are) and the Ontological (i.e. That things are). Operating from the everyday mode of existence, we tend to focus on appearance, autonomy, accomplishments, possessions, and prestige. Operating from an Ontological mode of existence, we tend to focus less on everyday concerns and more on our authenticity, connectivity with others, the larger meaning of things, and self-fulfillment. Another way to understand an Ontological mode of existence is through Yalom's own words:

> ... one marvels not about the way things are but that they are. To exist in this mode means to be continually aware of being. In this mode, which is often referred to as the ontological (from the Greek ontos, means 'existence'), one remains mindful of being, not only mindful of the fragility of being but mindful, too... of one's responsibility for one's own being (p. 31).

It is not the doing that creates issues with our existential responsibility, but rather the unforgiving, uncritical judgmental attitude we manifest in the doing. The results of judgment – not ever being good 'enough' for instance – can be crippling to our wellness over time. We are not, after all, our mistakes.

A Brief Case

The finite lines we draw are the roots of virtually all organizational dysfunction. As a consultant moves from observing the individual, to team, to organizational level, they may observe that adversarial lines spread quickly, like a crack in a car's windshield. Such was the case for a consulting engagement I was brought in on, the first I had ever attempted with a religious institution. Some noteworthy differences in opinion revealed themselves when Pope Francis took the helm of the Catholic Church. Conservative Catholics who are reputed to hold a firm circle around their religion were reported to alienate many of the very people they serve outside of the circle. One example was a ministry group, a client whose mission was to spread the word of love across a university campus. When new leadership arrived at the university, this group was tasked with becoming more inclusive and to transform its proselytizing behavior to one that invites dialogue around that which is universal between all religions. To use Scharmer's metaphor, for years this group had been operating in the center of their circle, inviting others to enter. Now, they were tasked with leaving the circle, demonstrating even greater faith, and engaging in what is known as the Catholic Intellectual Tradition, which includes critical dialogue that deepens, rather than confirms one's faith at face value.

In line with Transformative Learning Theory, I realized that no deeper understanding or thinking would help this group shift their behavior. What would be required is a disorienting dilemma that guided the group in letting go of all biases, at least temporarily through meditation, to enter the Presencing process. I chose to use what is known in the Transformative Learning field as the Mailbox Exercise, which I was first introduced to by John Dirkx, a professor of Higher, Adult and Lifelong education at Michigan State University. In this activity, I first asked the group to relax, close their eyes, and drop in on their sense of breathing moving in and out of the body, breath by breath. I facilitated breathing meditation for ten minutes before providing instruction that I would be saying words and phrases that would likely provoke immediate subjective insights. Rather than thinking about the words, I encouraged the group to simply hear them and focus more on capturing (in their imagined mailbox) the imagery, symbols, feelings, that arose. After the activity we would share what they collected for deeper reflection. Here are the phrases and words I shared:

1. The greatest of these is Love
2. Compassion toward all
3. Commitment to inclusion
4. Communion
5. Faith

At the close of this activity the majority shared exactly what fell in line with their existing belief system, both from the standpoint of symbols such as the crucifix, and convictions such as sacrifice. For instance, one member shared that when they heard the word inclusion, they felt fearful that dialogue with other religions could overshadow the convictions of the Catholic faith. A minority of members experienced worrisome insights that they might be approaching the ministry too narrow-mindedly. But it was one member of the group who brought up the most powerful imagery of all, that of a Muslim woman, who came to the room and could only look in from the outside, knocking on the door and attempting to open the locked door. Additionally, this individual saw that all members of the group were unwilling to move, and despite his own desire to open the door he was paralyzed in his seat.

Clearly, a strong visualization of separation existed, as did the stifling freedom to act in the context of a social system that had no will to assist. The group engaged in dialogue and my simple protocol was to gently pose the question "why" in the name of their faith tradition, they believe they received such imagery. The interpretation of the individual who saw the Muslim woman was powerful. Even if the group had been willing to invite others into dialogue, they were missing the first step: opening the door. The dialogue continued and at the end the group determined that opening the door was precisely the act of love that was required to "be" one's faith, rather than to attain or convince anyone to "have" the same faith.

I could only imagine how difficult this would be for those who had established the habit of mind that one must convert others, rather than accept them just as they are. In this sense, the group had witnessed transcendence in one of its members and talked about how the act of being one's faith is more than the act of demonstrating the "difference" in one's faith. Perhaps they suggested, communing with others around "the universal" would be the key to that stubborn door.

Conclusion

Presencing is a process that may become clearer and more relatable with the help of perspectives from Buddhist and Hindu traditions as well as Western Existential philosophy. This chapter began with the Hindu concept of Maya, suggesting that the narratives we sew create veils that obscure reality and finitize our very sense of being. In the language of Presencing, downloading is a process that only serves to reinforce this veil. Buddhist philosophy ostensibly suggests that downloading is a source of suffering, and that an important precursor to enlightenment is that we become aware of this process and its potentially harmful consequences. It is through this awareness that Existential philosophy suggests we realize our own existence, perhaps for the very first time. This realization can be experienced as both a dreaded void and liberating. At the end of the day however, existential psychologists suggest that we lean into this ontological way of being, as it frees us to contend with what Scharmer sometimes refers to as stuckness. Presencing draws us home, grounding us in the world, and heightens our respect for humanity.

Wisdom traditions as highlighted in this chapter also bring several important questions to mind in the organizational context for Presencing. What would it be like to work in an organization with leaders, teams, and individuals that are more present, compassionate, and selfless during a typical work week? What types of unhealthy attachments are prevalent in our organizational culture and how aware are individuals of their limiting and distorted nature? Lastly, perhaps for now, what is our organization currently doing, knowingly or unknowingly to impedes or enable a greater sense wakefulness and higher sense of purpose at work?

References

Barrett, W. (1958). Irrational Man: A Study in Existential Philosophy. Anchor Books, Random House.

Dalton, D. (1996). Gandhi: Selected political writings. Hackett Publishing. de Unamuno, M. (1925).

Essays and soliloquies. Harrap.

Easwaran, E. (2007). The Upanishads:(Classics of Indian Spirituality). Nilgiri Press.

Fromm, E. (1976). To Have or to Be? The nature of the psyche. Bloomsbury

Heidegger, M. (1962). Being and time. Harper Perennial

Huifeng, S. (2016). Is "Illusion" a Prajñāpāramitā Creation?: The Birth and Death of a Buddhist Cognitive Metaphor. Journal of Buddhist Philosophy, 2, 214-262

Presencing Institute Toolkit (2019). U Journaling Activity. Source: www.presencing.org/files/tools/PI_Tool_UJournaling.pdf

Sartre, J.-P. (1956). Being and nothingness. (H. E. Barnes, Trans.). Secaucus, NJ: Citadel Press. (Original work published 1943)

Schilpp, P. (1957). The Philosophy of Karl Jaspers. The Library of Living Philosophers.

Taylor, E., & Cranton, P. (2012). The handbook of transformative learning: Theory, research, and practice. John Wiley & Sons.

Kabat-Zinn, J. (1990). Full catastrophe living: Using the wisdom of your body and mind to face stress, pain, and illness. New York: Delacorte.

Loy, D. R. (2018). Lack & Transcendence: The Problem of Death and Life in Psychotherapy, Existentialism, and Buddhism. Wisdom

Publications.

Mezirow, J. (2000). Learning as Transformation. Jossey Bass, San Francisco

Nietzsche, F. (2003). Beyond good and evil. Penguin.

Yalom, I.D. (1980). Existential psychotherapy. Basic Books Inc.

Yalom, I. (2008). Staring at the sun: Overcoming the terror of death. San Francisco: Jossey-Bass.

CHAPTER 10

The U Process and *The Nile Project*:
Presencing with Music to Address the Water Crises in the Nile Basin Region

Kelly Mancini Becker

Introduction

The *Nile Project* is a musical collective that was founded in 2011 to find a solution to the dire water crisis facing East Africa. Musicians from each of the riparian counties on the Nile River were convened to share their musical traditions, dialogue, learn from each other, and co-create music to spark curiosity, raise awareness, and spur a solution to the crisis. The intent was to model a new way to collaborate in the region where collaboration has to date been unsuccessful.

In my interview with Mina Girgis (personal communication, April 16, 2015), producer and CEO of *The Nile Project*, he shared with me the concept of "zambaleta,"[1] an Egyptian slang word that he defines as "spontaneous cacophony." The idea is that one person or a group of people spontaneously begin to make noise, almost like a party. The noise gets so loud and so inviting that those at the periphery can no longer resist participation. They hear the

---

1 Quotes shared are from a qualitative study on *The Nile Project* (Becker, 2016). However, the ideas shared in this paper are solely of the researcher and not the organization.

noise, become curious about what is happening, are drawn to the source, and actually begin to participate. Girgis shared the concept of zambaleta in connection with the revolution that happened in Egypt in 2011. In his opinion, zambaleta helped to turn the tide in the revolution. Groups of young men created a ruckus so inviting that the citizens began to move from the periphery to the center tipping the scale so the political issues could no longer be ignored. The idea of zambaleta mimics how Scharmer (2009) describes what can happen with presencing:

> What I see rising is a new form of presence and power that starts to grow spontaneously from and through small groups and networks of people. It's a different quality of connection a different way of being present with one another and with what wants to emerge. When groups begin to operate from a real future possibility, they start to tap into a different social field from the one they normally experience. It manifests through a shift in the quality of thinking, conversing, and collective action. (p. 4)

The Nile Project, attests Girgis (personal interview, April 16, 2015), is "a sequence of pieces that is facilitating that same goal as zambaleta," creating a "magnetism that brings people from the periphery to the center". The project is creating what he calls a "hospitable environment" where such a phenomenon can happen as well as a community where people feel safe to participate. Speaking at the core of what *The Nile Project* is after, Girgis (personal interview, April 16, 2015) explains:

> So how can you use music to facilitate a sense of community among people in 11 countries, starting with musicians within those countries (…). If you try to understand what zambaleta is, you start seeing all these people that are participating in this almost on an ecosystems level, like this one person and then like all these people in the periphery, almost like a nucleus and atoms.

When a zambaleta occurs, there is not one leader per se; it

may begin with one leader, but as others join and are called to the source, the field changes. It becomes a collective experience making it almost impossible to locate the leader. As people move out and others in, the participants can see themselves as part of the whole. This is similar to how presencing is described: "turning inside out and outside in" (p. 191). Interachangable leadership is central to zambaleta and might provide another way of thinking about presencing:"When a group operates from such a place, its participants also begin to see their relationship to the system and how they collectively enact it" (Scharmer, 2009, p. 147). Maybe creating such an energy, "noise," or magnetism mimicking zambaleta could help ignite presencing for organizations.

The Nile Project (2011) is attempting to generate a similar energy by bringing together musicians from various countries to co-create, attune to each other, and learn in effort to find a solution to the water crisis in East Africa. *The Nile Project* (2011) is creating a synergy where groups of people, be it musicians, students, or researchers are having conversations, conducting workshops, performing for audiences and making some "noise." This is enacted to encourage stakeholders on all levels to get curious and come to the source to find a solution to this issue. As musicians are transformed by the process, they move out to the periphery, not only to see how they play an integral role in the problem and the sollution, but also to attract others to the source by spurring curiosity.

The U process framework was fundamental to *The Nile Project* (2011). Girgis utilized the process to guide citizens, starting with the musicians in the collective, towards a new way of addressing the complex issue of the water crisis in the Nile Basin region. Girgis recognized that old paradigms failed to solve to the crisis currently facing East Africa, and that a new way of thinking and operating was essential to finding solutions. Girgis (personal interview, April 16, 2015) in the following excerpt, makes it clear how this occurs:

> *The Nile Project* is working on two levels. There is like this very simple level. In order for these people of the Nile Basin to even realize they have anything in common, they

need to become curious about each other. And if they're curious about each other, they're going to learn about each other. And if they learn about each other they're going to start understanding each other. If they understand each other, they are going to become more empathetic to one another. And once they are empathetic to one another, they can have the hard- core conversations about water.

This process described by Girgis aligns with the U process in many ways. This chapter will discuss how the leadership of *The Nile Project* (2011) utilized the U process in their aim to move stakeholders from "co-initiating to co-evolving, from low cooperation to high cooperation, from disconnected neighbors to connected neighbors, and from disengaged Nile citizens to engaged Nile citizens" (see Figure 1). The quotes and data shared in this chapter are from a qualitative, arts-informed research study on *The Nile Project* (Becker, 2016) that focused on how a group of musicians with different languages, musical traditions, and political views collaborated to create music. I will begin with some background on *The Nile Project*, a brief overview of the conflict in East Africa, and then share some findings from my study that demonstrate alignment between the efforts and outcomes of the work of *The Nile Project* and the U process.

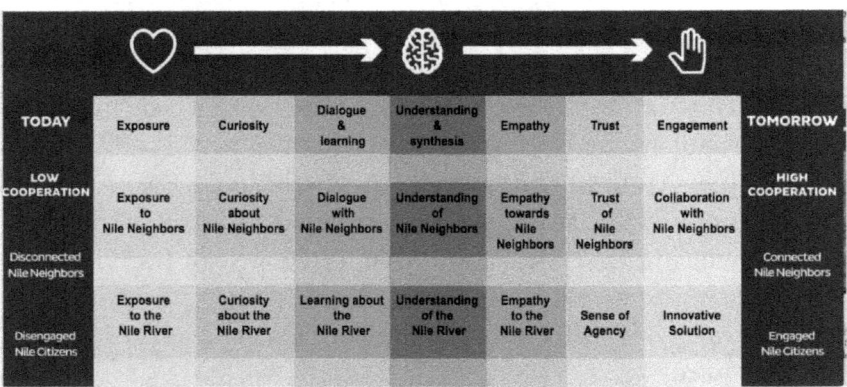

Figure 1: Chart from The Nile Project website (http://nileproject.org/about/) with the title: "Solution: Bring people together and help them find the solutions we need." The connection to the U process: open heart, open mind, open will are evident.

The Nile Project

"The essence of leadership is to shift the inner place from which we operate both individually and collectively" (Scharmer, 2009, p. 11).

The Nile Project (2011) seeks to encourage action from citizens, starting with the musicians who participate in music residencies. Girgis (observation, March 13, 2015) explains: "We wanted to find a way to have all 400 million inhabitants of the Nile Basin be a part of the solution, not the load". Mina Girgis developed *The Nile Project* to explore how the process of music making might model ways to collaborate and inspire an out-of-the-box solution to the crisis. There are multiple levels of the project (see Figure 2). On one level, the organization performs for the public with an aim to spur curiosity and then action from audiences. The second level is to engage university students in the process. The organization provides residencies on college campuses where they perform and present in classes. They also sponsor university fellows that undergo a 12-month leadership program for students to develop skills to create regional networks aimed at finding innovative solutions to sustainability issues in the Nile Region. The first level provides an avenue for musicians to work together to co-create a musical album and prepare for a tour. This chapter focuses mainly on this level of the program.

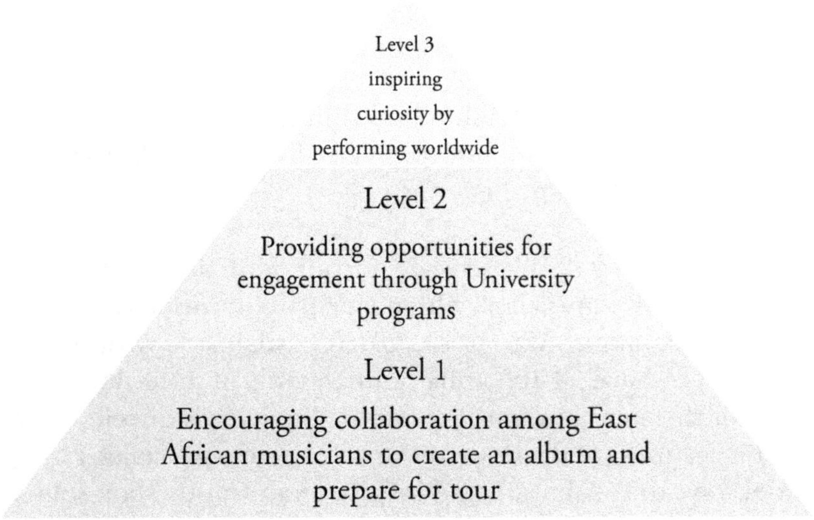

Level 3

inspiring

curiosity by

performing worldwide

Level 2

Providing opportunities for
engagement through University
programs

Level 1

Encouraging collaboration among East
African musicians to create an album and
prepare for tour

Figure 2: Pyramid figure demonstrates the different intentions of The Nile Project (Becker, 2017)

The Nile Project brings well-known musicians from all of the countries that line the Nile River to what they call a "gathering." The gatherings allow musicians to engage with their fellow Africans as neighbors and colleagues rather than adversaries, share their musical traditions, and work together to create a unified sound. The musicians were also able to share their music, instruments, and musical traditions. The first gathering took place in Aswan, Egypt in 2014 over the course of nineteen days. Musicians spent the first four days in workshops where they participated in dialogue sessions and activities with various leaders, innovators, and entrepreneurs with knowledge of the Nile River conflict (see Figure 3).

Figure 3: Dialogue session at the 2016 Gathering in Aswan, Egypt. Mina Girgis facilitates dialogue using a talking stick to ensure that everyone speaks and that all give their full attention to the speaker. (To see snippets of the dialogue session, see https://vimeo.com/197796895) (Quino, 2016)

The Water Crisis in the Nile Basin

Over 400 million people depend on water from the Nile River for their life and livelihood. Within the next 25 years, the population will likely double, creating a concern for the sufficiency of the water supply to serve all the inhabitants of the basin. Other mounting concerns include poverty, growing agriculture and industry, all of which are exacerbating and accelerating the issue (Kameri-Mbote, 2007). The crisis in the Nile Basin is complex with no foreseeable solution. The limited supply of water needs to be shared among eleven countries: Burundi, Egypt, Eritrea, Ethiopia, Kenya, Rwanda, Sudan, South Sudan, Tanzania, Uganda, and the Democratic Republic of the Congo; however, Egypt currently maintains water rights. Despite some attempts at collaboration in the region, the authorities have not been able to agree on a viable and equitable way to share the water. Those in power are currently engaging in what Scharmer (2009) calls "downloading," using the same processes that have failed to make change in the past.

Downloading

"What we do is often based on habitual patterns of action and thought. A familiar stimulus triggers a familiar response. Moving toward a future possibility requires us to become aware of- and abandon- the dominant mode of downloading that cause us to continuously reproduce the patterns of the past." (Scharmer, 2009, p. 119)

Habitual patterns of action and thought as well as a prevalent power dynamics appear to be at play in East Africa. Egypt has maintained sole rights to the water from the Nile River and a position of power. The Nile Water Agreement established by Britain under colonial rule in 1929 granted Egypt rights to the majority of the water and complete control over the Nile River. This policy requires all British colonies to refrain from any action that might affect flow of water to Egypt. Other countries such as Ethiopia and Sudan have little to no power. Dialogue, negotiations, and cooperation among the nations in the Nile Basin are essential to finding a solution, but there is currently no means to accomplish this. Countries still harbor mistrust since the treaty of 1929 that gave the sole rights to the water from the Nile River to Egypt (Tawfik, 2016). Despite attempts to find an equitable solution, no agreements have been accomplished. An international treaty to govern water use, the Nile Cooperative Framework Agreement (NCFA) has been drafted, but it has yet to gain consensus (The Nile Basin Initiative, 2012). Tensions and conflict escalated in 2013 when the Ethiopian government began construction on The Renaissance Dam that will divert the Blue Nile and has raised concerns for Egypt who fears it may diminish their water flow. This dire situation could lead not only to a humanitarian crisis, but to war. As Egyptian President Anwar Sadat said in 1979, "The only matter that could take Egypt to war again is water" (Kameri-Mbote, 2007, p. 1). It seems as if those in power and the politicians involved are downloading, attempting to use the same processes that have failed in the past. The status quo with Egypt in power and other countries at a disadvantage continues to be an acting force preventing authorities from finding a solution to the crisis and working together for a solution (Kameri-Mbote, 2007). Perhaps what is needed in the region is a new way of "seeing" both the conflict and each other. *The Nile Project* hopes music making may act as a new way to move forward in a more effective way towards a solution.

Seeing

"When we stop the habit of downloading, we move into the state of seeing. Our perceptions become more acute, and we become aware of the reality we are up against" (Scharmer, 2009, p. 129).

How does an organization or group stop downloading or break free from "habitual patterns of action and thought" (Scharmer, 2009, p. 119). Otto Scharmer (2009) suggests we shift to what he calls "seeing." We do this by "(1) clarifying questions and intent (2) moving into the contexts that matter, and (3) suspending judgement and connecting to wonder" (Scharmer, 2009, p.131). If we can move past our old habits of "downloading" or simply reacting to issues as we have always done, we can move towards "seeing." In this stage, suggests Scharmer (2009), we become much more in tune, perceptive, and we see more clearly the issue we have to face. *The Nile Project's* response to the water crisis through music may be an attempt to "see" in a new way. Instead of reacting similarly to the politicians who have acted in repeated patterns with no positive results, *The Nile Project* is offering a new way to sharpen perceptions and attune to each other and the problem.

The first *shift* that Girgis aimed to encourage in the residency was how musicians' viewed themselves; a shift from thinking of themselves as advesaries (or on opposite sides of the political divide) to thinking of themselves as neighbors. At the start of the residency, the musicians were distinct individuals representing the 11 riparian countries on the Nile River. Each came with their own beliefs about the political dynamics, varying degrees of knowledge of the water crisis, and a wide-range of cultural backgrounds. As one musician affirmed, they also had their own set of "cultural baggage" (Alsarah, personal interview, April 15, 2015). As Alsarah, a Sudanese born singer affirmed, some musicians brought bias:

> We all come with our cultural baggage. I had my own prejudices that I had needed to get rid of. They had prejudices that they had to get rid of. But that's part of it. That's part of becoming a band.

As Alsarah (personal interview, April 15, 2015) continues, it becomes evident that assumptions about "the other," built on existing tensions between the two countries, were brought to the project:

> Egypt and Sudan were under the same colonial rule. So the border between Egypt and Sudan were open until like 1950 something. So Egypt thought of Sudan as belonging to them. So it's a huge point of tension for me with Egyptians usually. But not with these guys, because these guys are more educated. Also because I check all them: 'Ah... don't get aggressive..'

Jorga (personal communication, April 15, 2015) affirmed the tensions that currently exist in Africa between the people living there: "In fact, like...everything is getting even more strained now across religious lines, ethnic lines, and so this concept of unity was something that was a seed, but you didn't know if it was going to grow or not."

As the residency progressed, however, musicians began to see each other differently, even to go as far as considering each other as family. Observing these musicians in a variety of settings including class visits, performances, and casually hanging out, it was clear that they have built strong relationships with each other as a result of the project. Jorga (personal communication, April 14, 2015) affirms: "We are like family." At an informal performance in a professors' home, their enjoyment of each other was palpable. The way they looked at each other, smiled, and joked made it clear that they have formed a strong bond and truly enjoyed each other's company.

At a class visit, one of the musicians maintained that a special bond had been created between the musicians despite their political divide. (This excerpt was transcribed at the time of the class and may not be verbatim):

> How can your community grow? I think that is a lot of the process that we've experienced. The grown sense of we and beyond that. The fact that when it comes to growing that musically. It is love; the collectiveness that we are reaching towards. Personally, that's an on-going journey. The people on stage truly love each other – that kind of feeling of the cross-cultural experience. We have all learned a lot of different words from each other. (Meklit Hadero, personal communication, March 30, 2015)

Another musician offered a similar sentiment:

> We all got more than what we expected – having so much a neighbor and didn't know it existed – great musicians – and it's kind of like – I wish every Ethiopian could have the opportunity to meet – really knowing each other. (Jorga, personal communication, March 30, 2015)

Alsarah (personal interview, April 15, 2015) affirms that "knowing each other" was an outcome of this musical process. There is evidence in the following quote that the project allowed her to see people, who were previously seen as enemies, now as neighbors:

> Change starts at home. Starts in you and being the kind of

musicians that goes out to get to know fellow musicians from like my neighbors and my community. [Considering all people] on the Nile now as my neighbors and my country, neighbors and my region.

Opportunities to Work Together with other Africans

One finding of the study that was particularly noteworthy, was that *The Nile Project* offered African musicians the rare opportunity to work together with other Africans. This opportunity was something participants suggested was a need, but was lacking, and yet essential if perceptions of "the other" are going to be transformed. One musician (personal communication, April 13, 2015) confirmed this idea in an interview on National Public Radio (NPR): [I have] "no chance in Egypt to cooperate with any other African musicians, usually we participate with European and American musicians" (Eyre, 2015). For Girgis, this opportunity is essential to finding solutions to the crisis: [The project is] "really a way to get people – a way to introduce all of these different people and different cultures – together in a part of the world that we need to talk together." Another musician, Abozekry (personal communication, field notes, March 30, 2015), shared how working with other African musicians was a new experience for him. (This excerpt was transcribed at the time of the class and may not be verbatim):

> In Egypt, we have a big problem. We have been divided socially and culturally – a lot more Arabic culture, then African. Certain peoples have been treated very badly. I didn't know anything about my African Identity. [*The Nile Project*] is where I met African musicians; [the] first step to discovering my African identity, to meet other musicians.

The common interest in music enticed these musicians from all over East Africa to collaborate, offering them the rare opportunity to work with and learn from and about each other. The residencies provided an opportunity to spur musical curiosity, which Girgis believes is essential for these musicians to undergo a transformation from "disconnected Nile neighbors to connected Nile neighbors, low cooperation to high cooperation" and "disengaged Nile citizens to engaged citizens" (see Figure 1).

Music, in my opinion, was the catalyst for a new way of "seeing" as it provided a safe environment to explore trying new things and doing things differently starting with the ways in which the musicians made music together. In the following pages, I will explain how music was used by *The Nile Project* to spur curiosity, connect to wonder, and create a conducive enviroment for open and honest dialogue that led to "seeing." As musicians created music in a new way, using instruments in ways that had never been done before, or creating a sound that fused multiple styles in new ways, musicians were able to "see" how music could be done differently and ultimately paved the way for new learning and new perspectives.

Curiosity and Connecting to Wonder

"We started with musical curiosity. The realization that we don't really get exposed to other cultures in Africa. I grew up in Egypt and never heard any Sudanese music. Music can drive peoples' curiosity, from there- there is understanding, from there is empathy. Music is the engine of that curiosity- getting people to ask the question- it's not just about water- it's about identity (...) the music was the opening" (Girgis, classroom observation, April 15, 2015)

Spurring curiosity is central to *The Nile Project's* mission and foregrounded in the work with the musicians. In an effort to change musicians' perceptions of "the other," eliminate bias, and provide a means to "see" in a new way, Girgis (personal communication, field notes, April 15, 2015) began the process by having the musicians share their musical instruments with each other (see Figure 4). Girgis, an ethnomusicologist, studies how instruments migrate from one place to another. He thought that if musicians were able to see that they used common instruments, despite their cultural, musical, and geographic difference, it would spur their curiosity. One example of a common instrument that migrated across the African continent is the lyre. All of the musicians had seen a lyre, but they did not call it by the same name or realize that it was played in various countries across Africa. Additionally, Girgis (observation, March 13, 2015) shared that the inanga, which found its way to Uganda, reminded him of an instrument seen on the ancient walls in Egypt: "These instruments demonstrate a connection between people – how much we share that we don't see because the world has not taught us to think that way".

Kasiva, the female drummer for the collective, was amazed by the realization that many Africans played similar instruments. When she met another musician from the region that played an instrument almost identical to one from her country, but called it something different, it was a staggering revelation: "I didn't even know that they were the same thing until I met and I was in *The Nile Project*. And then being in here and discovering …oh my god, these people have fiddles, lyres (…). We literally share instruments" (personal interview, April 15, 2015). For Kasiva, this commonality acted as a bridging agent. She began to see that she had similarities with other Africans that were previously unknown to her. In this quote, a sense of "wonder" is evident which can act to spur curiosity as well as be an outcome of being curious. As musicians learned about their commonalities, they often expressed amazement and wonder.

Figure 4: Mina Girgis, CEO and co-founder, and Rapasa Nyatrapasa Rapwapwa, from Uganda, discuss Rapasa's traditional instrument.

Connecting to Wonder

"Wonder is about noticing that there is a world beyond our patterns of downloading. Wonder can be thought of as the seed from which the U process grows. Without the capacity for wonder, we will most likely remain stuck in the prison of our mental constructs" (Scharmer, p. 134).

It was clear that the project created an opportunity for the musicians to "connect to wonder." Kasiva, the percussionist from Kenya, was filled with wonder the minute she was united with the other Nile Project musicians. She recognized many of the traditional instruments they played, but was surprised by how they played them:

We have similar, almost the same instruments, you know,

but we call them different names. And maybe they choose to put like different skin over the top. We literally share instruments. The method of playing is very different and the method of tuning is sort of very different. (...) It blew my mind. (Kasiva, personal communication, April 15, 2015)

Wonder also emerged as musicians played together. They were amazed at the talent, the unique abilities, and the skills each of the musicians brought to the project. Jorga, the saxophonist, shared his interest in the project: "So for me, music is like, a very spiritual thing, and when musicians connect musically, it's very powerful." As the interview continued, Jorga (personal communication, April 15, 2015) shares a sense of wonder at what it means to play together:

So good music excites people to start with. So when you have good musicians living together for three weeks and you hear music, and it was like, you realize for example on percussion. When I hear Mohamed play, I realize I am hearing the best that there is on ute. When I hear them play, I know, they are the best. Everybody is the best. So it's like a great concert that doesn't end. It has been a joyous thing.

Kasiva also shared her reason for getting involved in the project. It is evident that making music, specifically the collaborative process created for her a sense of wonder and excitement:

The main reason why I applied is because, so – in short, he told me it was like a collaborative kind of space, (...). So being able to actually collaborate with other people and see what, sort of, the world has to offer was like – it was eye opening for me (...). So when Rock told me about *The Nile Project* and told me it was a collaborative space, instantly I was like excited. I had like stars in my eyes. I was like, another opportunity to have like this kind of feeling and this kind of experience. I really want this. (Kasiva, personal communication, April 15, 2015)

As the musicians began to play together and create music, the issues, problems and perhaps even bias of "the other" were suspended in effort to create a new sound. The members took a step back from defining each other as Egyptians or Ethiopians, and instead worked together as singers and musicians.

Suspended judgement: Sharing Stories and Encouraging Dialogue

Once a connection is established, there is the opportunity for "suspended judgement." Scharmer (2009) suggests, "one of the most effective mechanisms for suspending judgement and connecting to wonder is to draw people into one another's first person stories" (p. 142). In *The Nile Project*, the sharing of stories was facilitated through music. The first step in the collaborative process was to pair musicians up in cross-cultural groups. These groups of two to three musicians were from different countries, might speak different languages, and potentially be on different sides of the water issue. After they shared their instrument, they were asked to play their instrument for each other. It was clear that their music, be it their musical tradition, the way they play their instrument, or what instrument they played is closely linked to their identity. Whether they shared the name of their instrument that may be unknown to their musical partner or a traditional song from their country, they shared a part of their personal selves. They each had a story to share. Sophie Nzavisenga, for example, from Rwanda, plays the inanga. She shared that she is the first female player of the instrument in her country. Her father, who was one of the most renowned players in Rwanda, taught her. Kasiva, the percussionist, plays many types of drums from African, despite it being taboo to play as a female. Michael Bazibu is a walking history of music and musical traditions of Uganda. He plays multiple indigenous percussion, stringed, and wind instruments, and performs authentic Ugandan dances and songs. These stories surfaced as the musicians worked closely together and shared what they hold sacred: their music and their musical traditions. These sessions were catalysts for dialogue, another key outcome of the project.

Dialogue

"Dialogue: enter the space of seeing together" (Scharmer, 2009, p. 142).

Dialogue is essential in the U process and is an avenue by which participants "see" together. The process begins by participants listening to each other's stories and then relating these to their own and other people's experience in small- group discussions. Dialogue was also central to the mission of *The Nile Project* as expressed in the following interview responses:

Hadero: We can be a kind of model for the world that we want to see and in the Nile Basin that we'd like to see.

Girgis: Is it a music project? Is it an environment project? Is it a dialogue project? In reality, it's all of those things. (Caine, 2014)

Dialogue was encouraged on all levels of the program. Tours included discussion sessions after performances for audience members and musicians, and residencies at the universities included class visits that encouraged dialogue between students, faculty, and the musicians. Dialogue was a natural outcome of the musical collaboration sessions as part of the gatherings (see Figure 3) and are key to understanding how the organization used the U process to "see together."

A Glimpse of the 2016 Gathering

On the banks of the Nile River in Aswan Egypt, a group of

musicians who speak multiple different languages from 11 of the riparian countries in East Africa sat in a circle. It was closing circle after a long day of rehearsals for their upcoming concert for the community. Closing circle ended each rehearsal day and gave the musicians an opportunity to talk about the day, to address areas of concern, to acknowledge each other, and to discuss any unfinished business (see Figure 5). On that day, Girgis, CEO and facilitator, asked the musicians for their thoughts on the morning dialogue session on the crisis facing the Nile Basin area. He passed the talking stick, which is used to ensure that one person is speaking at a time and that all attention is on the speaker. After many of the musicians had spoken up, including most of the Egyptian musicians, Girgis requested that some of the Ethiopians speak, as none had offered their thoughts on the subject. After the Ethiopians denied the talking stick again, Girgis rephrased the question, hoping to encourage one of them to speak. He then insisted that at least one representative speak for the group. Finally, one of the Ethiopian musicians shared her thoughts. At the end of the meeting, Girgis reminded the musicians how imperative it is for everyone to participate in dialogue so that all the countries are represented and varied perspectives are heard.

This exchange was significant. It demonstrated the foundational place that dialogue holds in the program. Additionally, Girgis' insistence that musicians from all the countries participate in discussions is noteworthy as it demonstrates the core beliefs with which *The Nile Project* was created- a dedication to egalitarian conversations and to engaging all stakeholders in finding solutions to the water crisis in the Nile Basin region. Had Girgis relinquished and not demanded that all of the countries contribute, this dialogue session would have mimicked what was happening politically, with the Egyptians having all the power and the Ethiopians at a disadvantage. Girgis was adamant that this should not occur because this music project intends to model effective ways for groups in conflict to work together.

These dialogue sessions allowed musicians to share their stories about their lives, how they began playing music, and how and why they got involved with *The Nile Project*. Kasiva, the female percussionist, shared that before she ever touched a drum, her grandmother taught her about rhythm by encouraging her to listen to nature. Alsarah, one of the female vocalist, shared about her interest in a style of music from Sudan called Aghani Albanat which translates into something close to "girl music" and is a genre of music that is "for women, by women, about women" (class observation, April 14, 2015). Songs in this genre are practiced in social gatherings, sung at weddings, and often about love (see Alsarah sing one at https://youtu.be/dPOnonHh6a4). Dina brought to the project a specific genre of songs about war and heroes that are traditional in Egypt. She is one of the only women who sings these types of songs in Egypt. Sharing personal stories is one of the stages of the U process and key to what Scharmer (2009) calls a "collective field shift" (p. 148) and necessary if the group is going to move towards collectively "seeing" in a new way.

Figure 5; Closing circle of the 2016 Gathering in Aswan, Egypt

Music and Sensing

While traditional forms of dialogue were an important aspect of *The Nile Project*, their inclusion of music in the process may have helped to make "sensing" more effective. What does the use of music in this context teach us about the U process and what *The Nile Project* was accomplishing in their work? It is clear when reading Scharmer (2009) that he reveres the artist mentality. He calls indivuals and groups who innitiate change, "the artists" as they "create something new and bring it into the world" (p. 22). Scharmer (2009) was influenced by Chinese and Japanese artists and the avante guard painter, Josepju Beuys. He applauds artists' "other ways of knowing" and argues that the process comes more naturally to creative people. Scharmer (2009) uses the anology of "tunning our instruments" when he articulates: open mind, open heart, and open will (p. 40). How, then does music come into play in the process of *The Nile Project's* journey towards change? As I considered Scharmer's (2009) "Evolution of Conversational Field Structures," I began to see a close connection to what occurred as the musicians in *The Nile Project* co-created music together (see Figure 6).

Stage	Downloading	Debate	Dialogue	Presencing
1	*Listening 1:* *Downloading-: habitual patterns of the past:* Musicians Listen to each other's music as separate- do not see a connection yet	*Listening 2:* *Factual connection*	*Listening 3:* *Personal connection*	*Listening 4:* *Source connection*
2		**Debate:** *Stating differences:* Each musician plays for each other, displaying their unique and different sound/ way of playing; musicians are ready to listen	*sharing and listening to each other*	*authentic sharing and listening to each other*
3			**Dialogue:** Inquiry, thinking together: Musicians are asked to play together, find a way to merge their two sounds to create one	*dialogue: Attending to the deeper space*
4				**Collective Presence:** *connecting to source; collective flow:* Musicians find the space that exists between their two ways of playing, adapt, play in the same key-creating opening for a new sound.

Figure 6: Adapted from Scharmer's (2009) "Evolution of Conversationsl Field Structures" with a connection to the music process occurring through The Nile Project (p. 296).

In Scharmers' (2009) "Evolution of Conversation," there is a movement from dowloading where dialogue repeats typical patterns of the past towards "debate" where each particpant in the conversation shares their different opinions. Next comes dialogue where the participants begin to actually listen to each other. As the particpants authentically listen to each other, attending to what Scharmer (2009) calls a "deeper space," they connect with the source. This attunement leads to a collective flow of ideas and new learning. The process by which *The Nile Project* co-created music followed a similar pattern. First musicians played for each other, in an "I play," "you play" format. In this way old patterns were repeated. There was an "us" and "them" or "other" mentality. When the musicians were asked to create a musical dialogue, and acutally merge their two musical lines into a musical conversation, a shift had to take place. Musicians had to adapt and change in effort to play together. (This process will be articluated more fully in the next section.) This type of musical dialogue required the musicans to listen in a deeper way, to find the ways where they could connect. This mimics how Scharmer (2009) suggests dialogue progresses with mutual thinking and inquiry. As the musicans continue to explore, listen deeply to each other, and find a way to connect musically, a flow happens. When this occurs a new sound is created.

Musical Conversations Create Space for New Opportunities

When interviewing some of the musicians about the process of making music together, it became evident that it was not an easy process. To the general public, the notion of bringing a group of musicians together to make music may not seem like much of a challenge. This is what musicians do, come together with all their instruments and "jam," which usually involves improvisation based on common chords or playing commonly known songs. However, in the case of these musicians, particularly those from Egypt versus other African countries like Ethiopia and Kenya, the musical languages are completely different. Musicians from these countries actually use different musical scales. Music of Egypt is based on a pentatonic scale, typical of eastern music, which means they use a five-note scale. The other countries' music is based on the western scale, which is built using seven notes. These musicians would not be able to play together until one or more of the musicians changed how they played, altering the very core of what they do.

When the musicians from *The Nile Project* with their diverse musical traditions came together to make their first album, Aswan, what scale did the musicians agree upon? Would those from Ethiopia and Sudan play in the Egyptian scale? Changing scales would demand that the musicians deny their traditions and "musical language" in an effort to play together. In taking on the pentatonic scale, the music would sound more like Egyptian music and lose the identity of the other musical traditions. As Alsarah claimed, she was not interested in making Egyptian music or allowing one identity to take over. Moreover, this relinquishing of their musical language would mirror the political relinquishing, giving Egypt control over both water rights and musical scales. This concession would not lend itself to conflict transformation or positive feelings among the musicians. Learning a new scale and playing in an entirely different way was very challenging for some of the musicians[2]:

Miles Jay: We asked them to re-tune their instrument in an Egyptian way – and I wanted to ask you – how did that feel?

M. Bazibu: Imagine you play an instrument for 16 years, and then you have to play a different scale?

So how did these musicians negotiate through this challenge? They learned each other's musical language. As Jorga (personal communication, field notes, April 14, 2015) affirmed, "I wanted to have this conversation between the Ethiopian and Egyptian scales". But this process was far from easy. One of the musicians

---

2 This conversation was taken from a class visit on April 14, 2015 and was between the current musical director and a musician from the project.

expressed how difficult it was for him. He described it as actually "disturbing" and that he felt very limited at first – "could not find his flow" – "It's totally different."[3] The learning of new scales and styles offered, however, was powerful for some. Jorga claimed it created an opportunity to experience something new with his music. In a classroom observation, the musical director explained that when these two alternative scales are played together (ones used by Egyptians and the other by Ethiopians), the musicians are not only encouraged to play in new ways, but there are "holes" created – and more space to go musically, which creates a different way of interpreting the music. As the musical director (personal communication, April 14, 20015) affirmed: "If you engaged in the music of Uganda – adding a line here (which he shows on the board) you'd be listening in a whole new way". He used the example of the Egyptian oud player who started to make "big jumps" in the music.[4] When learning to play new notes not typical of his scale system, Danny Mekkonnen, Ethiopian- American saxophonist claimed: "When I was with Nedar, learning to hear those quarter tones was very difficult. And I really feel there were a few moments today where I just kind of opened up and reached a new place" (2016 Nile Gathering - Musical Speed Dating, 2016). The process required both musicians to "bend" and alter their styles, but in the end, something entirely new was created through this type of musical collaboration. This musical conversation progressed from individual tunes to co-created piece, mimicking how Scharmer (2009) describes "redirecting attention":

> You try to move into the field of each example that you study, you stay with it, and, as you do this, you *hold* the earlier examples in your mind. You do that with one example after another. You listen deeply to one view after another. As your listening deepens, you also begin to pay attention

---

3 This conversation was gathered in an observation of the organization at a classroom visit on April 14, 2015.

4 This quote was also taken from a classroom observation on April 14, 2015. When quotes are used, it means that I took notes during the class visit, and they are as close as possible to verbatim.

to the space in between the different views. You stay with it, and then, when you are just about to follow the next example, suddenly a shift takes place that allows you to see the collective pattern that gives rise to all of the specific examples in front of you- you see the formative forces that is connecting them. (p.148)

The act of co-creating music appears to have created a unique opportunity for these musicians to negotiate, balance power dynamics, and practice creating something new instead of furthering old paradigms or downloading, which resulted in a new way of seeing. In this way, the musicians began to open their minds, hearts, and wills.

Open Mind- Open Heart- Open Will
Exposure of Nile Neighbors leads to Collaboration of Nile Neighbors

The goal of transforming these Nile neighbors (the musicians) to neighbors that collaborate was accomplished in the project. Their musical collaboration generated an album which was toured across Africa and the US (see Figure 7). It was evident from my observations and interviews that these separate entities that arrived to the 2016 Gathering underwent a transformation. The opportunity to share stories, suspend judgement, and dialogue encouraged learning. Scharmer (2009) suggests there are two types of learning- "learning from the past which is based on a traditional learning cycle of act, observe, reflect, plan, and act. Learning from the future, however, is based on suspending, redirection, letting go, letting come, envisioning, enacting, and embodying" (p. 467).

Learning

The process of learning about each other's musical styles and traditions provided an opportunity for deeper understanding about each other. A prominent theme that emerged from the interviews was that *The Nile Project* gave musicians a chance to learn about their fellow Africans, essential to building collaboration amongst them. Participants affirmed that they knew very little about each other. Alsarah admits, "Our knowledge of each other is just really limited." Girgis (personal communication, field notes, April 15, 2015), in the introduction to a panel on water, affirms this notion:

> We started at the place of musical curiosity, the realization that we don't really get exposed to other cultures in Africa. I grew up in Egypt and never heard any Sudanese music, and only knew about three countries on the Nile before I started.

Alsarah suggested that this lack of knowledge of each other is partly a result of colonization, which made the continent so divided. She believes that the infrastructure on the continent makes it difficult to travel across Africa. In her mind, this has prevented Africans from knowing each other, an important step towards cooperation amongst them.

In an observation of a class visit, Nadar (personal communication, field notes, March 30, 2015), one of the musicians, shared his lack of knowledge about other African musicians: "I had no understanding of any countries in the Nile Basin". Nadar, a flute player from Egypt, explained that it was an opportunity for him to learn about all these different countries and cultures. He also expanded his knowledge musically. He admitted that he used to only play Egyptian music, but now he has learned a lot of different musical styles from all of the other countries involved in the project. Alsarah (personal communication, April 16, 2015) made it clear that learning is an essential aspect of the project, "It's like music, like languages. Every country has its own language and within that country every sub group has its own accents in its language and so learning all of that from each other, that's the point". As the interview continues, Alsarah shares, "I think it's a brilliant initiative and, I believe that music is the ultimate way to educate people about each other."

In some cases, the learning led to a new understanding of African identity. As an interviewer shared on NPR, "The Nile Project has enlarged her [Dina's] sense of what it means to be Egyptian and African." Dina affirms this when she said, "I started to love so much the African Identity" (Eyre, 2015). Seeing each other as Africans, and understanding that unifier, was key to seeing themselves as neighbors.

This learning was essential to building relationships, especially when musicians take the time to learn about other musicians, their language, and their musical traditions. The saxophone player (Ethiopian) shared in a class visit that he was so impressed that the flute player (Egyptian) took the time and effort to not only learn a lot of the Ethiopian language, but how to play like an Ethiopian (Jorga, personal communication, March 30, 2015). For the Ethiopian saxophone player, this effort made a lasting impact and paved the way for a deeper relationship between the two, and perhaps a change in perceptions about the "other".

Figure 7: The Nile Project performs.

Building Relationships

As Girgis (personal communication, field notes, April 15, 2015) suggested in an interview, relationship building is essential to a resolution in the conflict:

> [IT] starts with the sustainability of the Nile Basin, but it has to start with the people; start[ing] with the cultural sustainability of the relationships among the people of the Nile Basin and then we can talk about environmental sustainability.

Observing these musicians in a variety of settings including class visits, performances, and casually hanging out, it was clear that they have built strong relationships with each other as a result of the project. Jorga (personal communication, April 14, 2015) affirms: "We are like family". At a class visit, one of the musicians maintained that a special bond has been created between the musicians despite their political divide:[5]

> How can your community grow? I think that is a lot of the process that we've experienced. The grown sense of *we* and beyond that. The fact that when it comes to growing that musically. It is love; the collectiveness that we are reaching towards. Personally, that's an on-going journey. The people on stage truly love each other – that kind of feeling of the cross-cultural experience. We have all learned a lot of different words from each other. (Meklit Hadero, personal communication, March 30, 2015)

Another musician offered a similar sentiment:

> We all got more than what we expected – having so much a neighbor and didn't know it existed – great musicians – and it's kind of like – I wish every Ethiopian could have

---

5 This excerpt was transcribed at the time of the class and may not be verbatim.

the opportunity to meet – really knowing each other. (Jorga, personal communication, March 30, 2015)

Girgis (personal communication, March 30, 2015) affirmed the importance of knowing each other:

> We have seen the most change in the countries – that people from this region (are) starting to see each other as neighbors. How can you start to have a conversation and collaboration if you don't even know each other? If you don't even understand that you are part of one region?

It appears that the format of the residencies encouraged the forming of new relationships, through what Alsarah (personal communication, April 14, 2015) called "cross pollination": "This intentional cross pollination, is what I love best about this project. When every person brings something into it – I love it".

The goal of the project was to make music that combined musical traditions, required musicians to work together, learn about each other, and find ways to collaborate. But it may not have been a natural process. At one of the class visits, a student asked about how the "mixing" happened in the residencies, and one of the musicians shared that at first, there was not a lot of "mixing" of people. She admitted that in the beginning, for example, all the Ethiopians hung together. They did not, for example, see all the drummers or singers hanging out together (Meklit Hadero, personal communication, March 30, 2015). Through different processes encouraged by the project, musicians from other traditions were paired together and encouraged to collaborate musically, which led to new relationships. The residencies offered an opportunity to really listen to each other. As Hadero acknowledged: "The fact that folks from everywhere are in those places means that we can hear each other's music, we can grow beyond being strangers in a very everyday way" (Caine, 2014). As Girgis (personal communication, March 30, 2015) affirmed: "We didn't know what the music was going to sound like- but what we saw on stage was relationships (...) a model of how we could solve problems – models the kind of relationships and partnerships we'd like to see in the Nile Basin." Alsarah (personal communication, April 14, 2015) supported the importance of "knowing each other" in this process. There is evidence in the following quote that the project allowed her to see people, who were previously seen as enemies, now as neighbors: "Change starts at home. Starts in you and being the kind of musicians that goes out to get to know fellow musicians from like my neighbors and my community. [Considering all people] on the Nile now as my neighbors and my country, neighbors and my region."

Letting Come: Envisioning the Future that You Want to Create

Scharmer (2009) defines the stage of letting come as "the capacity to crystallize and envision the future that you want to create while staying connected to the source of your inspiration" (p. 467). It is clear from the following quote from Kasiva (personal communication, interview, April 15, 2015) that music was helping her to envision a new future:

> I actually felt we were not curious enough as a country. Because seriously, like all we do with some of the instruments is tune it to the pentatonic scale and get comfortable in the pentatonic scale. For sure we're going to find something unique with that instrument. You mind as well pluck it with your toes, pour water on it. I don't know play it upside down (…) but we are so comfortable with the pentatonic scale, I mean, something that really blows my mind.(...) I don't even have words, to like measure how I really appreciate instruments fitting into traditions that they're not really meant to be fitting into- it really blows my mind.(...) seeing the inanga tuned to an Ethiopian scale is like- hell yeah- this is what were supposed to do. We're going to do this until we find quarter tones in an instrument that has never played quarter tones in. This is the start of discovering new sounds. This is the start of putting curiosity and making us do things with our instru-

ments that are like "we're not going to do this" it will force you to do this. We're going to get there.

This ability to see things in a new way, by playing music in a new way, began to be used as a metaphor for politics:

So the fact that we are actually wired to think like that-these are the ideologies that are bringing problems along the Nile Basin basically the people there, this is why fights will never end- and misunderstanding because we are not allowing ourselves to start thinking in other creative ways to be able to co-exist basically. (Jorga personal communication, interview, April 15 2015)

This transformation of thought resembles what Scharmer (2009) describes as a "shift in the attention field." Scharmer (2009) sees this as an essential step towards change: "How can we as a group shift our attention field so that we connect to our best future potential instead of continuing to operate from the experiences of our past?" (p. 49). It was clear from this study that learning and a shift of attention was happening for many of these musicians. Kasiva (personal communication, interview, April 15, 2015) makes this shift evident:

Just like this instrument is like used to playing a pentatonic scale, and rather it's us who make it play like that. It is us who make it like that. For example, if you never had tuners in the world, we would always find a way to play without tuners and you would come up with like a weird scale that doesn't have a name right now, but you would work with that. Same applies to people. Because we are used to doing things in a certain way, we feel obliged to do them in that way. And don't give ourselves space to start thinking of other ways of doing something.

Figure 8: Morning activity to start the day. Musicians play the rock passing game from Ghana.

How might an organization accomplish this learning from the future as it emerges? Scharmer (2009) foregrounds the importance of "changing the container". This is one aspect of the process that *The Nile Project* accomplished effectively.

Changing the Container

"Weaving the collective body of co-sensing happens in places: physical space, time space, relationship space, and intentional space" (Scharmer, 2009, p. 147).

Scharmer (2009) argues that an intentionality of space is essential to creating the type of atmosphere that is conducive to the U process. He suggests (1) creating a physical space that is free from a lot of distractions (2) having an "energetic timeline" (3) encouraging a relational space where personal connections are made prior to the meeting, and (4) being intentional with the space, ensuring that participants are clear about the purpose of their work. From my observations of *The Nile Project* in multiple settings, and most specifically at the gathering in Aswan, Egypt, they were both intentional and successful at creating a conducive environment for their work and transformation.

Girgis (personal interview, April 16, 2015) found inspiration for creating a conducive environment for transformation from his work in hospitality and the study of experience economy (Pine & Gilmore, 1999) which he saw as intrinsically linked to creating the kind of environment necessary for dialogue, collaboration, and change:

> I'm interested in what you might call a grass roots experience design that allows for people to be themselves and to have an experience that they wouldn't have had otherwise. And for me the hospitality is about facilitating that temporary sense of community in a space that would allow for these spontaneous experiences to happen naturally through music.

Girgis (personal interview, April 16, 2015) sees a direct connection between the two that is essential to the process:

> So for me this is like the environment to allow for this to happen is like an art of itself and that's my combination of hospitality and music. This is why I studied hospitality and music, and I consider my work now in *The Nile Project* and the music school to be hospitality. It's not furniture and fabrics, so it's designing experiences. In this case designing participatory and spontaneous experiences.

Jorga (personal interview, April 15, 2015) made it clear that *The Nile Project* did an amazing job setting the stage for a warm and welcoming environment for their work:

It was like a family reunion – the place was set up – it was a big tent – it was on the banks of the Nile – it had a camp atmosphere – we met and we started partying – like there was music, dancing, food, all people partying. It was in the middle of the revolution at the same time. So it was crazy like – but it was like every musician had worked at his own game for a long time. So good music excites people to start with – so when you have good musicians living together for three weeks (...). It has been a joyous thing.

There were many practices that *The Nile Project* utilized to create this conducive environment. First and foremost, the gathering was on the banks of the Nile River (see Figure 9). There seems no better way for the group to "facilitate a shared seeing and sense-making of what is actually going on in the larger surrounding ecosystem" (Scharmer, 2009, p. 44) then to be at the very source of their mission. Schedules were created each day to ensure "an energetic timeline." Each day ended with a closing circle where musicians could talk about the day and share how they were feeling, both good and bad (see Figure 5). The building of relationships before, in, and between workshop sessions was noteworthy. Often the day started with an activity to build relationships, understanding, empathy, or interdependence. For example, one day the musicians were challenged to play the rock passing game from Ghana. The only way to accomplish the goal of this game is for each member to be fully engaged and ready and for all members to move the rocks to the exact same rhythm (see Figure 8). Finally, outings were planned throughout the gathering, from visits to local markets and group meals to boat trips on the Nile. A noteworthy outing was a visit to the Renaissance Dam, a key issue that was addressed in the week's dialogue session.

Figure 9: View from the studio where the collaboration and workshops convened as well as the hotel where all the musicians stayed.

Presencing: The Future Coming into Being

When I consider how *The Nile Project* created a conducive environment for transformation, the idea of "zambaleta" resurfaces. In an interview, Girgis (personal communication, April 16, 2015) denied that *The Nile Project* was a zambaleta, or a "party or noise" that created a magnetism that pulled on-lookers into the center. Girgis asserted that a zambaleta had to be spontaneous and unplanned. But Girgis hoped that the project would create an opportunity for one. When I think about my involvement in the project, it very much acted as such for me. I saw a performance of *The Nile Project* in my hometown, not once but twice, and was immediately pulled as if by a magnetic force to talk to the creators. After waiting back stage and connecting with the organization that brought *The Nile Project* to Vermont, I went to hear them speak at the local college. I spoke with Girgis after the talk and embarked on a journey that led to following them to another college and finally to Egypt. The project worked for me just how Girgis hoped it would. It spurred curiosity, which led to investigation, learning, and ultimately action. Hopefully the writing I have done about the project will reach more stakeholders who help to find a solution to the water crisis in the area.

While research has not been done on the outcomes of the project, *The Nile Project* is producing a magnetism beyond that which occurred with the musicians. They are creating an energy "that starts to grow spontaneously from and through small groups and networks of people" (Scharmer, 2009, p. 4). Each musician that participated in the gatherings will return back to their home countries and hopefully share their new found learning and perceptions. At each gathering, new musicians are cycled into the project exposing more people to the process. The University fellowship program is cultivating youth leadership, and the project continues to reach new audiences with each year and tour. While there is no current solution to the water crisis facing the Nile Basin region, I am confident that change is coming as *The Nile Project* has demonstrated that change is possible.

References

2016 Nile Gathering - Musical Speed Dating. (2016). Aswan, Egypt. Retrieved from https://www.youtube.com/watch?v=THtnRv8V7-A

Becker, K. M. (2016). *The Nile Project: Creating harmony through music in the Nile Basin region*. (Unpublished doctoral dissertation). The University of Vermont, Ann Arbor. Retrieved from http://search. proquest.com.ezproxy.uvm.edu/ docview/1779282468?accountid=14679

Becker, K. M. (2017). The Nile Project: Making music for peace in the Nile Basin region. *Music & Arts in Action*, 6(1), 80–98.

Caine, J. (2014, September 14). *The Nile Project: Producing harmony in a divided region* [Radio broadcast]. National Public Radio Music. Retrieved from https://www.npr.org/2014/09/14/347733976/ the-nile-project-producing-harmony-in-a-divided-region

Eyre, B. (2015, March 19). All Things Considered. *Egyptian singer, meet*

Burundi bassist. Play among yourselves! [Radio Broadcast]. National Public Radio. Retrieved from http://www.npr.org/sections/ goatsandsoda/2015/03/19/393834758/ egyptian-singer-meet-burundi-bassist-play-among-yourselves

Kameri-Mbote, P. (2007). *Navigating peace. water, conflict, and cooperation: Lessons from the Nile River basin* (pp. 1–6). Washington, DC: Woodrow Wilson International Center for Scholars.

Nile Projects Vision, http://www.nileprojects.com/en-us/nileprojects/vission/vision-mission)

Pine, B. J., & Gilmore, J. H. (1999). *The experience economy: Work is theater and every business a stage.* Boston, MA: Harvard Business School Press.

Quino, P. (2016). *The Nile Project 2016.* [Internet presentation] Solysombra Recordings. Retrieved from https://vimeo.com/197796895)

Scharmer, C. O. (2009). *Theory U: Leading from the future as it emerges: The social technology of presencing.* San Francisco, CA: Berrett-Koehler Publishers, inc.

Tawfik, R. (2016). Reconsidering counter-hegemonic dam projects: The case of the Grand Ethiopian Renaissance Dam. *Water Policy, 18,* 1033–1052.

CHAPTER 11

Presence of Theory U in the Communities of Practice Process of Knowledge Creation

Jacqueline B. Saldana

Presence of Theory U in the Communities of Practice Process of Knowledge Creation

Contemporary organizations seek to produce solutions to complex problems as environments become incredibly competitive, and new solutions are necessary to achieve the sustainability and survival of these institutions. Theory U presents a practice frame that allows practitioners to evaluate problems through a process of connection within themselves (and others), resulting in new solutions that come as new processes, creative methods that promote work improvement, and quality practices. As part of this "U" process of connection, transcendence, and innovation, solutions to problems emerge with "real" connections to the practitioners, fitting into their context, and resonating with root problems. Through time, organizations have tried to explain their problem-solution processes through Theory U, including learning new skills (Fisk, 2015), change management (Dirani, 2011), operationalization of diaconal duties (Zeitler, 2014), or proposing entrepreneurial solutions (Scharmer & Kaeufer, 2010).

Theory U augments the capabilities of groups within organizations to adapt to change and increase innovation. It has been said that "Theory U approach presents organizational transformation as a journey where the desired outcome is the result of a deep understanding of the problem and underlying need for change," (Temple, 2014, p. 4). Furthermore, the power of the Theory U is that it can be applied to both small-scale self-improvement projects and global phenomena such as global warming or world hunger (Arthur et al., 2004).

The term Communities of Practice (CoPs) was coined by Wenger (2000), who defined CoPs as, "...groups of people who share a concern, a set of problems, or a passion about a topic, and who deepen their knowledge and expertise in this area by interacting on an ongoing basis" (p. 4). Members of the CoP come together because they share a passion for their "craft" and are interested in solving common problems, and as result of their work together, shared repertoire (i.e., new methods and practices) emerges as the result. It is the "domain" or area of expertise what keeps a CoP of professionals wanting to collaborate. Wenger (2004) predicted that the CoP ceases to exist if the "domain" becomes irrelevant so that members must sustain a common interest for any of these communities to survive. Wenger emphasized that CoPs are not social clubs or organizational units, but spontaneous groups self-organized and motivated by their commitment to common problems. Although CoPs are not technical teams or formal groups appointed by the organization, numerous organizations around the world from a vast diversity of fields have promoted CoP from within a strategy to promote innovation. Because CoPs replicate the main attributes of a high-performance team (e.g., interdependency, shared leadership, and co-reflectivity), organizations have recurred to them to facilitate knowledge creation (West, 2009). The processes of socialization and articulation of knowledge among the members of a CoP often results in a common language and epistemology, or their "own way" to see the world. Wenger alerted that the repertoire of the community transcends the borders of the traditional organization and that CoPs that become "institutionalized" are no longer "pure CoPs" as the interests of the community cannot be compromised by institutional goals. CoPs emerge in small and significant scale contexts and environments. For example, from neighborhood watch cohorts seeking to improve local safety to pharmaceutical engineers seeking to decrease the global cost of manufacturing medications, members of a professional community can elevate their reflective practice to accommodating different ways of producing knowledge, taking risks, and establishing new procedures even in the middle of a crisis (Stauffacher & Moser, 2010).

The "Reflective CoP" and Theory U

Research on CoPs (Saldana, 2014; 2016) demonstrated that their members operate from an inner state of connectivity (and connectivity with others) with visible behaviors, such as reflective behavior, spontaneous networking, mutual engagement, trust, and empathy. Just as with Theory U, members of a CoP use reflective strategies to create a moment of connection and transcendence in which creativity flourishes. Theory U allows members of the community to use previous knowledge of a field into a state of "not-yet-embodied" knowledge as well as a state of knowledge creation, in order to transform situations and problems (see Figure 1).

Figure 1: CoP Reflective Process for the Creation of Knowledge

In the context of a CoP, the "socialization" of a common problem promotes creativity to solve these issues through interconnection, mutual trust, communication, and the consideration of a diversity of epistemologies, discourses, and dialogues among the members of a collectivity of practitioners. Other authors (Lester & Kezar, 2017) have created parallel theoretical frames to Theory U by integrating constructs such as developing connections, "incubate" ideas," direction of energy, and letting go as part of the process of creating new ideas. Reflective practice is fundamental in the transformation of organizations. As practitioners act, reflect, and reframe new ways of doing things, they create the basis for continuous learning and improvement. Scholarly work (Sherwood & Horton-Deutsh, 1996) emphasized the numerous stories and examples in which reflective practice has become a powerful and effective means to create and change working methods in the field of nursing. Groundbreaking initiatives, such as the Institute of Medicine task force on the future of nursing, the Quality and Safety Education for Nurses project, and the Carnegie report on nursing education are all examples of how practitioners who engaged in reflective practice could create and disseminate fast changes among working communities. These positive results have increased the desire to reconsider reflective practice and dialogue among nurses to reframe their professional mindset. Theory U suggests that unconventional connections through intuition and awareness between individuals could increase cognition and critical thinking, or the "crystallizing" of new mental states (Scharmer, 2007). Furthermore, Theory U can contribute to the work of the CoPs in general, where deep connections are necessary to guide the inquiry-brainstorming-creation process.

Members of CoPs use reflective practice over time to enact mechanisms of open dialogue of prosocial theory that confront different viewpoints toward the solution of a common problem. Collaborative reflection happens at the micro level (individual-to-individual), at the meso-level (individuals and specific circumstances), and at the macro-levels (groups to groups) (Penner-Dovidio, Piliavin, & Schroeder, 2005). In studying reflective practice, scholars must consider the effects of dyadic relationships or the influence that one individual has over another individual during the process of reflective practice. For example, the level of involvement and personality of the member of the CoP has implications for both the ability to communicate and to learn. Scharmer's core concepts, such as co-initiating, co-sensing, presencing, co-creating, and co-evolving are similar to reflective practice theories that aim to explain how practitioners achieve innovation through mental processes similar to those in reflection-in-action

(Schon, 1989). These iterative frames place introspection and practice in iterative cycles of reflection-in-action as a method for analytical thinking. In his reflection-in-action proposal, Schon suggested that technical rationality must be leveraged with our "capability of reflecting on what we know as revealed by what we do" (p. 30).

As individuals engage in a collaborative performance, they remember a shared repertoire of skills and methods that elevate their practice and allow producing increased innovation. Reflection-in-action conforms to a cycle of appreciation, action, and re-appreciation (Schon, 1989). Appreciation happens when practitioners reflect on the tacit norms and methods of production, and how they would approach problems based on their feelings, intuition, and "know-how;" not only individually but as part of a broader context (Visser, 2010). Action encompasses doing as experiential action, allowing practitioners to produce and evaluate the quality of practice results. Re-appreciation happens when individuals use their professional's expertise as appreciate system (skills, values, and perceptions) to assess the effectiveness of used strategies and outcomes, with the capability of guiding future practice (Schon, 1989). In the reflection-in-action process, "doing and thinking are complementary" (p. 135). Scholars agree that reflection-in-action is a structured practice-based concept to improve the quality of work based on the duality of thinking and action, individual and collective inquiry, and the replication of effort, procedures, and artifacts (Visser, 2010).

Potter (2015) agreed with Schon in that people need to access their inner intelligence rather than conscious thought while collaborating to find novel solutions and presents Theory U as a model that combines the necessary elements to accomplish this level of innovation. Reflection should be considered as a "legitimate" managerial practice to solve organizational problems, suggesting that Theory U could be a reasonable substitute. Potter's research supports the idea that reflective analysis (the quality of attention) during the solution of problems facilitates a decision-making process and is fundamental to leadership success. On the other hand, Moffatt, George, Lee, and McGrath (2005) exposed that CoP groups learn and create solutions as reflective practitioners. Studies seem to validate that reflection is a driving force for knowledge to go from the individual to the group and then to the rest of the organization. Thus, that collective inquiry results manifests as *reflective learning at work*, which is necessary to change mental models, continuous improvement, and innovation (Sherwood & Horton-Deutsch, 2015). In the context of the CoP, learners open to a process of reflective learning within a dialogue in which each communicates a perspective, affecting the perspective of others consequently. The more transparent is the relationship between CoP members, the more significant the changes for these individuals to enrich a field or create knowledge (Potter, 2015). Furthermore, reflective practice allows members of a group to disclosure biases, prejudices, and oppressive forces that can curtail knowledge creation. By confronting conflicting viewpoints, the members make manifest troubling social relationships (Moffat et al., 2005) before engaging in collaboration.

Scharmer's Theory U provides with a sturdy reflective practice frame, as listening is a core element of this paradigm. Scharmer (2007) described listening as downloading, factual, empathic, and generative;" a "panoramic type of perception (p. 3) that is boundless. In Scharmer's view, listening allows individual to move from reactive responses that deal with symptoms to generative responses that deal with problems in an integrated way (Martin, 2000). CoPs, concurrently, are groups of individuals seeking solutions to problems using a reflective practice, active listening, and epistemic dialogue. CoPs use epistemic reflexivity and critical reflection to adopt new practices through inquiry and advocacy (Brown, 1990). The "inner dimensions" of individuals enhance their abilities from the "inside out." Such as athletes can "train mentally" and enhance their physical abilities, organizations can train their managers and employees to implement specific techniques to enhance performance from the inside out or even to explore the benefits of a reflective practice. Scharmer compared this knowledge insufficiency among managers and leaders a "blind spot." Their inability to connect to a deeper dimension of transformational change stuck these individuals and organization to operate with a higher risk of failure or to accomplish a mediocre or "average" at best level of productivity. The ability to connect these two, formal awareness training and every-day awareness as people perform, could provide organizations with the competitive advantage of individuals able to operate individually and collectively from the inside out, which can benefit the organizational culture in many ways, including improved relationships, tolerance for different epistemologies, and creative thinking.

Theory U in the Communities of Practice

Theory U (Scharmer, 2007) relates intrinsically to the way members of a community are connected by establishing negotiation-and-dialogue mechanisms that often result in new institutional infrastructures. CoPs can overcome environmental changes that alter the intensity and direction of knowledge creation by establishing strong leadership structures to promote active listening, conscious competence, and authenticity (Cashman, 1998). Such is the case of virtuoso teams (Boynton & Fisher, 2005), groups of individuals who accomplished remarkable innovation in the arts and sciences by engaging in a continual inquiry of the method. When circumstances place a group of experts in a situation where they are required to listen and think as they go through intensive socialization, radical innovation could happen. Strong leadership structures reflect community behaviors such as spontaneous networking and reflective practice could explain how individuals become willing and available to internalize and transform knowledge from tacit to explicit, promoting new spirals of knowledge and innovation. Nonaka and Takeuchi (1991) proposed that the socialization, externalization, combination, and internationalization (SECI) of knowledge in the organizations is the basis for learning organizations to develop their competitive advantage. The SECI model begins in the "ba," which is translated as "place," and it represents the location where inner knowledge resides. A place for knowledge can be physical, virtual, or mental. In the mental space, shared experiences, ideas, and values combine to enlighten people's capacity to think and act in the workplace. The application of "ba" is rooted on traditional

Japanese philosophies and proposes a platform for transcendental perspectives that integrates what all that people need to create knowledge. Furthermore, Nonaka and Konno (1998) proposed, "If knowledge is separated from ba, it turns into information, which can be communicated independently than ba." (p. 41). "Ba" has been observed to conform themselves from the individual perspective to global networks, as the organization that manages "ba" allows people to embrace the self in collective ways. Reported benefits of organizations that use the concept of "ba" included the successful accumulation of customer research knowledge base, capitalization of project teams, intensify a sense of speed and agility, change the "fiscal year" mindset, create boundary-less operations and partnerships, and the early creation for emerging markets. All these processes, Theory U, reflective dialogue, and SECI allow individuals to "let go" a previous mindset to adopt new and more significant perspectives and ideas and therefore new practices, resulting in an organization that is more adaptive and innovative.

Wenger (1998, pp. 125-126) defined the community of practice (CoP) as "a group that coheres through 'mutual engagement' on an 'indigenous' (or appropriated) enterprise and creating a common repertoire." Communities of Practice (CoPs) exemplify the utilization of Theory U in that they engage in a socialization and knowledge-sharing processes that allow the development of a common discourse to understand discipline and become a source of legitimate knowledge (Price, 2005). Members of the CoP who enact cohesive collaboration demonstrate relationships that transcend the boundaries of contemporary teamwork, which augments the capabilities of knowledge creation. Group cohesiveness is known as a dynamic process that increases the tendency of a group to "stick together and seek help among members to solve problems. Kratzer, Leenders, and van Engelen, (2006) reported that cohesive cohorts in research and technology presented higher willingness to collaborate, communicate, make parallel decisions, and coordinate tasks. CoP members who engage on this level of prosocial behavior collectively deploy competences of situational perception and the intuitive grasp of situations using deep tacit understanding (Hayward, 2002). Members of a CoP called to solve a problem purposefully combine analytic approaches with a higher level of understanding and a vision that many possibilities exist in the creation of new methods that would help to advance an industry. CoPs demonstrate a documented history of reflective collaboration and knowledge creation (Bach & Carroll, 2010; Lee & Cole, 2003).

This process of knowledge creation follows a sequence of interconnected dynamics comparable to those of Theory U (see Figure 2). Vast literature (Bach & Carroll, 2010; Carey, Smith, & Martin, 2009; De Palma & Teague 2008; Koutropoulos, 2010) demonstrates how members of CoPs engage in joint enterprise (pairing based on a similar profession or ability), find common purpose (finding commonalities), and use reflective collaboration to emerge from this process (i.e. innovation) with a shared repertoire of methods and tools that are later "normalized" in the community of practitioners. Li (2010) compared this process of knowledge creation to the work of multidisciplinary healthcare practitioners, in which the talent of different professionals are called by a sense of common purpose to engage in series of connections, and reflections that will allow the ideation and implementation of a "perfect" treatment plan. CoP studies demonstrate that members of a CoP can demonstrate similar levels of common purpose despite their time in the collectivity (Saldana, 2014, 2016). The "shared need" becomes an incentive strong enough to create loyalty and trust among the all (new and old) members of a CoP.

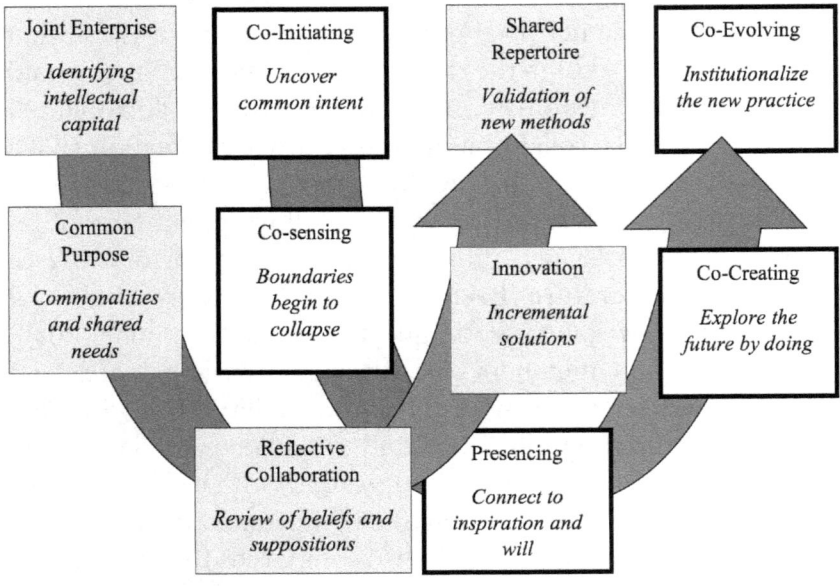

Figure 2 Presence of Theory U in the CoP Process of Knowledge Creation

Matching Theory U with the CoP Process of Knowledge Creation

The definitions of joint enterprise, sense of common purpose, reflective collaboration, innovation, and shared repertoire were aligned with the descriptions of co-initiating, co-sensing, presencing, co-creating, and co-evolving, respectively (see Table 1) to compare the CoP knowledge creation stages and the core elements of the Theory U. While the Theory U core concepts used Scharmer's definitions, the CoP knowledge creation stages were based on constructs validated by previous research.

CoP Knowledge Creation Process	Behavior	CoP Knowledge Creation Process	Behavior
Mutual Engagement	A shared discourse reflecting a certain perspective on the world (Li et al., 2009)	Co-Initiating	Build common intent through attentive listening to others and the self
Sense of Common Purpose	Bonds of solidarity, a reciprocal identification, commitment, and shared leadership structures (Fominaya, 2010). Members matter and believe they will satisfy shared needs through mutual commitment (Townley, Kloos, Green, & Franco, 2011)	Co-Sensing	The boundary between observer and the observed begins to collapse
Reflective Collaboration	Understanding of new realities through looking at the past to find new solutions (Tal & Morag, 2009); the careful, persistent, and active, consideration of any knowledge, belief, or supposition (Kinsella & Whiteford, 2010)	Presencing	Connecting a most profound source of inspiration and stillness—and to the place from which the future possibility begins to arise
Innovation	Incremental solutions to subject matter problems as expansion or refinement of existing knowledge (Dane, 2010)	Co-Creating	Explore the future by doing; enacting prototypes fast-cycle feedback from all stakeholders in real time.

Shared repertoire	The ability to assess the appropriateness of actions and products with specific tools, representations, and other artifacts (Li et al., 2010)	Co-Evolving	Interweave and link with the broader ecosystem around; practitioners begin to see, strategize, and act from a new mindset.

Table 1: Comparison of Theory U and CoP Knowledge Creation Process Behaviors

Once these constructs were aligned, formal review of the CoP literature conducted to observe the presence of co-initiating, co-sensing, presencing, co-creating, and co-evolving behaviors from CoP literature published from 2010 to 2016. Attributes in the selection of 110 articles included academic articles published with a research methodology and formal research results. The sample of articles included studies from 23 countries in 22 industry sectors (see Table 2).

Table 2

Countries and Industries Represented in the CoP Academic Literature

Country	f	%
Australia	3	0.03
Brazil	1	0.01
Canada	5	0.05
Germany	3	0.03
Greece	1	0.01
Hong Kong	1	0.01
Israel	2	0.02
Italy	3	0.03
Korea	1	0.01
Malaysia	2	0.02
Malaysia	1	0.01
Multinational	18	0.16
Netherlands	1	0.01
New Zealand	2	0.02
Norway	2	0.02
Scotland	1	0.01
Singapore	3	0.03
South Africa	4	0.04
Spain	1	0.01
Sweden	1	0.01
Taiwan	2	0.02
The Netherlands	1	0.01
United Kingdom	19	0.17
United States	32	0.29
Total	**110**	**1**

Industry	f	%
Agriculture	1	0.01
Banking	2	0.02
Call Center	1	0.01
Construction	4	0.04
Consulting Firms	6	0.05
Creative industries	2	0.02
Disaster Management	2	0.02
Education	40	0.36
Engineering	3	0.03
Forest/Steel	2	0.02
Healthcare	4	0.04
Hospitality	1	0.01
Insurance	1	0.01
Legal Services	1	0.01
Management	2	0.02
Military	1	0.01
Nonprofit	3	0.03
Nursing	1	0.01
Oil industry	1	0.01
Public Service/Politics	8	0.07
Real State	1	0.01
Safety	1	0.01
Technology	22	0.2
	110	**1**

The literature reflected the presence of visible expressions of the Theory U core elements co-initiating, co-sensing, presencing, co-creating, and co-evolving (see Table 3). This analysis considered the number of cases in which the expressions manifested, and not the number of times inside the same situation. It is important to notice here that the results compiled in these studies did not have the intention to measure constructs such as reflective practice, for which one cannot discard that these phenomena were present more times than what the results reported.[6]

Table 3

Presence of Theory U Core Element among CoP Members

CoP Knowledge Creation Process		Theory U Core Elements	f	%	Cumulative %
Joint Enterprise	=	Co-Initiating	33	14	17
Sense of Common Purpose	=	Co-Sensing	49	22	36
Reflective Collaboration	=	Presencing	22	10	46
Innovation	=	Co-Creating	57	25	71
Shared repertoire	=	Co-Evolving	66	29	100
			227	100	

6 For a complete 'Distribution of Theory U Expressions within the CoP Literature 2001-2015,' you can contact the author at jsaldana@devry.edu.

Joint Enterprise is Co-Initiating

CoP members who exhibit joint enterprise create a shared understanding that "bonds" them together. A community of practitioners would consider these shared understandings as their consequential practice domain. Joint enterprise goes beyond the concept of mutual engagement in that "intention" to collaborate is introduced. Wenger (1988) emphasized that joint enterprise is not only about sharing goals but also to accepting mutual accountability. Joint enterprise resembles attributes of "craft intimacy" (Wenger et al., 2002, p. 122), or the moment in which people realize that they share a common goal, challenge, or an issue to confront together. CoP members who experience joint enterprise are more adept to make a substantial contribution to the collectivity of practitioners (Gau, 2016). Co-initiating brings people together Co-initiating brings people together through attentive listening. As Scharmer (2018) reported that individuals in the co-initiating stage uncover shared intentions and an initial set of inquiries to explore, co-initiating was observed as joint enterprise (refer to Table 1). Joint enterprise promotes creative thinking as shown in documented cases of innovation. Surveyed members in CoPs (Saldana, 2014) reported that they were able to produce artifacts and group policies, transfer behaviors, and develop common semantics after participating in a joint enterprise. Documented cases of innovation (Bach & Carroll, 2010), such as the open source technology group that created Linux, reported how individuals who embrace reflective practice could unleash powerful capabilities to maximize intellectual capital and provide insight about the utility of innovation processes.

Co-Sensing is Sense of Common Purpose

A sense of common purpose suggests an alignment in the way members of the same group act and thinks (Townley et al., 2011). Wenger et al. (2002), on the other hand, warned how a growth paradox exists over sense of common purpose. As an organization becomes prominent, it loses the intimacy necessary to collaborate and create knowledge, risking to become institutionalized. In those conditions, a person can have a sense of common purpose and lack of the connections required to innovate. Nevertheless, Fominaya (2010) emphasized that sense of common purpose is critical to sustaining ideas over time through reciprocal identification, bonds of solidarity, and commitment. Fominaya suggested that this process of identity formation is what strengthens group cohesiveness, preparing them for reflective collaboration and future innovation. Co-sensing was observed in the literature of CoPs as sense of common purpose (refer to Table 1). Scharmer (2018) defines co-sensing as seeing realities to establish "horizontal" connections. Co-sensing happens when participants become immersed in new contexts. Outcomes of co-sensing include a set of personal relationships and an improved capacity for creating regenerative relationships. Sense of common purpose has been reported as a fundamental piece in work innovation to the point that the identity a collective group of practitioners can supersede can supersede both the culture and limits of the organization. Orr's (1996) *Talking about Machines* on the work of Xerox technicians suggested tensions between technicians and the organization because the collective views of what should be done and how it must be done were different from the established organizational politics. Experts tend to rebel when if they perceive that policies are against the collective expertise of a community. On the other hand, cases on CoP performance have shown that practitioners who share a stronger sense of common purpose can nurture routines, become familiarized with the tasks, understand clear responsibility lines, and verbalize their working rationale (Adkins, Bartczak, Griffin, & Downey, 2010; Topousis, Murphy, Holm 2008; Bowen, 2010). Furthermore, new research seems to indicate that individuals in communities of practice experience a strong sense of common purpose since the inception of the group as opposed to being built throughout time (Saldana, 2014).

Presencing is Reflective Collaboration

Presencing comes from using the "higher self" as a channel to connect with possibilities not seen before. "Presencing connects us to those who surround us" (Scharmer, 2018, p. 127), and is rooted in broader intention, curiosity, compassion, and courage. Reflective collaboration, concurrently, emerges from the increased consciousness about the elements that hold a community of practitioners through time (Carey et al., 2009). Defined as, the careful, persistent, and active, consideration of any knowledge, belief, or supposition within an area of expertise (Kinsella & Whiteford, 2010), reflective collaboration is also associated with the internalization and transformation of ideas through the understanding of diverse epistemologies. Price (2005) reported that CoP leaders use reflection to develop a holistic assessment of values, beliefs, and contexts. Scholars (Gausdal, 2008; Warhust, 2008) agreed that reflective collaboration increases collective learning as long as participants enact their power of intention. Individuals must engage actively and deliberately on thoughtful partnership (Machles, Bonkemeyer, & McMichael, 2010), and can leverage their passion for their ideas with their compassion for others to have the open discussion of contrasting views. Presencing was observed in the existing literature through reflective collaboration (refer to Table 1). Members of CoP often experience higher levels of cognitive understanding, improved expertise, and learn from others after practicing reflective collaboration (Saldana, 2014). Additional outcomes of reflective practice included thinking continually about how to use good practices, objects, and scientific knowledge. Documented cases of reflective practice reported that experts who engage in reflective collaboration were able to develop in-depth understating of existing problems (Blanton & Stylianou, 2009), elevated practice to new benchmarks of excellence (Wright, 2007), capitalize the use of information and technology (Murugaiah, Azman, Ya'acob, &

Thang, 2010), and improve their cognitive abilities (Vavasseur & MacGregor, 2008).

Co-Creating is Innovation

Dane (2010) defined innovation as the incremental solutions to subject matter problems as expansion or refinement of existing knowledge, whereas Anand, Gardner, and Morris (2007) described it as the capacity of creating structural paths to propitiate leading-edge ideas. Innovation is a socially interactive and spatially embedded within cultural processes (Strambach, 2002). Innovation requires the appropriate quantity and quality of expertise related to a specific social system to emerge. The literature on innovation and imitation (Semadeni & Anderson, 2010) reported that ledge edge action initiates a chain reaction of behaviors in which a first mover initiates action and a follower replicates an innovative practice. Innovation marks the path of progress and imitation supports the use of the best method. As CoPs mature, members tend to mentor newer participants to engage in reflective collaboration (Wenger et al., 2002). Co-creating is exploring the future by doing and "by iterating through the guidance of fast-cycle feedback from all stakeholders in real time" (Presencing Institute, 2015, para. 15). The outcomes of co-creating include "enhanced leadership and innovation capabilities for dealing with disruptive innovation" (Scharmer, 2018, p. 149). The five principles of co-creating are defined as core teams, places, and platforms, intention, listening to the universe, and prototyping. CoPs, in general, have been associated with innovation through the co-creation of new ideas and industry improvements. Members of CoPs were able to identify best practices, structure knowledge management processes, build new skills, and achieve collective improvement (Saldana, 2014). Like in the concept prototyping, innovation facilitates that practitioners engage in discovery through error-and-trial, peer-to-peer consultation, and networks of knowledge. Consulting companies have used CoP structures to identify new working methods, discovering during this effort that groups of practitioners develop distinctive behavioral paths conducive to knowledge creation (Anand et al., 2007). CoP members leverage their expertise with a collective inquiry to achieve professional progress (Ash, Brown, Kluger-Bell, & Hunter, 2009), learn new working methods, and break old paradigms (Bosa, 2008).

Co-Evolving is Shared Repertoire

A shared repertoire encompasses the capabilities produced by members of a CoP to through the process of knowledge creation (Wenger, 2004). It concerns the routines, stories, vocabulary, and new ways of addressing problems after the member of a CoP have experienced a period of innovation. Co-evolving is embodying and institutionalizing a new reality (Scharmer, 2018). Individuals begin to see, strategize, and act from that new reality as an emerging whole. After a period of innovation, co-evolving helps to "close the loop" between awareness and collective impact. Co-evolving outcomes include reviewing prototypes and sharing learned experiences, and embedding infrastructures, newly formed generative alliances, and new work narratives (Scharmer, 2018). The CoP literature demonstrated co-evolving as embedded communication roadmaps, best practices, and new knowledge management processes. Pharmaceutical communities of practice have been successful in creating shared repertoire of best practices that have resulted in trademarks and patents disseminated globally (DeSpautz, Kovacs & Werling, 2008). Part of these initiatives is the Good Automated Manufacturing Practice (GAMP), a series of books that compiles manufacturing practices embedding quality in each step of the production process as opposed to test quality randomly. Access to a shared repertoire of language and tools in CoPs happen as members learn-by-doing, create and transfer new working methods, and create knowledge repositories. Technology augments the capabilities of creating a shared repertoire because groups of practitioners can collaborate with greater agility and fewer boundaries. However, Gau (2016) emphasized that the success of CoP members in building a shared repertoire is the ability to connect to each other and to commit enthusiastically to the collective goals. Values such as open-mind-edness, ontological humility, and passion for the truth are neces-sary to overcome the challenges that emerge when people with different epistemologies and backgrounds engage in innovative practices. The shared repertoire is co-evolving in the sense that members of the community will continue to test prototypes until they coalesce into solutions. Even when a solution is found, the desire to apply and extend applications can keep the members of the CoP within spirals of knowledge creation.

Conclusion

As groups of practitioners in all types of organizations face the contemporary challenges of globalization, Theory U provides op-portunities for CoP members to connect with each other at deep-er levels of understanding that permit the flourishing of creative ideas. Although scholars have aligned the core principles of The-ory U to different professional fields, the power of self-conscious-ness applied to the creation of knowledge and innovation can be further explored into specific paths to accelerate innovation. In a time when society in general experiences high uncertainty, The-ory U has the capability of an application at the micro and the macro environments both locally and globally, promoting a change management paradigm from the inside out. The objec-tive of this chapter was to establish a direct link between Theory U core elements and the CoP process of knowledge creation. Members of CoPs engage on processes of socialization similar to the process of co-initiating, co-sensing, presencing, co-creating, and co-evolving, but in the jargon of the CoP world, these core elements transform into a joint enterprise, sense of common pur-pose, reflective collaboration, innovation, and shared repertoire. Nonetheless, mental transcendence, reflective practice, and mu-tual engagement facilitate "real" connections with root-cause problems and methods that fit the unique conditions of a field of expertise. Although Theory U increases the ability of CoP mem-ber to adapt to change to think creatively, previous research and theory presented a strong case for reflective practice to improve collective performance in the works of Schon (1989) and Nonaka and Takeuchi (1991).

By a method of operationalization, this chapter aligned the stages of knowledge creation to the Theory U core elements (co-initiating, co-sensing, presencing, co-initiating, and co-evolving), and then identified these elements on 110 academic articles on CoP academic literature published from 2010 to 2016. The formal review yielded parallelisms between how the CoP stages of knowledge creation unfold, creating a similar configuration, direction, and synergy than those observed through the Theory U. In comparing the stages of knowledge creation with the core elements of the Theory U, a joint enterprise was translated into co-initiating, sense of common purpose into co-sending, reflective collaboration into presencing, innovation into co-creation, and shared repertoire into co-evolving. Both co-initiating and joint enterprise happens when CoP members purposefully listen to each other, find commonalities, and establish a set of initial inquiries. This moment of co-initiation is when practitioners recognize that they have a common challenge or issue of interest, and they show a willingness to listen attentively. Co-sensing and sense of common purpose relate to the way members of a CoP reduce silos and become more cohesive through reciprocal identification. Co-sensing sets the grounds for reflective collaboration because CoP members will experience reciprocal identification, bonds of solidarity, and commitment. Presencing and reflective collaboration are both the connection with the higher self (from within and with others) through the awareness of new ideas and possibilities. Presencing facilitates that internalization and transformation of ideas into comprehensive practice through the connection of different suppositions, contrasting views, and epistemologies, and increases the ability to see situations from broader and holistic perspectives and frames. It is after this careful and persistent consideration of belief that co-creation emerges. Co-creation or innovation is a series of new ideas and prototypes that result from this deep level of connection. However, the literature on innovation and imitation (Semadeni & Anderson, 2010) reports that previous experience feeds intuition and creative thinking. In the case of CoPs, this is targeted knowledge on a specific field, contrary to

Theory U, which aspires to bring self-awareness that comes from personal rather than professional experience. Finally, co-evolving is the equivalent to share repertoire in that both facilitate the validation of best practices knowledge. Co-evolving happens as continue to engage in hands-on practice and repeated actions that become best practice when the outcomes continually positive. Pharmaceutical communities of practitioners have been successful in co-evolving practice methods into an explicit body of knowledge. Both co-evolving and shared repertoire presume that continuous communication will allow CoP members to ideate new working routines that are soon embedded into the existing field and organizational practices.

Contrary to the documented application of Theory U (Sharmer, 2004), CoPs operate outside the realms of the formal organization, as "pure" CoPs emerge spontaneously among a group of practitioners, are self-maintain, and refuse to be "institutionalized" as teams or organizational committees. Still, they are favorable environments for Theory U core elements to flourish because members must learn how to connect with each other, listen attentively, and expedite the learning that they acquire from each other and from other members of the community to create new solutions to existing problems. Visible behaviors during the CoP knowledge creation process include reflective behavior, spontaneous networking, trust, and empathy, which align with Theory U dynamics. The inner connections between these individuals facilitate that incubated ideas that incubate in the minds of practitioners can be revealed after a moment of collaborative reflection. Innovation theory identifies reflection as a "legitimate" managerial practice to solve organizational problems. Theory U provides with a strong frame for reflective practice because active listening, empathy, and connecting with the "blind spot" allow practitioners to use their perceptions, intuition, and tacit understandings to produce knowledge and adapt to change. Reflective practice is fundamental, consequently, to observe the integration of Theory U elements into the CoP knowledge creation process. Members of a community of practitioners must "socialize" their problems before they can find solutions or achieve continuous improvement, for which reflective practice is increasingly becoming a legitimate practice among organizations and professional communities. Documented outcomes on reflection-in-action applied to professional fields demonstrated that developing connections, active listening, and reflective practice is fundamental in the reframing of thinking systems and organizational transformation. Scharmer's Theory U facilitates boundless thinking from which CoP members can connect with their inner self and—from that place of connection—collaborate with peers to elevate professional practice. When several members of the community engage in reflective practice, CoPs not only are more productive and innovative but also can promote improved relationships and an environment of cultural inclusivity.

References

Anand, N., Gardner, H. K., & Morris, T. (2007). Knowledge-based innovation: Emergence and embedding of new practice areas in management consulting firms. *Academy of Management Journal, 50*(2), 406-428.

Arthur, W. B., Day, J., Jaworski, J., Jung, M., Nonaka, I., Scharmer, C. O., & Senge, P. (2002, April). Illuminating the blind spot. *Leader to Leader, 2002*(24), 11-14.

Bach, P. M., & Carroll, J. M. (2010). Characterizing the dynamics of open user experience design: The cases of Firefox and OpenOffice. org. *Journal of the Association for Information Systems, 11*(12), 902-925.

Boynton, A., & Fisher, B. (2005). *Virtuoso Teams: Lessons from Teams That Changed Their Worlds*. Mishawaka, IN: Better World Books.

Brown, R. H. (1990). Rhetoric, textuality, and the postmodern turn in sociological theory. *Sociological Theory, 8*(2), 188-197.

Carey, C., Smith, K., & Martin, L. M. (2009). Cross-university enterprise education collaboration as a community of practice. *Education & Training, 51*(8/9), 696-706. doi: 10.1108/00400910911005244

Cashman, K. (1998). *Leadership from the Inside Out: Becoming a Leader for Life*. Provo, UT: Executive Excellence Publishing.

DeSpautz, J., Kovacs, K. S., & Werling, G. (2008). GAMP standards for validation of automated systems. *Pharmaceutical Processing, 23*(3), 23-26.

De Palma, R., & Teague, L. (2008, December). A democratic community of practice: Unpicking all those words. *Educational Action Research, 16*(4), 441-456.

Dirani, K. (2011). Theory U: Leading from the future as it emerges. *Journal of European Industrial Training, 35*(3), 291-293. https://doi-org.contentproxy.phoenix.edu/10.1108/03090591111120430

Egger, M., Smith, G., & Phillips, A. (1997). Meta-Analysis: Principles and Procedures. *BMJ: British Medical Journal, 315*(7121), 1533-1537. Retrieved from http://www.jstor.org/stable/25176454

Fisk, N. (2015). *Building individual trust, tacit knowledge transfer, and theory U: A phenomenological study* (Order No. 3689909). Available from ProQuest Dissertations & Theses Global. (1678209966).

Fominaya, C. F. (2010). Creating cohesion from diversity: The challenge of collective identity formation in the global justice movement. *Sociological Inquiry, 80*(3), 377-404. doi: 10.1111/j.1475-682X.2010.00339.x

Gau, W. (2016). How to Construct Shared Repertoire in Older Adults' Communities of Practice. *Journal of Adult Development, 23*(3), 129-139. doi:10.1007/s10804-016-9229-6

Gausdal, A. H. (2008). Developing regional communities of practice by network reflection: The case of the Norwegian electronics industry. *Entrepreneurship & Regional Development, 20*(3), 209-235. doi: 10.1080/08985620701748367

Hayward, R. (2002). Discourse and the undiscussed: towards a framework for developing a little reflective theory for practice. *Urban Design International, 7*(3/4), 217.

Kinsella, E. A., & Whiteford, G. E. (2009). Knowledge generation and utilization in occupational therapy: Towards epistemic reflexivity. *Australian Occupational Therapy Journal, 56*(4), 249-258. doi: 10.1111/j.1440-1630.2007.00726.x

Koutropoulos, K. (2010, Spring). Creating networking communities beyond the classroom. *Human Architecture, 8*(1), 71-79.

Kratzer, J., Leenders, R. J., & van Engelen, J. L. (2006). Team Polarity and Creative Performance in Innovation Teams. *Creativity & Innovation Management,15*(1),96-104.doi:10.1111/j.1467-8691.2006.00372.

Lee, G. K., & Cole, R. E. (2003). From a firm-based to a community-based model of knowledge creation: The case of the Linux Kernel development. *Organization Science, 14*(6), 633-649. doi: 10.1287/orsc.14.6.633.24866

Lester, J., & Kezar, A. (2017). Strategies and Challenges for Distributing Leadership in Communities of Practice. *Journal of Leadership Studies, 10*(4), 17-34. doi: 10.1002/jls.21499

Li, L., Grimshaw, J. M., Nielsen, C., Judd, M., Coyote, P. C., & Graham, I. D. (2009). Use of communities of practice in business and health care sectors: A systematic review. *Implementation Science, 4*, 1-9. doi: 10.1186/1748 -5908-4-27

Machles, D., Bonkemeyer, E., & McMichael, J. (2010). Community of Practice. *Professional Safety, 55*(1), 46-52.

Martin, L. A. (2000, May). Effective data collection. *Total Quality Management, 11*(3), 341-344.

Moffatt, K., George, U., Lee, B., McGrath, S. (2005). Community Practice Researchers as Reflective Learners. *The British Journal of Social Work*, 35(1), 89–104. https://doi-org.contentproxy.phoenix.edu/10.1093/bjsw/bch164

Nonaka, I., & Konno, N. (1998). The concept of "Ba": Building a foundation for knowledge creation. *California Management Review, 40*(3), 40-54.

Nonaka, I., & Takeuchi, H. (1995) *The knowledge-creating company. How Japanese companies create the dynamics of innovation*. Oxford University Press, Oxford.

Orr, J. E. (1996). *Talking about machines: An ethnography of a modern job*. Ithaca, NY: Cornell University Press.

Penner, L. A., Dovidio, J. F., Piliavin, J. A., & Schroeder, D. A. (2005). Prosocial behavior: Multilevel perspectives. *Annual Review of Psychology, 56*(1), 365-392. doi: 10.1146/annurev.psych.56.091103.070141

Potter, C. (2015). Leadership development: an applied comparison of Gibbs' Reflective Cycle and Scharmer's Theory U. *Industrial and Commercial Training, 47*(6), 336-342. doi: org/10.1108/ICT-03-2015-0024

Price, M. (2005). Assessment standards: The role of communities of practice and the scholarship of assessment. *Assessment & Evaluation in Higher Education, 30*(3), 215-230. doi: 10.1080/02602930500063793

Presencing Institute. (2015). Principles and Glossary of Presencing. Retrieved from https://www.presencing.com/principles

Saldana, J. (2016). Meta-Analysis on the Presence of Leadership Expressions among Global Communities of Practice. *DeVry University Journal of Scholarly Research, 3*(1), 22-37.

Saldana, J. B. (2014). *Comparison of community, practice, domain, and leadership expressions among professional communities of practice* (Order No. 3647745). Available from Dissertations & Theses @ University of Phoenix; ProQuest Dissertations & Theses.

Scharmer, C. O. (2018). *Essentials of Theory U*. San Francisco, CA:

Berrett-Koehler.

Scharmer, C. O. (2007). *Theory U: Leading from the future as it emerges.* San Francisco, CA: Berrett-Koehler.

Scharmer, C. O., & Kaeufer, K. (2010). In front of the blank canvas: Sensing emerging futures. *The Journal of Business Strategy, 31*(4), 21-29.

Schon, D. A. (1989). A symposium on Scbön's Concept of Reflective Practice: Critiques, commentaries, illustrations. *Journal of Curriculum & Supervision, 5*(1), 6-9.

Sherwood, G., & Horton-Deutsch, S. (2015). Reflective Organizations; On the Front Lines of QSEN and Reflective Practice Implementation: On the Front Lines of QSEN and *Reflective Practice Implementation*, Sigma Theta Tau International.

Semadeni, M., & Anderson, B. S. (2010). The follower's dilemma: Innovation and imitation in the professional services industry. *Academy of Management Journal, 53*(5), 1175-1193.

Stauffacher, M. & Moser, C. (2010). A new 'epistemic community' in nuclear waste governance? Theoretical reflections and empirical observations on some fundamental challenges. *Catalan Journal of Communication & Cultural Studies, 2*(2), 197-211. doi: 10.1386/cjcs.2.2.197_1

Strambach, S. (2002). Change in the innovation process: New knowledge production and competitive cities--the case of Stuttgart. *European Planning Studies, 10*(2), 215-231. 10.1080/09654310120114508

Townley, G., Kloos, B., Green, E. P., & Franco, M. M. (2011). Reconcilable differences? Human diversity, cultural relativity, and sense of community. *American Journal of Community Psychology, 47*(1/2), 69-85. doi: 10.1007/s10464-010-9379-9

Temple, K. L. (2014). *Transformational process mapping to theory U: A case study of a united states city government's information technology and innovation branch transformational alignment to improve business service* (Order No. 3670204). Available from ProQuest Dissertations & Theses Global. (1649198288). Retrieved from https://search-proquest-com.contentproxy.phoenix.edu/docview/1649198288?accountid=134061

Terry, R., Hing, W., Orr, R., & Milne, N. (2017). Do coursework summative assessments predict clinical performance? A systematic review. *BMC Medical Education, 17.* doi: http://dx.doi.org/10.1186/s12909-017-0878-3

Vavasseur, C. B., & MacGregor, K. (2008, Summer). Extending content-focused professional development through online communities of practice. *Journal of Research on Technology in Education, 40*(4), 517-538.

Visser, W. (2010). Schön: Design as a reflective practice. Collection, Parsons Paris School of art and design. *Art + Design & Psychology*, pp.21-25.

Warhurst, R. P. (2008). Cigars on the flight-deck': new lecturers' participatory learning within workplace communities of practice. *Studies in Higher Education, 33*(4), 453-467. doi: 10.1080/03075070802211828

Wenger, E. (2004). *Communities of Practice: Learning, Meaning, and Identity* (7th Ed.). Cambridge, UK: Cambridge University Press.

West, R. (2009, June). What is shared? A framework for understanding shared innovation within communities. *Educational Technology Research & Development*, 57(3), 315-332. doi: 10.1007/s11423-008-9107-4

Weil, J. (2014). Crisis of Leadership. *Foot & Ankle Specialist, 8*(1), 6-7. doi: 10.1177/1938640014565091

Zeitler, U. (2014). Spirituality in diaconia: A reinterpretation of diaconal professionalism within the framework of Theory U. Scandinavian. *Journal for Leadership & Theology, 1*(1), 1-1.

CHAPTER 12

Exploring the use of Inward Looking in Theory U

Kriyanka Moodley

Eco-system awareness

This chapter proposes a refining of Theory U's download-ing stage using the behavioral intervention Inward Looking created by John Sherman. It argues that, in moving to-wards eco-system awareness, it is imperative to suspend and let go of mental models that obscure recognition of non-separation. This calls for much deeper engagement in mindful dissipation of the egoic structures that block access to Source.

Scharmer and Kaufer (2013) maintain that eco-system aware-ness does not mean removing the self during cognitive processes but involves "decoupling of structures of eco-system reality from the structures of ego-system awareness", including the well-being of others, nature, and the self (Scharmer & Kaufer, 2013). It is critical to be mindfully cognizant of the self when embracing a mind-set change.

The shift of awareness from ego- to eco- requires a journey through the U-process that involves seeing, sensing and presenc-ing other experiences. It is the modification mechanism through which consciousness is created by an open mind, "intellectual in-telligence", an open heart, "emotional intelligence", and an open will, "spiritual intelligence" (Kimmie, 2012). I expand on these concepts using eco-system awareness (Scharmer & Kaufer, 2013), as follows:

- An open mind represents the capacity to see the world with fresh eyes and to suspend old habits of thought.
- An open heart means the capacity to empathize, to see any situation through the eyes of someone else.
- An open will is the capacity of letting-go and "letting-come:" letting-go of old identities (like "us versus them") and letting-come a new sense of self and what that shift can make possible.

The inclusion of Inward Looking in Theory U

It is important to reiterate that, from a Theory U perspective, personal transformation effects social transformation; however, the latter is not entirely dependent on the former. Social transformation can be achieved provided that individuals are willing to suspend their mental models. However, these suspended models are likely to obscure recognition of non-separation; more insidiously, old mental models may resurface and subvert positive social gains (the many degradations of positive social revolutions attest to this). Inward Looking enables one to suspend and let go of mental models that obscure the recognition of non-separation by reconstructing the context of fear. Simply suspending such models is not a long-term solution; their dissolution could support the other stages of the process.

It is proposed that Inward Looking be included in Theory U model as follows:

1. Downloading (download habitual behaviors)
2. *Inward Looking (moving the beam of attention inward)*
3. Seeing (build common intent)
4. Sensing (observe, observe, observe)
5. Presencing (connect to the source or Source of inspiration)

6. Crystalizing (vision and intention)
7. Prototyping (link the mind, heart and will)
8. Performing (operating from the whole)

The graphic representation below shows the addition to the U-process. This is followed by a discussion on the use of Inward Looking.

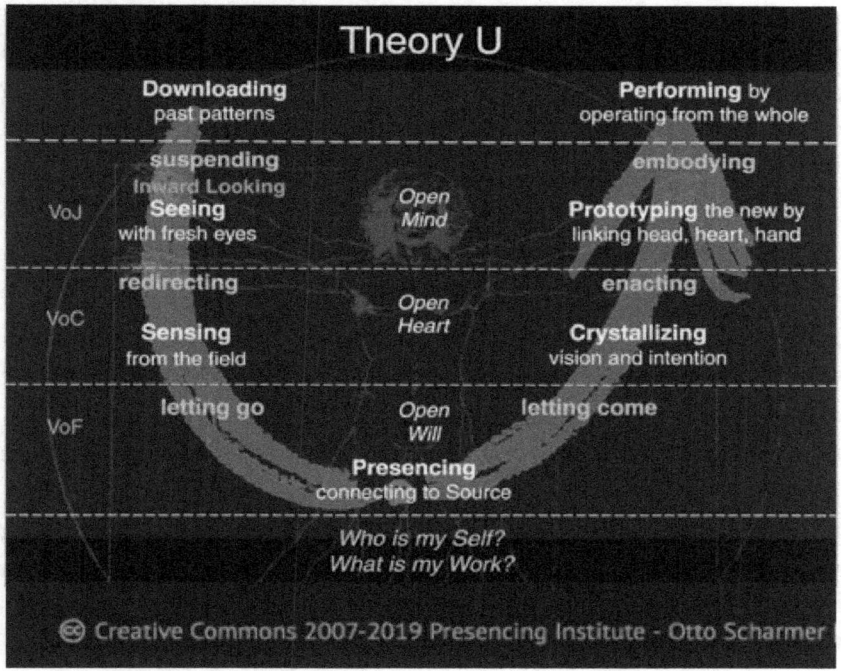

Figure 1: The U process (Scharmer)

Scharmer (2007) argues that we should download and suspend old patterns of thinking, as these could lead to excessive disapproval and fragmented communication with others (Hardman & Hardman, 2013). In the state of awareness that downloading creates we are unable to engage with habitual thinking, which leads to resistance to new ideas. Hardman and Hardman (2013) note that, in holistic cognitive action, we use:

...different parts of our brain, left and right hemispheres, frontal and occipital lobes, so that our minds can operate coherently and effectively, engaging fresh perspectives and ideas creatively and without judgment (p. 8).

In some cases these effects occur after a period of time and can be debilitating during the recovery period, often resulting in reversion to old methodologies or patterns of behavior. Theory U is a continuous process; thus, recurrence of past behavioral patterns may only occur toward the end of the process, or a certain amount of time after it. I therefore explore a generative framing of the use of Inward Looking in facilitating the breaking down of mental models.

Scholarly perspectives on Inward Looking

I argue that by suspending our mental models we are not necessarily letting go of them, a resounding feature of how Inward Looking would facilitate the Theory U process. During the experiential components of this research, it was found that mental models were likely to surface, or the issues confronting the participants might re-surface or recur either during or after completion of the U-process. This could result in the process being ineffective either during the process or in one's field of action. During the Presencing Foundation Program (2014), participants appeared to be hiding from what arose during and after the program. I thus recognized that participants' personal experiences likely motivated them to engage with the program, or were possibly brought out by the program.

It is argued that if the U-process addresses the root cause of these mental models, identified as fear and separation, by letting go of them rather than merely suspending them, it is likely that individual or collective resistance, which obscures recognition of non-separation and thereby the opportunity for holistic action, will be avoided.

This can be achieved by focusing attention on the self, by looking inward. Following the downloading stage, Inward Looking would allow individuals to face and put an end to the psychological barriers of fear and separation, which could not only be inhibiting us from effectively going through the rest of the U-process, but can lead to excessive disconnection and fragmented interaction with others (Hardman & Hardman, 2013). Therefore, Hardman and Hardman (2013) suggest that we remove the barriers inhibiting us in a healthy way by quietening the mind, focusing on breathing and attention, and by moving the beam of attention inwards once we have identified these habitual behaviors.

Inward Looking has been selected as an exemplar; a very direct one that explores the various forms of mindfulness, mindful practice and research into mindfulness. Theoretically, conceptually and experientially, it a simple, clear and direct method to achieve this. It facilitates what Hardman and Hardman seek to achieve with various contemplative practices. Although Scharmer pays less attention to this stage than other processes, he alludes to the notion of deep personal transformation, that is, *seeing the world differently, or when one's paradigm has changed.*

Inward Looking is proposed as it is what "we do naturally, when we focus our attention on anything present in our consciousness" (Sherman, 2011). The following is abstracted from Sherman's (2011) work: right now, your attention (as the reader) is focused for the most part on this text, essentially ignoring everything else around you. Inward Looking provides participants with a skill that brings about self-reliance; specifically during the most difficult periods that follow the breakdown of the *context of fear* and separation that can be molded in every aspect and psychological mechanism of our minds.

Conceptually and experientially, Inward Looking is directed at quietening our mind, freeing it from internal and external distractions, and establishing the present place and moment as we focus our attention. Bearing in mind that the *context of fear* (Sherman, 2013) controls almost every facet and psychological mechanism of our mind, one way to develop self-reliance is to nurture our ability to direct and focus attention. The exercise of looking inward will reinforce our "ability to focus attention on a single object, ignoring everything else, as a means to develop a natural skillfulness in the intelligent use of this power," to focus on attention and intention. Inward Looking causes the senses to be activated, further ensuring a sense of presence and openness.

Non-separation, non-dualism and mindfulness

Elaborating on how this notion came about brings to light the perennial wisdom lineage of non-separation, non-duality and mindfulness which shapes the overreaching theme of this chapter, without simply laying out the facts, not on the grounds of empiricism, but from a consciousness point of view.

The Story of Separation

An underlying motivation for this chapter is the dominant cultural narrative articulated in detail by Charles Eisenstein (2013). Eisenstein's (2013) use of the concepts of the "story of separation" and "story of Interbeing" clearly articulates these ideas. The story of separation recognizes the narrative of the individual as a separate self, isolated from others, in a universe that is also separate. Eisenstein's (2013) story of Interbeing recognizes the relationship between individuals and their physical environment. Theory U unknowingly mirrors the story of Interbeing. In the arguments presented in this chapter we can begin to see how the term eco-system awareness resonates with Interbeing.

This research examines the discontinuation of the story of separation which we perpetuate through the core manifestations of human hatred, ill-will, greed and violence, which leads to fearful separation from our own life (Loy, 2003; Sherman, 2011), and influences all our systems – economic, political, cultural, and educational (Pillay, 2016).

Eisenstein (2013) argues that we perpetuate the story of separation in a myriad of ways through holding one unchallenged precept which Pillay (2016) describes as the notion "that there exist separate and solid things apart from me and that I am another solid and separate thing" (Pillay, 2016; Goode, 2016).

The underlying context of fearfulness is not the experience of fear with which we are all familiar. The term "fear of life", coined by Sherman (2011) is explained through the symptoms of hatred of the self and others, greed, aggression, ill-will and apprehension that derive from fearful separation from others as well as from our own lives. Sherman asserts that:

> This underlying context of fearfulness is not the experience of fear with which we are all familiar. It is below the level of conscious awareness, and it is mostly inaccessible to us, except through its symptoms. The fear of life is more like an autoimmune disease. It spoils life for us by corrupting every component of the developing structure of personality through which we have the experience of life (Sherman, 2013).

This research considers that suspending but also letting go of these psychological barriers of fear and separation during the U-process will enable more efficient movement towards eco-system awareness.

Non-separation

While non-separateness is a fact, it is challenging to verify; hence, it is not widely understood as factual, at least not in the conventional academic sense of the term. I therefore acknowledge that experiential apperception of non-separation is already a fact – that there is "no separate, solid, physical world that exists independently of consciousness" (Pillay, 2016; Goode, 2016).

I experientially, conceptually and theoretically explored the ontological models Theory U and Inward Looking through my doctoral research. A central component of both is the experiential act of being mindful. It was by exploring the self that the main focus was developed, which is the understanding that the mental models that obscure recognition of non-separation can be broken down to attain eco-system awareness.

Non-dualism

Eugene Fernandez (2014) articulated that the intent of non-dualism is to peel away the valence mask and show the world, including the self, as one essentially inseparable whole. I recognize that nonduality implies that the observer is not separate from the observed. For instance, "fear is an actuality, and trying to understand a fact with an abstraction" is not possible (Krishnamurti, 1973). In part, I allude that the observer is fear, and when one sees that they are in fact part of fear, not separate from it, fear comes to an end (Krishnamurti, 1973).

Nonduality is currently emerging as a viable paradigm. This can be seen in the world's only peer-reviewed, academic journal that discusses the intersection of nondual philosophy and psychology, entitled *Undivided Journal, The Online Journal of Nonduality and Psychology*. Furthermore conferences organized by Science and Nonduality (SAND) aim to nurture a new relationship to spirituality, free from religious doctrine, but based on ageless traditions of wisdom, educated by cutting-edge science, and grounded in direct experience. These examples show that non-dualism is emerging as a strong presence in other disciplines and can be regarded as an interdisciplinary phenomenon.

The nondual perspective or argument is based on the premise that suffering has to do with dualism's effects – "dualism leads to suffering and misery" – that Sherman (2011) describes as the "fear of life." From a nondual perspective, a dualistic and divided experience of the world results in feelings of separation, which can be expanded upon as separation from what we take to be external objects, other people and the world. I argue that this can lead to feelings of separation, which result in one feeling restricted and vulnerable, leading to suffering. This can be lessened by a deep, intuitive understanding of our nondual, continuous experience, which is the end of the experience of separation; that which is necessary to end suffering.

Non-dualism provides a worldview and an experiential practice to shift our self-perspective from the sense of separation towards apperception of non-separation, where awareness is the state of being in which no experiential division can be found, where self, other and nature are one (Katz & Pillay, 2014). I argue that this is the most conceptually appropriate theoretical framework to understand and affirm the effectiveness of Theory U.

Non-dualism and Theory U

The central ontological question is: "What is my Being?" This question is emphasized by the school of non-dualism, encouraging an individual to awaken to their true nature, out of which, it is asserted, intellect, ingenuity, and the right relationship will emerge. A comprehensive picture of nondual ontology can only be achieved by unpacking nondual perception, action, and thinking, because these acts conventionally describe "how we experience ourselves and the world" (Loy, 1997).

Similar questions arise in the presencing stage of Theory U, "Who is my Self?" and "What is my Work?" giving rise to ontological assertions of acumen, ingenuity, and the right relationship to others and the world. Loy (1997) uses the terms nondual perception, nondual action and nondual thinking, which, according to Pillay (2007), are imperative in defining ontological status.

The separation created in our lives can be attributed as the structure of thought, which is the action of the observer who thinks of themselves as separate. They think of themselves as a thinker, which is regarded as something different from their thought. In seeking to explain this, I recognize that there can be no thought without the thinker and no thinker without the thought. Similarly, the experiencer tends to separate themselves from the things experienced. Thus, the observer, the thinker, and the experiencer are no different from the observed, the thought, and the experienced (Krishnamurti, 1973).

In a related example arising from Interbeing, Thich Nhat Hanh (1987) uses roses and garbage to show that nothing in the world is either pure or ruined; these are empty concepts. Without a rose, there can be no garbage, and without garbage, there can be no rose; these objects co-exist and are therefore equal. This further illustrates the connection between non-dualism and Interbeing. In elaborating on this, I look to Krishnamurti (1969) who emphasizes the outcome of attaining this nondual perception, nondual action and nondual thinking.

Nondual perception collapses the habitual distinction between the observer and the observed (Loy, 1997). This is seen experientially during the seeing and sensing stages of the U-process. This process challenges habitual behaviors and allows the observer and the observed to be one.

Loy recognized that "nondual action arises when the mind, based on experience, is not guiding action: when thought, based on experience, is not shaping action" (Loy, 1997). In Theory U the action, being processes, does not force but yields. The action is passive, or acts by means of applying slight action at the right time and place, in order to effect radical transformation in oneself and subsequently society. The action is natural.

Nondual thinking is experienced through the U-Process by means of engagement. The delusion of separation is illustrated through intense interaction and engagement with others, more often than not resulting in the ending of fear, because the notion that we are ultimately one with others and nature is driven with vigor throughout the process (adapted from Loy, 1997). Theoretically, nondual thinking is most evident in Scharmer and Kaufer's (2013) concept of eco-system awareness. This state of awareness is characterized by the totality of being one, as opposed to the ego-centric way of thinking and being.

Goode (2007) explains that non-dualism focuses on the complex connectedness of the self with reality. It collapses the "spectator" perspective of the perceiver perceiving the perceived and places the self at the core of radical transformation. Theory U holds the observer and observing at the forefront of the processes, locating the self through various experiences within one's reality. It addresses the observer and the observing in unique yet complementary ways. Scharmer's Theory U is a transformative, procreative field of potential, allowing one to suspend mental models of the past and to be able to move into a space of non-phenomenal awareness before emerging into the new (adapted from Senge, 1990). It further considers movement from ego-system awareness by moving the egoic self to eco-system awareness, through considering the self, others and the environment, which is supported by the notion of Interbeing.

Mindfulness and Eco-system awareness

Kelly (2015) asserts that while awareness is vital, human beings have limited knowledge of it. We tend to focus on awareness of things rather than awareness itself. There is a parallel in Kelly's (2015) assertion on Theory U's presencing in that "the awareness we seek is right here, right now, and equally available to each of us" (p. 1). He recognizes that awake awareness is like any other human function. At a basic level of awareness, it reveals the foundation of "how we know and who we are" (Kelly, 2015); in shifting our identity and knowing, we undergo what Kelly labelled as a journey of awake awareness. This is further identified as the "transformation of consciousness" identified as "awakening". By doing so, we open ourselves up to the ability to be liberated, content and interconnected. Awake awareness is at the core of Being and mindfulness.

Mindfulness encourages one to utilize all one's senses in perceptions of situations experienced, rather than relying on and paying attention to the words that another individual speaks (Langer, 1989). Seeing situations from numerous perspectives, that is, with an open mind, and attending to our surroundings help us to understand all that is happening and to construct innovative mental maps of other peoples' personalities to assist us to respond appropriately. According to Langer (1989), being mindful involves awareness of our own conventions, thoughts, emotions and the selective acuity, attribution and classification that should be adopted (Langer, 1989). Mindfulness creates a sense of observing what is apparent about another individual and changing their assumptions, opinions and behavior. Mindfulness engages with:

> empathy – the ability to mentally put ourselves in the other person's shoes as a means of understanding the situation and their feelings toward it, from the perspective of their cultural background rather than ours (Langer, 1989).

I concur with Scharmer and Kaufer (2013) that it is not possible to move from an ego-centered economy to an eco-centered model without the shift in consciousness that is postulated. Scharmer adds that simply shifting individual consciousness is not enough; a threefold revolution is required including individual, relational, and institutional processes of inversion.

Scharmer and Kaufer (2013) elaborate on the processes of inversion as follows:

- Individual inversion means opening up our thinking, feeling, and will so that we can act as instruments for the future that already wants to emerge.
- Relational inversion means opening up our communicative capacities and shifting from a focus on conformity and defensiveness to generative dialogue, so that groups can enter a space of thinking together, of collective creativity and flow.
- Institutional inversion means opening up traditional geometries of power that are characterized by centralized hierarchies and decentralized competition and re-focusing institutions around co-creative stakeholder relationships in eco-systems that can generate wellbeing for all.

Southern (2013) created the notion of "Being in Care" (p. 62) which resonates with the concepts cited above. She used the theory of transformative learning and change to create a shared capacity to reconsider, reform and reshape new constructs and developments that assist in identifying innovative ways of existing and operating together that protect individuals as well as the natural resources required to sustain life on earth.

Southern (2013) maintains that this type of learning mainly involves interpersonal work, which necessitates self-examination and "personal development along with a shift in the Western assumption of the separate individual self". Her view extends to the self as a relational being which is formed through relationships. Becoming more present in the moment, being alive, and being skillful in working with complex situations while determining a future we see emerging, is relational work.

Southern (2013) states that:

> ...it is both inner and outer work, which includes the ability to place oneself in a vulnerable place, opening up opportunities to be influenced, and then coming back to self in a centered way to reflect and learn from one's engagement with others and in the world (p. 62).

Southern's (2013) notion of Being in Care is based on the premise of "holding others, ourselves, our relationships and our environment in care." This is a similar approach to Heidegger's (1962) philosophical stance on a relational way of being, providing a perspective which informs a radical shift from an individualist orientation. The individualist orientation influences how we design processes and models that inform our thinking and being, thus reinforcing a way of being that may no longer appropriately serve collective needs. Sustainability of the environment's resources and the interconnectedness of human life on the planet should be understood as relational as this is critical to constructing the transformational changes required today (Southern, 2013). Southern (2013) draws on Bateson's (2004) work to describe this shift to relational self:

> More and more it has seemed to me that the idea of a separate individual, the idea that there is someone to be known, separate from the relationship is simply an error... we come to create each other, bring each other into being by being part of the matrix in which the other exists (p. 63).

I therefore argue for a deeper shift in consciousness so that we can create, reflect and act for the interests of the self, others and the physical environment. It should be noted that there is a risk that these externalities could be left unmitigated while the mindfulness that shaped them is left intact, allowing the same inadequacies to re-surface in a number of different ways.

To successfully move from ego-system awareness to eco-system awareness, a model is required that is:

- Simple and easily grasped.
- Applicable in various change contexts including educational, organizational and societal forums.
- Able to remove the sense of separation experienced in moving toward eco-system awareness.

Conclusion

This chapter proposed a refining of Theory U's downloading stage using the behavioral intervention Inward Looking. The downloading stage needs to be refined to facilitate the move from ego-system awareness to eco-system awareness. The chapter suggests a deeper process of not merely suspending, but undoing the mental models held in place by dual thinking habits and well-worn conditioning. This requires significant practice to shift deeper structural conditioning. The chapter therefore proposes a process like Inward Looking, which accelerates the breaking down of mental models as opposed to simply suspending them. The psychological barriers of fear and separation usually associated with fragmentation and conflict, which are reflected in our various social structures, need to be dissolved to attain eco-system awareness. Facing and ending these mental models could avert falling into past patterns of behavior.

References

Bateson, G. (2004). *Willing to learn: Passages of personal discovery*. Hanover, New Hampshire: Steerford Press.

Eisenstein, C. (2013). *The more beautiful world our hearts know is possible*. Berkeley, CA: North Atlantic Books. Retrieved from http://charleseisenstein.net/project/the-more-beautiful-world-our-hearts-know-is-possible/. Date accessed: 12 February 2015.

Fernandez, E.C. (2014). *Doors to Reflection* (Unpublished doctoral thesis). University of Technology, Sydney.

Hanh, T. N. (1987). *Being Peace*. Berkley, California: Parallax Press.

Hardman, J., & Hardman, P. (2013). Traveling the U: Contemplative practices for consciousness development for corporate and social transformation. In O. Gunnlaugson, C Baron, M. Cayer (Eds.), *Perspectives on Theory U: Insights from the field* (pp. 1-13). Hershey, P. A: IGI Global.

Heidegger, M. (1962). *Being in time*. San Francisco, CA: Harper-Collins.

Goode, G. (2016). *After Awareness: The End of the Path*. Non-Duality.

Katz, J., & Pillay, K. (2014). #5223 – Dr. Kriben Pillay: Interview and Article. Retrieved from https://nonduality. org/2014/05/29/5223-dr-kriben-pillay-interview-and-article/. Date accessed: 23 March 2016.

Kelly, L. (2015). *Shift into freedom: The science and practice of open-hearted awareness*. Colorado. Sounds True. [Kindle DX version]. Retrieved from Amazon.com. Date accessed: 15 February 2016.

Krishnamurti, J. (1969). *Freedom from the Known*. Ebury Publishing. Retrieved from https://books.google.co.za/books?id=43aiO8V7HQg-C&pg=PA105& lpg=PA105&dq. Date accessed: 24 May 2016.

Krishnamurti, J. (1973). *Education and the significance of life*. Bombay: B.I Publications.

Langer, E.J. (1989). Minding matters: The consequences of mindlessness-mindfulness. *Advances in Experimental Social Psychology*, 22.

Loy, D. R. (1997). *Nonduality: A study in comparative philosophy*. Atlantic Highlands, NJ: Humanities Press.

Loy, D R. (2003). *The Great Awakening: A Buddhist Social Theory*. Boston: Wisdom Publications.

Moodley, Source: Author's conception in her doctoral study

Pillay, K. (2007). *Nondualism and educational drama and theatre: A perspective for transformative training*.

Wandsbeck, South Africa: The Noumenon Press.

Pillay, K. (2016). Learning and the Illusion of Solid and Separate Things: Troublesome Knowledge and the Curriculum. Unpublished paper. Durban: University of KwaZulu-Natal.

Scharmer, C. O. (2007). *Theory U: Leading from the future as it emerges*. San Francisco, CA: Berrett-Koehler. [Kindle DX version]. Available from Amazon.com.

Scharmer, C. O., & Kaufer, K. (2013). *Leading from the emerging future: From ego-system to eco-system economics*. San Francisco, CA: Berrett-Koehler.

Senge, P. (1990). Towards an ecology of leadership: development journeys of three leaders, change and development journeys into a pluralistic world. Annual Meeting of the Academy of Management, Chicago.

Sherman, J. (2011). *The fear of life and the simple Act of Inward Looking that snuffs it out.* Ojai, CA: Silent Heart Press.

Sherman, J. (2013). The Looking. Retrieved from http://www.justone-look.org/downloads/JOHN_SHERMAN_The_Looking.pdf. Date accessed: 10 November 2015.

Southern, N. (2013). Presencing as being in care: Extending Theory U through a relational framework. In O. Gunnlaugson, C. Baron, M. Cayer (Eds.), *Perspectives on Theory U: Insights from the field* (pp. 61-76). Hershey, P. A: IGI Global.

CHAPTER 13:

Transforming u.lab: Redesigning a Social Technology from a Strategic Sustainable Perspective

Florentina Bajraktari, Rosamund Mosse and Gabriel Neira Voto

Introduction

> I used to think that top environmental problems were biodiversity loss, ecosystem collapse and climate change. I thought that thirty years of good science could address these problems. I was wrong. The top environmental problems are selfishness, greed and apathy, and to deal with these we need a cultural and spiritual transformation. And we scientists don't know how to do that. (Gus Speth, 2015)

Currently society is facing a set of interconnected challenges, known collectively as the sustainability challenge, which are systematically increasing socio-ecological unsustainability on a scale never experienced before. In order to address the sustainability challenge, u.lab's experiential response inspires participants to question their paradigms of thought and societal norms. By providing an approach that is systemic, participatory and emergent, u.lab enables solutions that are responsive to the dynamic nature of those interconnected challenges. The authors saw an opportunity to create a u.lab course specifically designed for sustainability that combines the strength of the U process and a strategic sustainable development approach. Using the framework for strategic sustainable development, designed to help practitioners facilitate society's transition towards sustainable development, our research explores how u.lab can be re-designed in order to move society strategically toward a sustainable future.

Getting Started

In August 2015, we were meeting for the first time. We had left jobs and lives and travelled to the picturesque and fairly tiny town of Karlskrona, in Sweden, to be students once again. Enrolled in the Masters in Strategic Leadership towards Sustainability (MSLS) programme at the Blekinge Institute of Technology, we were joined by fifty-one fellow change-makers from around the world.

Florentina had travelled from Brussels, Belgium, leaving her role as an Equal Opportunities Project Manager. Wide-eyed and with her heart on her sleeve, she settled into the MSLS community, drawing people to her with her authenticity and laughter.

Rosamund had come from New Brunswick, Canada. Having been working in community and international development, she landed in Karlskrona with only the fiercest and most absolute knowledge that she needed to be there - for some reason. With cautious optimism and reserving judgement, she stepped into the experience.

Gabriel made his way to Europe from Rio de Janiero, Brazil, where he had been working with Favela Verde - an environmental and educational NGO he founded in Favela da Rocinha, the biggest favela in Latin America. Full of energy, enthusiasm and joy, Gabriel brought his whole self to MSLS.

Karlskrona is small in size but, largely due to MSLS, is a big player in the realm of innovative education. We may have come from diverse backgrounds, but we were united in our desire to understand and find solutions to tackle the problems we were seeing in our various corners of the globe. MSLS gave us a grounding in sustainability science as well as the framework for strategic sustainable development (FSSD), a framework for sustainability created by two Swedish scholars - Karl-Henrick Robèrt and Göran Broman. The FSSD is a framework designed to help practitioners to facilitate society's transition towards sustainable development. Strategic sustainable development, or SSD, can be defined as the shift from our current, globally unsustainable systems, structures and practices towards sustainable ones in a strategic way (Robèrt & Broman, 2015).

MSLS 2016 was made up of fifty-four people from thirty-two countries. We were idealists and skeptics, engineers and philosophers, new grads and those who had long ago entered the workforce. We were not fast friends, necessarily, but what followed in those first few months was a series of moments that showcased our unique talents and aptitudes, and our strength when united. Before we came together to begin the process of writing our thesis, we had opportunity to see each other shine, and developed a deep respect for the skillsets we each brought to the table. MSLS provided us with a knowledge of the FSSD, yes, but we were also pushed to be collaborative and caring leaders and to find a sense of purpose. We were asked not only to think systematically, but also to develop creative problem-solving approaches to complex issues. We were encouraged to be curious, to cross-pollinate different theories and lead new initiatives within the local context. We took this so seriously that by the end of our year together, we had already run a u.lab hub for our local community, helped organise an Art of Hosting training for 110+ participants from all over the world, and written our thesis together.

You might say that theory U and u.lab brought us together - there certainly are direct causal links to how and why each of us arrived in Karlskrona as a part of MSLS 2016. Mostly, we believe that our collaboration and shared work was as much emergent as it was preordained. Each of us was responding to what we came to understand as a shared way of wanting to work and be with others in the world.

Observe, Observe, Observe

The Call: The Sustainability Challenge

We are currently facing exponential population growth, increasing demand on and for natural resources, and social and economic inequality, as well as ecological problems such as ocean acidification, ozone depletion, chemical pollution, biodiversity loss and climate change. As we learned about one challenge after another, we were overwhelmed by the impact that we, as humans, were having on the planet, which we all rely on for survival as a species (Robèrt & Broman, 2015; Rockström, 2010; Scharmer & Kaufer, 2013). We came to understand this interconnected and systemic set of challenges as the sustainability challenge.

To better comprehend the sustainability challenge, it is important to understand the pressure and the urgency we are facing, and so we use the metaphor of a funnel. The funnel becomes a representation of the systemic challenges we face, with the wall of the funnel representing Earth's capacity to carry life. As the funnel narrows, we have less room to maneuver towards a sustainable society, which puts increasing and exponential pressure on those social, ecological and economic capacities we rely on to sustain life.

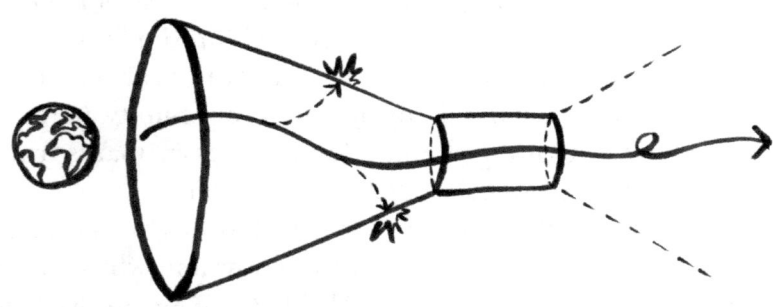

Figure 1: The funnel metaphor (Holmberg & Robèrt, 2000). Adapted from a design by Beltrame, Rootes and Serrure, 2013. Image by Rosamund Mosse.

As increased pressure is felt worldwide, it will result in more social, ecological and financial crises and less room and time for us to alter our course in the direction of a sustainable future. Over time and without drastically adjusting our behaviour to limit our impact on the earth, we will end up crashing into the wall of the funnel, surpassing the limits of the planet and leading to irrevocable damage to social and ecological systems (Robèrt & Broman, 2015).

By November, our understanding of the challenges we were facing was beginning to weigh on us. The shortening of the Swedish days did not help. What were we doing to the planet and ourselves? We deliberated in the classroom during the day, and often debated late into the evening in someone's cottage. Fifty-four inspired change-agents in one small Swedish town? We did not have much else to do but try to find answers. However, as is often the case, the more you learn, and grow, the more questions you seem to have. We were beginning to realise that we had only peeled back the first layer of our understanding of the sustainability challenge, and many more layers were yet to be uncovered.

We were beginning to see the sustainability challenge as a "wicked problem" (Rittel & Webber, 1973; Xiang 2013, 1; Scharmer & Kaufer, 2013). Wicked problems have no clear definition, those involved have radically different points of view, the solutions do not fit into binaries of yes/no or true/false, and approaches to solutions are dynamic and change over time (Rittel & Webber, 1973). The sustainability challenge, as with other wicked problems is an "expression of diverse and conflicting values of interests" (Norton 2011, p. 447). Resolving wicked problems, then, requires flexible, process-oriented and holistic approaches instead of linear and reductive strategies (Xiang, 2013). And, as we try to solve these wicked, systemic challenges, the solutions we develop continue to impact and influence one another, adding even more complexity to the system (Frensch & Funke, 1995).

The sustainability challenge and other wicked problems are unpredictable and current ways of dealing with them have failed to address their interconnectivity, complexity and emergence

(Mintzberg, 1994). As there is no clear relationship between the cause and the most appropriate solution, adaptive solutions are the best course of action. Adaptive solutions are flexible, there is no best practice and many solutions are possible in a given time. Instead of focused silos of inquiry and action, specialisation and expertise (Burge, 1993), they require a dispersed and internalised learning approach throughout organisations and systems (Heifetz & Linsky, 2002).

The Seed: U.lab as a Response to all this Complexity?

MSLS was not only about the science of sustainability though. It was also a course on leadership, and we were asked to question and curate our assumptions and beliefs, as well as our relationships with ourselves, our communities and our planet. Pushed to dive into other theories and find our own creative solutions, we started a u.lab hub that ran parallel to the programme. We quickly realised that the process, container and tools of u.lab had the potential to address big, sticky, wicked problems as it left room for emergence, complexity, urgency, a shift in belief systems, and adaptive solutions. The wheels in our heads started turning, and we began to imagine what combining u.lab and the FSSD might look like.

U.lab: Transforming Business, Society and Self was an experimental and innovative massive open online course that ran for eight weeks and followed the U process. More than 100.000 people took the class worldwide, gathering into self-organised hubs that developed innovative approaches to the course. U.lab is a social technology that fosters social innovation across sectors and cultures and cross-cuts hierarchy.

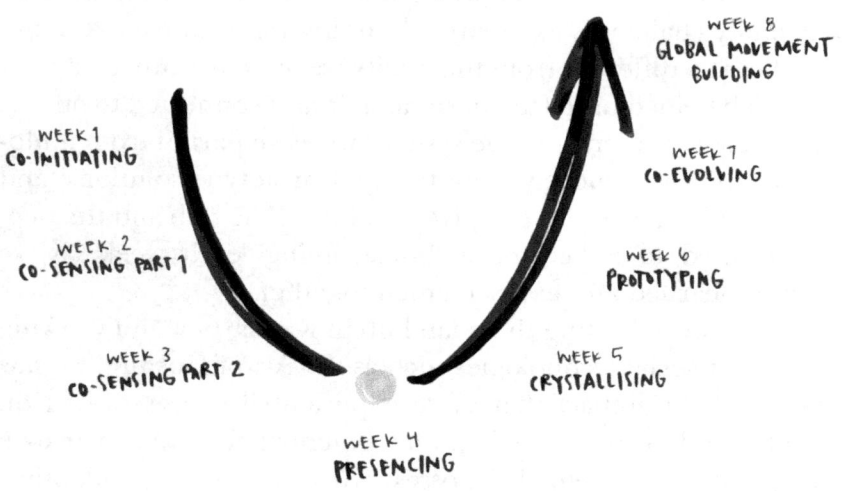

Figure 2: U.lab track. Adapted from u.lab (MITx, 2015).
Image by Rosamund Mosse.

What we saw in u.lab, its intention and approach, was a hybrid of a social lab which aims to address complex and systemic challenges and an open-source educational platform. It merges the teaching of theory U with a transformative, experiential process to inspire individuals to take action towards creating a future that we all want (MITx, 2015). The design and popularity of u. lab not only highlights the shift in higher education models, but also the potential for yet another breed of social labs - one that can include diverse experiences and involve hundreds of thousands of people, no matter their background.

Theory U, and subsequently u.lab, came into being as responses to the permanent increase of complexity in our current environment (Scharmer & Kaufer, 2010). Scharmer and Kaufer (2010) argue that the more complex a challenge or situation, the more ineffective it is to rely on only our past experience to inform solutions. They asked themselves: "what if the future is different from the past? What if one's past experiences aren't relevant to

319

the emerging challenges? Is it possible, instead, to learn from the emerging future?" (Scharmer & Kaufer, 2010, p. 22). It therefore is fitting that u.lab be used as a platform for addressing the sustainability challenge, as we are all hoping for a future that looks significantly different from the reality we are currently living.

U.lab helped us to feel more capable and connected to others, more able to understand the systems we were part of from multiple perspectives, more willing to rapid-prototype solutions, and more keen to reflect on our given realities. The hub and the people devoted to it became a 'homecoming' each week, as we worked, learned and experimented together.

As we were hosting the u.lab hub in Karlskrona and working with other social technologies such as the Art of Hosting, we saw first-hand the impact that these experiential processes had on people, and were excited at the potential for transformative change that they seemed to possess. We saw u.lab as an adaptive, emergent and dynamic tool with the potential to address the sustainability challenge. However, by not having a scientific understanding of sustainability, the transformation fostered by u.lab *as it was* did not necessarily encourage sustainable development. We hypothesized that the addition of strategic sustainable development concepts could enhance u.lab to help it *necessarily* move society towards sustainability.

The Framework: Conceptual Architecture

We came to Karlskrona to study the framework for strategic sustainable development (FSSD), as well as leadership in complexity, so it only felt right to use the FSSD, along with strategic sustainable development (SSD) concepts in order to assess and design a u.lab that would necessarily move society towards sustainability.

Strategic sustainable development incorporates concepts that are designed to address complex and systemic challenges such as the sustainability challenge. In essence, strategic sustainable development encompasses the shift from current, globally unsustainable systems and practices towards a sustainable society in a strategic way (Robèrt & Broman, 2015). As defined by Holmberg and Robèrt (2000), to be strategic on the path toward sustainable development is to use a 'simplicity without reduction' approach. This methodology presents first-order principles or principles that define the system at its most essential level. The first-order principles that explain the systems of society within the biosphere are the first and second laws of thermodynamics, photosynthesis as a biogeochemical process and trust as an essential bond to societal systems (Holmberg & Robèrt, 2000). The first law of thermodynamics states that all the matter that will ever exist on earth is currently here, as earth can be seen as a closed system to matter. The second law states that disorder (entropy) increases in all closed systems. While the Earth is a closed system to matter, it is an open system to energy as it receives energy from the sun. Sunlight is responsible for almost all increases in net material quality on the planet. The flow of energy from the sun creates structure and order from the disorder through photosynthesis and the effects of solar heating. Plants receive energy from sunlight through chloroplasts and in turn, provide energy for other forms of life, such as animals (Robèrt & Broman, 2015). With regard to society as a system, trust is a necessary condition for economic, political and social sustainability, and is therefore a fundamental human need (Missimer, 2015).

Establishing these first-order principles gives us a enough of a shared vision of what a sustainable society should look like, but provides no specific details, symptoms or consequences, which can sometimes confuse and fracture different sets of stakeholders (Holmberg & Robèrt, 2000). A "common principled framing would allow for identification of common challenges, possible synergies and coordinated collaboration over sectors...for reaching sustainability" (Robèrt & Broman 2015, p. 4) that is "independent of scale and context" (Robèrt & Broman 2015, p. 3). According to Robèrt and Broman (2015), the sustainability principles of the FSSD are the only such principles to observe these criteria.

The framework for strategic sustainable development outlines a scientific and principled definition of sustainability, helps us to take a systems perspective, understand complexity and avoid the pitfall of reductionism (Holmberg & Robèrt, 2000; Ny, MacDonald & Broman, 2008). The FSSD provides an understanding of the global socio-ecological system, eight principles for sustainable development - or sustainability principles (SPs), backcasting from a vision of success, and actions and tools to help us move towards sustainability (Robèrt & Broman, 2015).

In our research, we decided to focus on the following concepts from the FSSD: systems thinking, the sustainability challenge, a clear, singular and unifying definition of sustainability, boundary conditions for sustainable development, and a vision of success and backcasting.

Systems thinking.

Systems thinking is a discipline for understanding and interpreting whole systems, seeing the interrelationships and patterns as opposed to a static reality made up of individual parts. If a given system is broken down or pieced out, innate properties of that system disappear. This means that we can only gain a real understanding of a system when we take into consideration that system as a whole, embedded within its context, and inclusive of the relationships between its components (Senge, 1980).

The sustainability challenge.

The sustainability challenge can be defined by the rising complexity and interconnection of systemic socio-ecological issues such as population growth, the ever expanding gap between the rich and the poor, civil war, increasing and fatally damaging land use, nitrogen and phosphorus inputs into the biosphere, and the symptoms of climate change (Robèrt & Broman, 2015). It is one of the most complex challenges the human race has ever faced, and finding a solution is urgent, if we - and many other species - are to survive.

A clear, singular and unifying definition of sustainability.

The concepts that make up the definition of sustainability in the FSSD are the result of scientific consensus, are based on common and widely understood language and are comprehensible to diverse audiences (Robèrt & Broman, 2015). Having a clear, singular and unifying definition of sustainability means that everyone approaching a particular challenge can start from a common understanding of what success (i.e. a sustainable society) means.

Boundary conditions for sustainable development.

The sustainability principles are stated as exclusion criteria - in that they tell you what you *cannot* do, not *what to do*. This allows for many versions of a vision of a successful sustainable society as they simply serve as "the boundary conditions within which society can continue to function and evolve, outside of which it cannot" (Robèrt & Broman, 2015, p. 7). As Robèrt and Broman conclude, "[i]t is difficult to know whether any given scenario is truly sustainable or not if it is not framed by and assessed against a principled definition of sustainability. While specific initiatives and actions can have beneficial impacts, without proper framing, the likelihood of unintended negative consequences is significant" (p. 3).

Each sustainability principle is necessary and sufficient for a sustainable society, as well as general enough to be used in different contexts and by different actors. They are also concrete enough to allow for actions to be developed and non-overlapping and non-mutually exclusive (Robèrt & Broman, 2015).

The eight sustainability principles are as follows (p. 7):

- *In a sustainable society, nature is not subject to systematically increasing...*

- *...concentrations of substances from the earth's crust (such as CO_2 and heavy metals),*

- *...concentrations of substances produced by society (such as endo-*

crine disruptors, chlorine and bromine),

- *...degradation by physical means (such as deforestation and draining of groundwater tables).*

- *In a sustainable society, people are not subject to social conditions that systematically hinder...*

- *... their health (mental, physical and emotional),*

- *...their influence (participating in shaping social systems they are a part of),*

- *...their competence (developing competence/learning individually or collectively),*

- *...their impartiality (discrimination, fairness, equity) and,*

- *...meaning-making (creating individual or common meaning).*

A vision of success and backcasting.

Once we have determined the system and our vision of success, there is a need to shape how we are going to get there. The FSSD uses an approach called backcasting. A backcasting approach is different from forecasting which is when you use prior knowledge, current reality and existing mental patterns to make decisions about what is possible in the future. Backcasting instead starts with the vision, prompts us to ask how we might get there (indicating that more than one path is possible) and to answer by providing flexible, creative solutions that close the gap between the vision of success and the current reality (Robèrt & Broman, 2015).

As we have established that the sustainability challenge is complex and emergent, we know that predicting future events is nearly impossible, and the future that wants to emerge might not be what we can currently conceive, therefore a backcasting approach makes the most sense when establishing our next steps.

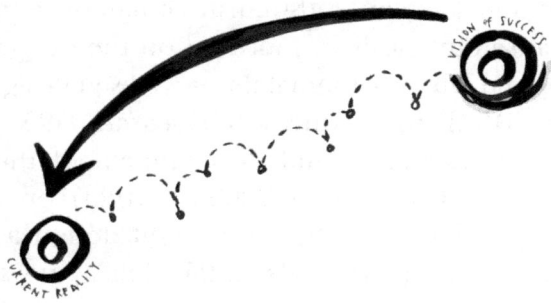

*Figure 3: Backcasting from a vision of success. Adapted from Robèrt &
Broman (2015). Image by Rosamund Mosse.*

The Potential: U.lab as a Niche

We believe that one of the most exciting aspects of u.lab - indeed why we have such hope for its potential - is that it can be seen as a niche. A niche is a protected space where users support emerging innovations and actors work on innovative and disruptive prototypes with the wish to replace existing (political, economic, social) systems and structures. Niches are particularly effective in inspiring societal transitions due to the prototypes they incubate which can lead to big waves of systemic change (Geels, 2011). We saw u.lab as a tool to address wicked problems like the sustainability challenge, but we were unsure if u.lab was explicit enough in how it framed sustainability, and that the prototypes to come out of it would indeed lead us toward a sustainable future.

Retreat and Reflect

The Inquiry: Laying a Foundation

We conducted the research for our thesis between December 2015 and June 2016, occupying various spaces at the university and around Karlskrona. These months were dark in Sweden, and begged for hibernation. Our thesis was fuelled by lots of coffee, tea, care and kanelbulle (Swedish cinnamon buns - a true staple!). Because our thesis was focused on the design of a new type of u.lab – a u.lab for sustainability – we used design research methodology (DRM) to conduct our research. DRM allows for the formulation, validation and development of theories and models (Blessing & Chakrabarti, 2009). Furthermore, our guiding research question asked how we might design a u.lab that necessarily moves society towards sustainability, and so we used concepts of strategic sustainable development to build the reference model. We analysed the ideology, strategy and vision of u. lab, and the interplay between the course and what it takes to be a sustainable society, as defined by the FSSD. This helped us in determining the areas in which u.lab had room for improvement in terms of being a vehicle to propel sustainable development.

In undertaking the work of writing a thesis together, we were intent that we learn not only from the content we read and generated, but the journey itself. The U process lent itself to the task and helped us to really embody the subject and experience the journey of learning and creating. After all, u.lab is all about breaking established paradigms and disrupting old patterns of behaviour and thought. As a team, we set an intention to walk our talk, and to support each other on the journey, knowing that the process of reinventing patterns and behaviours "only works when leaders and innovators and creative people who activate this source of knowing actually do some inner leadership work" (MITx, 2015, course video).

Collectively, we had fifty-four years of conventional education under our belts and knew, therefore, that we needed to take the time to completely immerse ourselves into the subject. We needed to stop downloading – operating from the old patterns and habits that our previous training had normalised in us. We turned to the U process, and realised that in order to stop downloading, we needed to engage in observation: Observe, observe, observe are the instructions for the first movement, or 'inner gesture', in order to change our patterns of thinking and being.

We spent weeks going through u.lab, reading the theory behind it, talking through the process and understanding the nuances, in order to be able to engage with the course as a whole (understanding that it is comprised of concepts, methodology, and theory). Ultimately, in the scoping of the topic, in order to undertake a manageable project, we decided to engage with u.lab on a theoretical level – establishing a thorough understanding of the systems within which it operates, the vision of success and the strategy of the course.

The second movement is to 'retreat and reflect.' As is often the case in life, when it rains, it pours, and we collectively (sometimes cumulatively) dealt with financial crises, personal struggles and the pull of other work. We took a week off – a literal and metaphorical retreat – in order to shake off these distractions, to let our inner knowledge emerge, and in the hopes of returning with a new perspective and sense of vigour - presenced.

The discussions around our thesis, our intentions, the process and methodology from that point on were fast-paced and very productive. Our focus and the ways that we went about answering our research questions changed multiple times, and rapidly – responding to that which wanted to emerge. Indeed, we acted very much in an instant – prototyping various ways of achieving our goal, and iterating the research questions and methodology as needed. This inner gesture of acting in the instant felt hectic and foreign, but the process of rapid-cycle iteration helped us in the refinement and evolution of our prototype.

A summary of our research, findings and conclusions constitutes the bulk of this chapter, which concludes with a theoretical model, or 2D prototype, of what *u.lab: Transforming Business, Society and Self towards Sustainability* might look like.

We did a review of the literature on u.lab, theory U and the FSSD, which allowed us to determine the criteria for success for both u.lab and the FSSD. We used concepts from Scharmer and Kaufer's (2013) written work to augment some of the theories that u.lab mentions but doesn't delve into, for example, society 4.0 and the shift from '*ego*-system' to '*eco*-system' awareness" (MITx 2015, course video). Society 4.0, with its eco-system awareness, includes awareness-based collective action, cross-sector co-creation, actions arising from a process of seeing the emerging whole and a dominant ideology of eco-system thought. We used these descriptors to detail the vision of success of u.lab, or where u.lab wants us to end up. We then created a reference model using the FSSD as a lens through which to analyse u.lab. A reference model is a representation of the current reality. Models generally "provide conceptual organisation" and highlight "significant relationships between... concepts or attributes" (Blessing & Chakrabarti, 2009, p. 20).

The reference model encapsulated the current reality of u.lab and served as the reference for what interventions should be developed. It really focused on the theoretical underpinnings of u.lab as opposed to specific actions and tools included in the course, which meant that we were looking to strengthen concepts such as the three divides as opposed to actions and tools such as the empathy walk or coaching circles, for example.

We were looking to see if the SSD concepts of systems thinking, the sustainability challenge, a clear, singular and unifying definition of sustainability, boundary conditions for sustainable development, and a vision of success and backcasting were already present in u.lab, and to what degree, so that we could then create an impact model (our vision of success - a u.lab for sustainability) which would enhance or include them as necessary. We had to concede that while those SSD concepts may not have been prevalent, or communicated in the same way as they were in the FSSD, some similar knowledge may be presented throughout the duration of the course. This is what we wanted to find out and verify.

After our own analysis of whether the five aforementioned SSD concepts were already inherent in the online course or not, we checked our assumptions with fifty-one fellow practitioners in order to validate our findings by using an online questionnaire distributed in various u.lab practitioners groups. The questionnaire was designed with both open- and close-ended questions to allow respondents to express themselves with greater accuracy and in greater detail, without being forced to put their responses into a category which might not feel right (Fink, 1995). This expression was important in our research because of the complexity of the concepts and the diversity of different individuals' potential understanding of sustainability. A self-administered electronic questionnaire was chosen for empirical data collection because it allowed for a large sample size and geographical diversity, and it was important for us to have a sample that reflected the international and emergent nature of the course.

We employed non-probability sampling, an approach that does "not guarantee that all eligible units have an equal chance of being included in a sample" (Fink 1995, p. 32). While we acknowledge that the number and breadth of responses cannot be considered as representational of the entire u.lab community, we consider the geographical diversity and anonymity of respondents, as well as the method of circulation, sufficient to validate the assumptions made in our reference model.

We used an ordinal scale to analyse the quantitative data (from the close-ended questions), and a combination of pre- and post-defined coding to analyse the qualitative data (from the open-ended questions). The coding was carried out by at least two members of the research team to ensure inter-encoder reliability (Blessing & Chakrabarti, 2009). The findings of our reference model are as follows:

Systems thinking.

We found that the systemic nature of our current reality was demonstrated quite well in u.lab by the iceberg model. The iceberg model is characterized by 'symptoms' above the water line (those events and activities that we see and interact with every day), which are the result of systems and structures immediately below the water line. Below those systems and structures, lie our unconscious values and beliefs which are deeply influenced by our current paradigms of thought (MITx, 2015, course material).

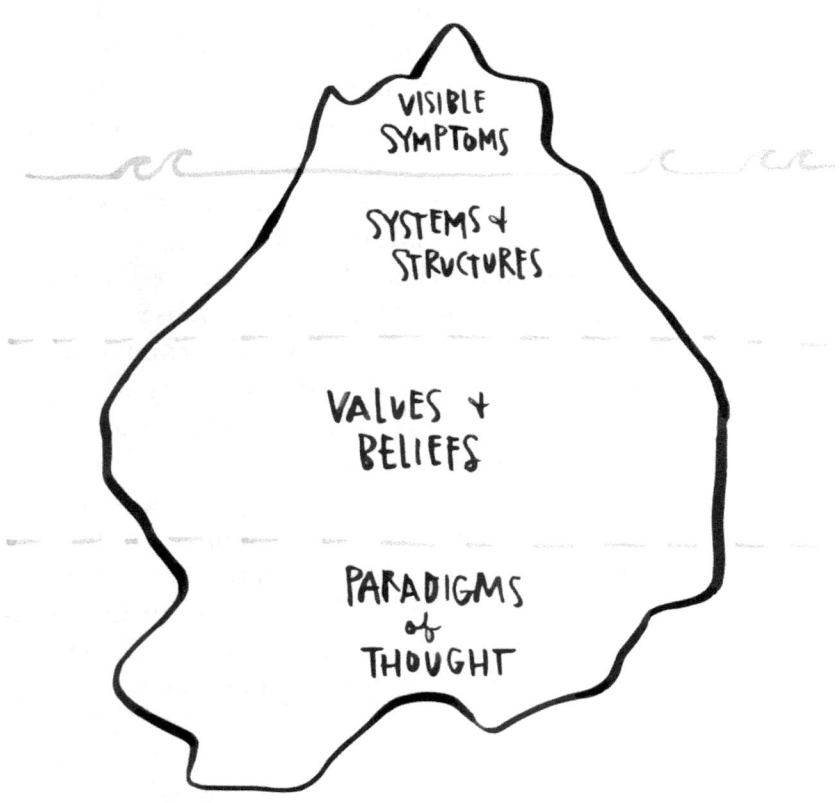

Figure 4: The iceberg model. Adapted from u.lab (MITx, 2015). Image by Rosamund Mosse.

There are other ways that systems thinking shows up in the course. For example, the three divides connect ecological, social and spiritual or cultural challenges, while the eight acupuncture points connect the symptoms of visible challenges, such as the sustainability challenge, with the underlying "structures, paradigms of thought, and sources that are responsible for creating them" (MITx, 2015, course video).

In *Leading from the Emerging Future: From ego-system to eco-sys-*

tem, Scharmer and Kaufer (2013) use the concept of eight 'acupuncture points' - leverage or pressure points within a system - to outline the underlying structural disconnects we are currently experiencing, and what society 4.0 would look like if we were to close the gap between those disconnects. The eight acupuncture points are as follow

- between the financial and the real economy...

- between the infinite growth imperative and the finite resources of Planet Earth...

- between the Haves and the Have Nots...

- between institutional leadership and people...

- between gross domestic product (GDP) and well-being...

- between governance and the voiceless in our systems...

- between actual ownership forms and best societal use of property...

- between technology and real societal needs (Scharmer & Kaufer, 2013).

In the first weeks of the course, participants are invited to "begin to see the system as a constellation of variables" (MITx 2015, course video) that includes them. Furthermore, Scharmer argues that we need to "[c]reate collective sensing mechanisms that make the system see itself" (MITx 2015, course video), which would imply a systems thinking perspective.

The reference model showed that the iceberg model exemplifies the interconnected and systemic nature of the challenges society faces. What was not clear was how well the concept was communicated, and how much of a systems thinking perspective participants took away from the course – especially if they did not have a prior knowledge of systems thinking.

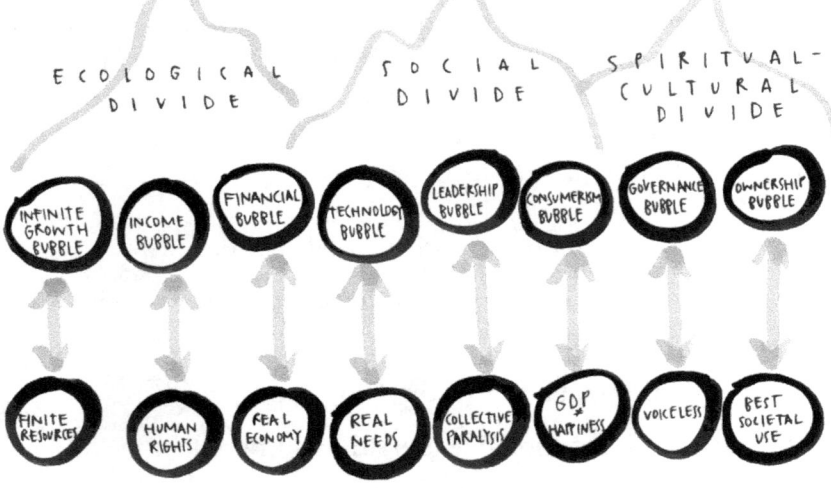

Figure 5: The three divides and the eight acupuncture points. Adapted from u. lab (MITx, 2015). Image by Rosamund Mosse.

The participants of our survey, however, did feel as if the challenges that u.lab seeks to address are explained in terms of systems thinking. Sixty percent of respondents believed the systemic nature of the challenges we face to be very well defined and thirty-three percent of respondents believed it to be fairly well defined. One respondent wrote of the "disconnection of thinking resulting in failure of decision [sic] regarding ecological and social problems, systems thinking" (Questionnaire respondent 8, April 28, 2016), in response to being asked about the challenges presented by u.Lab.

It was clear from our research that the current design of u.lab does communicate a systems thinking perspective quite clearly and there was no need to complement the design of u.lab with systems thinking concepts from SSD.

The sustainability challenge.

Although the language is different, aspects of the sustainability challenge show up in u.lab course content as externalities of the current economic system which, in turn, influence our paradigms of thought, according to Scharmer (MITx, 2015).

For example, the three divides speak to: environmental challenges such as destruction, resource scarcity, falling water tables, climate change, and soil erosion; social challenges such as inequality, polarisation and violence; and spiritual challenges, evidenced by current mental health trends and suicide rates (MITx, 2015, course video) which would all be included in the FSSD description of the sustainability challenge.

Many aspects of the sustainability challenge, as described by Robèrt and Broman, are included in course material, even if the language is non-specific. Results from the questionnaire indicated that u.lab participants felt that u.lab provided a good explanation of the ecological, social and spiritual/cultural struggles that our society is facing today, and respondents were able to regurgitate the examples easily, even using specific content, context and language from the course.

However, while participants demonstrated a good grasp of the three divides, the urgency of our current situation does not appear to be as apparent as in Robèrt and Broman's explanation of the sustainability challenge with the funnel metaphor. Even though we prefaced asking for an example of an ecological, social or spiritual struggle that u.lab highlights with an explanation of the sustainability challenge that included the pressure to solve the issues quickly due to increasing inequalities and scarcity of resources, no respondents spoke of urgency, pressure or a timeframe of any sort. The funnel metaphor is helpful in understanding the pressure to solve our environmental, social and spiritual issues quickly as the visual representation clearly communicates increasing inequalities and scarcity of resources over time (Robèrt & Broman, 2015). We concluded that, while the sustainability challenge is well communicated throughout u.lab, the urgency of our current situation could be better communicated. We decided to include supplementary concepts from SSD that would emphasize the *urgency* of the sustainability challenge in our impact model.

A clear, singular and unifying definition of sustainability.

While the inherent sustainability of u.lab's society 4.0 is implied, there is no unified and scientific definition of sustainability, which makes it "difficult to know whether any given scenario is truly sustainable" (Robèrt & Broman, 2015, p. 3).

A single definition of sustainability might feel prescriptive and exclusionary of the 'future that wants to emerge' (Scharmer & Kaufer, 2013), but Robèrt and Broman (2015) argue that outlining a principled definition of sustainability, framed as a set of boundary conditions, or things *not to do*, gives us more flexibility in making choices about the future. It means that "there are many possible sustainable societies (all complying with basic sustainability principles) and there are many routes to sustainability" (p. 11).

Our questionnaire respondents demonstrated that there was no consensus on whether sustainability was well defined. About one-third of respondents thought that sustainability was fairly well defined, but twenty-three percent were not sure or stated that it was not at all well-defined, and twenty-five percent felt that it was somewhat well defined. Furthermore, many participants couldn't remember any of the concepts included in the u.lab definition of sustainability. The complexity of the iceberg model and eight acupuncture points, which u.lab uses to explain the current ecological, social and spiritual struggles we are facing (and what the FSSD would understand as the sustainability challenge) might be a factor hindering participants' understanding. We believe that the complexity of the concepts may have caused participants to take a reductionist approach, memorising language but not understanding concepts fully. For example, many participants only mentioned "ego to eco" (Questionnaire respondents 5, 17, 18, 28, April 28, 2016) in their responses, but refrained from further explanation.

We noted with interest that the awareness and consciousness of the individual as a requirement for sustainability came up multiple times; a concept that is outside the realm of the FSSD definition of sustainability, but a main tenet of u.lab. It felt as though u.lab and SSD concepts were not only comparable but complementary and we saw potential for SSD concepts to strengthen u.lab in its redesign for sustainability. In the same way – and if we were redesigning the FSSD – we saw the potential for concepts from u.lab, particularly the internal condition of the individual, to augment and enrich the concept of strategic sustainable development.

Boundary conditions for sustainable development.

There are eight sustainability principles which act as boundary conditions in the development of a sustainable society. They are presented in the negative, and therefore dictate "exclusion criteria for redesign" (Robèrt & Broman, 2015, p. 7). In comparison, society 4.0, presented in the affirmative, proposes to lay out both the vision of success and (conflictingly) the future that is wanting to emerge. It is at once prescriptive, and without strategic guidelines for its realisation. The description of society 4.0 is also not based on scientifically-backed theory. It is missing key criteria that are necessary in order to establish a sustainable society, and the language used is not accessible to diverse audiences. Finally, the acupuncture points of society 4.0 are not non-overlapping, but tend to be interwoven, making following them as guidelines much more difficult.

If we are to look at u.lab's vision of success as a tool to "guide problem-solving and innovation" (Robèrt & Broman, 2015, p. 3), in the same way that the sustainability principles are, then we see that it is very much determined by forecasting from our past experiences, current reality and already established mental models. While society 4.0 offers some tangible examples of systems, processes or movements, the guidelines that u.lab provides in order to move us towards this vision are vague. For example, u.lab advocates for the respect and protection of the commons, but this requires that 'respect and protection of the commons', along with society's other pressing issues are universally understood to mean the same thing – to be normative, which is a potentially dangerous assumption.

When it comes to the prototyping phase of the course, the advice offered to participants is to have three dialogues: one with ourselves, one with our close circles, and one with the Universe, by connecting 'horizontally' and listening to how life responds to your intention (MITx, 2015). This is not bad advice, however it is the only direction for how we might move prototypes towards society 4.0 – and it is therefore insufficient.

What u.lab outlines well is the historical context and foundational understanding of the transformational nature of economic paradigms. The course focus is on the shift in individual leadership capacity, and u.lab advocates for personal transformation as a necessary pre-condition to changing the social systems we are a part of. While u.lab doesn't outline steps to transition to a sustainable society, the belief of the power of the individual to transform the social systems they are a part of is a great place to start. Therefore, we saw the potential of the course to help move society towards sustainability with the help of a few additional SSD concepts.

Our qualitative data showed that participants interpreted the quality of relationships with oneself and others as being some form of guideline offered by u.lab, as highlighted by a respondent when they wrote: "Ulab [sic] provides the attitude and awareness guideline needed to move towards sustainability. When we live from open heart, open mind and open will, mankind will take [sic] decisions and actions based on responsibility and care. Which will create completely different outcomes!" (Questionnaire respondent 35, May 1, 2016). However, we hesitate to assume that the outcomes created will necessarily move society towards a sustainable future without having been generated within clear boundary conditions.

On the other hand, participants didn't necessarily see clear guidelines as relevant or needed. For example, respondent 9 stated: "The focus on boundary conditions feels very inadequate and maybe even counter-productive. In my experience, what is needed is an affective [sic] experience of being connected in this amazing living system. To feel love and awe and connection and from there to act to create a more beautiful world" (April 28, 2016). And another respondent wrote that "the concept of proto-typing and trying and sensing...would be against the concept to provide clear guidelines" (Questionnaire respondent 6, April 28, 2016).

While u.lab is a powerful tool, inspiring reflection and moti-vating action, there is also the potential for prototypes, actions and processes to be inherently unsustainable as u.lab gives no clear boundary conditions for success. Furthermore, the respons-es from our questionnaire participants – even though they would appear to disagree with our premise – only serve to illustrate the need for a set of sustainable boundary conditions. Responses demonstrated no common perception of what sustainability means, as well as an almost zealous adherence to vague and ab-stract concepts that could be interpreted in numerous different ways. In order to really co-sense and co-create a future that we all want, we need a common language and a common understand-ing of where we want to go – or at least where we don't want to go. We therefore decided to introduce the sustainability princi-ples as boundary conditions for success in our impact model: *u.lab: Transforming Business, Society and Self towards Sustainability.*

A vision of success and backcasting.

The purpose of u.lab, is to "build the capacity to sense and actualize a future that we feel is possible, that we know is possible, but that isn't quite there yet..." (MITx, 2015, course material). But how, exactly? An affirmative vision of success, such as society 4.0, can be difficult for diverse groups to agree upon. A princi-ple-based definition of sustainability made up of exclusion crite-ria means that many different visions of success are possible. We found that some of the questionnaire respondents saw society 4.0 as prescriptive - a pre-determined vision of success which severe-ly limited participants' agency to build their own vision of success. One respondent wrote that "Since U lab [sic] is based on theory

U it is both a methodology and provides analysis of what is wrong today and which goals we should all thrive [sic] for - what is good (hence is normative). Methodology of co-creation and personal development is best implemented without normative implications...the mix of methodology and normative goals has a risk of being manipulative" (Questionnaire respondent 29, April 29, 2016).

Furthermore, society 4.0 was seemingly developed by forecasting, i.e. it is based on historical trajectories, as well as current trends, and opposed to backcasting, which would see individuals creating a vision of success and then developing a plan for how to reach it from their current position.

The idea of learning from the emerging future (MITx, 2015) parallels backcasting in the constant conceptualising and refining of a vision of success. But, society 4.0 as a long-term, and ultimate, envisioned future seems to be in contradiction with the idea of a "future that wants to emerge" (Scharmer and Kaufer, 2013, p. 3).

This conceptual confusion is reflected in our questionnaire respondents' understanding of their envisioned future. Respondents were inclined to build their own vision of success from concepts throughout the course that spoke to them, instead of using the concepts of society 4.0. When asked to provide examples of when the vision of society 4.0 impacted their prototyping process, half of our respondents skipped the question. While society 4.0 provides a vision of success that might work on a macro scale, it is not particularly helpful at the micro scale – the level of individual prototypes, and therefore cannot be seen as a sufficient guiding vision.

We saw reason to introduce a mechanism for visioning into u.lab, that would give participants more agency over the future they envisioned. This process of visioning would need to happen within the boundaries of the sustainability principles and alongside the methodology of backcasting in order to illustrate which parts of the process are rigid and which parts are flexible – as well as why.

Act in an Instant

The Prototype: Building an Impact Model

While some participants questioned the purpose of a sustainability-focussed u.lab and demonstrated a concern that boundary conditions or a single definition of sustainability might hinder one of the main teachings of u.lab which is to let things emerge, our analysis still demonstrated that designing *u.lab: Transforming Business, Society and Self towards Sustainability* could address some gaps in the current iteration of u.lab making it more effective in inspiring the systemic change necessary in the pursuit of sustainable development.

Based on our findings from the reference model and the data we collected, we built a prototype for an impact model that included the following SSD concepts: the urgency of the sustainability challenge, a clear, singular and unifying definition of sustainability, boundary conditions for sustainable development, and a process for creating a vision of success and backcasting. The impact model is a 2D prototype of *u.lab: Transforming Business, Society and Self towards Sustainability*, which would include the four recommended interventions presented below. Each intervention would include a lesson and workshop on the particular issue, developed and delivered in collaboration with FSSD and other sustainability practitioners.

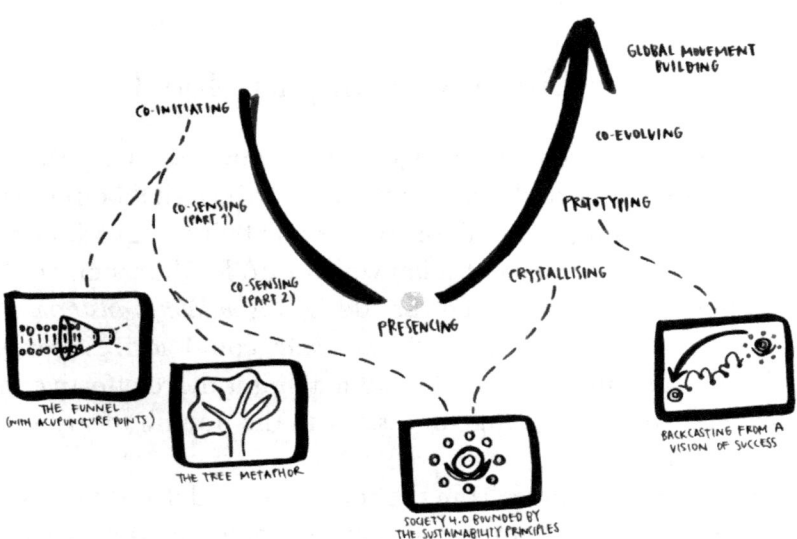

Figure 6: Our impact model of u.lab: Transforming Business, Society and Self towards Sustainability. Adapted from u.lab (MITx, 2015). Image by Rosamund Mosse.

The development of the four interventions was a creative process, and we recognise a need to prototype our impact model to allow for feedback that could be incorporated into further iterations. We also see an opportunity to explore how u.lab, theory U or specific tools of the course could benefit practitioners in implementing the FSSD or in communicating the sustainability challenge - but we will have to leave that for future research.

The urgency of the sustainability challenge.

We found that the iceberg model provided an effective and well-communicated visualisation of the sustainability challenge, but the questionnaire responses indicated that the urgency of the sustainability challenge was not apparent. Therefore, we felt that it would be necessary to slightly tweak it in order to effectively convey the urgency of the situation. We propose that u.lab introduce the concept of the funnel in the co-initiating phase. The outline of the funnel will follow the discussion of the three divides and eight acupuncture points to illustrate the urgency of action, as well as the limits that we are increasingly surpassing with our current actions and ways of thinking.

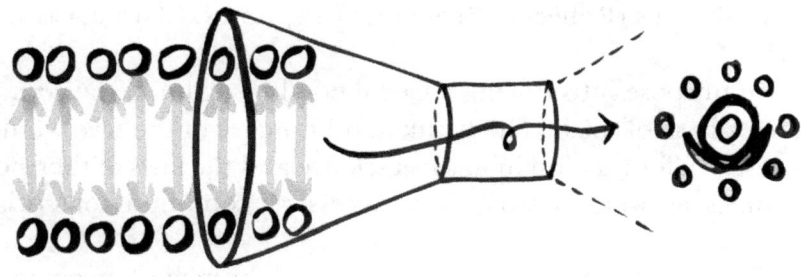

*Figure 7: The funnel with the eight acupuncture points and society 4.0.
Adapted from u.lab (MITx, 2015) and Robèrt & Broman (2015). Image by Rosamund Mosse.*

The wall of the funnel still represents the decreasing carrying capacity of the earth. As portrayed above, the eight acupuncture points and the disconnects currently will not pass through the contracting wall of the funnel, demonstrating the inherent unsustainability and urgency of our situation. We need to close the disconnects of each acupuncture point in order to keep from hitting the wall of the funnel and to move society towards a sustainable future, where the earth's carrying capacity remains in balance with society's actions and resource use. The vision of a sustainable society would include the concept of society 4.0, re-imagined and bounded by the eight sustainability principles, as described below, under 'boundary conditions for sustainable development'.

A clear, singular and unifying definition of sustainability.

Our research indicated a need for a clear definition of sustainability for our impact model. A common language around sustainability will help to allow a strategic coordination across different sectors and the design of more effective and streamlined solutions (Robèrt & Broman, 2015; Kates, Clark & Corell, 2001).

We propose introducing a tree metaphor, again in the co-initiating phase of u.lab. The trunk and branches of the tree would represent a foundation in natural science and the laws of thermodynamics as well as trust as a necessary condition for social systems.

The first-order principles (trunk and branches) provide a foundation for creating a shared vision of what a sustainable society should look like (Holmberg & Robèrt, 2000). Where the leaves represent a more nuanced and specialised understanding of specific disciplines of natural and social science, the trunk and branches of the tree represent a foundational understanding of sustainability science that people from many disciplines can understand, without 'getting lost in the leaves' (Holmberg & Robèrt, 2000).

Finally, the tree metaphor also reflects a systems thinking approach, reinforcing the idea that the components of the sustainability challenge interact and affect one another in multiple feedback loops (Robèrt & Broman 2015).

Figure 8: The tree metaphor. Adapted from Robèrt & Broman (2015). Image by Rosamund Mosse.

We believe that the tree metaphor will help to bridge a gap we saw in our research, as our data suggested that participants did not necessarily connect the details, or symptoms, of the sustainability challenge when presented with the iceberg model alone. In contrast, when those symptoms are presented as leaves, associated with a specific branch representing a specific law or discipline, participants can trace the symptom back to a first order principle in social or natural science. The tree metaphor, with its scientifically-based definition of sustainability, will also become a precursor to the boundary conditions explained in the prototyping phase of u.lab as detailed below.

Boundary conditions for sustainable development.

We recommend that *u.lab: Transforming Business, Society and Self towards Sustainability* adopt the sustainability principles, as explained by Robèrt and Broman (2015), as the boundary conditions for sustainable development. They will be explained in the co-initiating phase along with the tree metaphor and at the time of crystallizing, they will be discussed again in more detail in order to influence sustainable prototypes. The sustainability principles will appear twice - once with a reimagined society 4.0, to clarify u.lab's long-term vision of success, and again as guidelines for sustainability for the prototypes participants create.

Where society 4.0 is currently prescriptive as to the future we all want, we will reimagine society 4.0 as many potential visions of success, all falling within the boundaries of what a sustainable society is *not*. Furthermore, during the prototyping phase, when participants are invited to ideate, innovate and prototype new results, it is incredibly important that these 'new' results move society in the direction of sustainability, instead of contributing to our current unsustainability. Therefore, having tangible and accessible guidelines - or principles - is paramount. The eight sustainability principles will provide a more comprehensive understanding of the vision of success of society 4.0 as well as of the individual visions of success of each prototype.

Figure 9: Society 4.0 bounded by the eight sustainability principles. Image by Rosamund Mosse.

A vision of success and backcasting.

As described above, we proposed to reintroduce society 4.0 as bounded by the eight sustainability principles as the long-term vision of success of u.lab for sustainability. We also suggested a process whereby participants are invited to construct their own vision of success at the prototyping phase that is more specific to the desires of the participant and the sector of the prototype. This micro-scale vision of success should also be created with the eight sustainability principles as boundary conditions so that each prototype necessarily moves society towards sustainability.

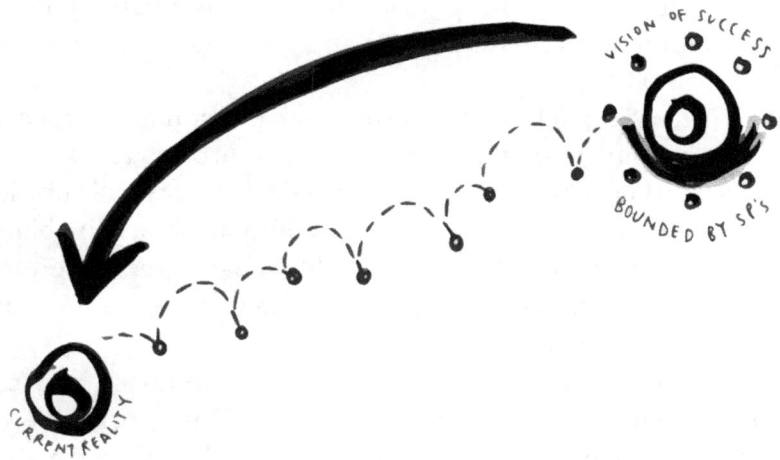

Figure 10: Backcasting from a vision of success (society 4.0) bounded by the sustainability principles. Adapted from Robèrt & Broman (2015). Image by Rosamund Mosse.

The Presencing Institute 'Toolkit for Prototyping' asks, "[w]hat is wanting to born in my life and work right now?" and "[w]hat future do I want to create?" (Presencing Institute, 2015). However, Robèrt and Broman (2015) claim that backcasting from a vision of success framed by a principled definition of sustainability will constitute a more intuitive and practical approach to sustainable development.

The Aim: Scaling up

Scaling up a niche requires expanding the resource base for participation and innovation as well as developing a common language and explicit expectations (Geels, 2011). Scaling up a u.lab for sustainability would involve: boosting support from external actors by clearly articulating expectations and visions; providing guidance for innovation activities; expanding the resource base of niche-innovations through expanded social networks guaranteeing the enrolment of more actors, and; a multi-dimensional and iterative process of learning and articulation (Geels, 2011). We believe that our interventions serve to improve the efficacy of u.lab as a structure in moving society towards sustainability, lending momentum to its current design and growing it beyond niche status (Geels, 2011).

The impact model clarifies a sustainable vision and expectations by using language that is precise and more broadly accepted (Geels, 2011). The introduction of SSD concepts will supplement u.lab with a clear and unified definition of sustainability, relay the urgency of the sustainability challenge, introduce boundary conditions and a principled vision of success, and communicate the benefits of backcasting.

Geels argues that one can improve the legitimacy and resources to niche-innovations by enlarging their networks, thereby increasing the potential of the participation of powerful actors (2011). One of u.lab's current strengths is its reach and networks, as demonstrated by the great diversity of stakeholders, powerful and not, from individual actors in the majority world to the Scottish government, for example.

However, we believe that our impact model, with its scientifically-backed concepts and language, could make *u.lab: Transforming Business, Society and Self towards Sustainability* accessible to further communities of participants. For instance, our re-design recommends collaboration with FSSD and other sustainability practitioners, which has the potential to expand u.lab's stakeholders and participants as sustainability practitioners could forge a link with sustainability-focussed corporations, academic institutions, not-for-profit organisations and municipalities.

Our impact model acknowledges the power of experiential learning processes, as well as the benefits of diversifying content, methodologies and language. We have recommended the supplementary information in order to ground the content of u.lab in natural science, thereby 'stabilising' the course (Geels, 2011). While u.lab wasn't developed specifically with sustainability in mind, we believe we have demonstrated the need and potential for designing a u.lab for sustainability.

The Motive: A Summary

The global sustainability challenges we are facing today are urgent, complex and systemic. We therefore need to develop new ways of tackling them. We need to develop solutions that encourage broad-scale participation, address underlying structures that reenact results that nobody wants, and embrace innovation and experimentation. We are running out of time and we need to fail fast to learn fast.

U.lab has a structure that empowers change-makers to co-sense and co-create the future that is wanting to be born, by shifting our learning processes from learning from the past to learning from the emergent future (MITx, 2015). U.lab also advocates that the only way to break the cycle of downloading in order to address the complex challenges of our time is by sensing into a deeper source of knowledge, understanding and acting (Scharmer & Kaufer, 2010).

We ourselves have experienced first-hand the deeply profound transformational process u.lab can inspire. Our findings demonstrate room for improvement in order to further inspire and aid u.lab practitioners and participants to move society strategically towards sustainability. Consequently, we have made suggestions for four interventions in the current design of u.lab and strongly believe that the FSSD can lend structure and clarity to the intention of a u.lab for sustainability.

And, as practitioners of the FSSD, we agree with Robèrt and Broman when they acknowledge the limitations of the FSSD and its role in sustainable development. They contend that they have always expected "that much more knowledge and competence will be developed on how the FSSD and other forms of support can be mutually supplemental" (2015). They go on to conclude that: "the purpose of the FSSD has never been to replace or exclude other forms of support for sustainable development, but the opposite; to provide a structure that allows for clarification of their respective strengths and that aids a coordinated use of them" (Robèrt & Broman, 2015, p. 12). As such, we also recognise the enormous potential for FSSD practitioners to explore how u.lab, theory U or specific tools of the course could aid them in communicating, designing for, and provoking innovations for sustainability.

The development of the interventions in our impact model was a creative process and a theoretical creation. It was an extrapolation of reality as defined by the literature review and empirical data and interpreted by us, and we recognise that it needs to be evaluated in the field to legitimate any assumptions we may have made (Blessing & Chakrabarti, 2009).

The dream has always been to put our research into practice. By workshopping the impact model with diverse stakeholders, we would hope to improve subsequent iterations that could eventually stand alone as *u.lab: Transforming Business, Society and Self towards Sustainability*!

The Next Breath: A Postscript

When we graduated in June 2016, we were determined that our experience together would not just end. We decided that our new-found knowledge and skill-sets, as well as our friendship, was something that needed to be explored. We wanted to have an impact on society by being the change or leading the change or changing *something*, but how the *heck* were we going to do that?

With diplomas in hand and after a well-deserved break, we began our second year in Karlskrona, ready to tackle our dream and co-create something together. After six months spent in a business incubator, we co-founded Transition Lab - a platform for designing and facilitating systemic change that would help people and organisations move towards more sustainable practices and collaborative leadership. Scaling highs and descending to lows, we committed to trying to understand how to do the work the world needed, crafting in response an answer that felt, more or less, like 'us'.

In June 2017, we were all contracted to help facilitate a u. prototype bootcamp, organised by the Hive Experiment in partnership with the Department of Strategic Sustainable Development (TISU) at BTH and the Presencing Institute (PI). The Hive Experiment is an MSLS alumni initiative focused on convening and leveraging a network of change agents from across the globe at the intersection of social innovation, sustainable development & emerging technology to support tangible action towards creating more sustainable and vibrant societies around the world.

Eight teams from all over the world (Israel, United States, Hungary, Sweden, and Holland) went through three days of a facilitated U process to accelerate their prototypes at the intersection of sustainable development, new technology and social innovation.

The thirty-five participants had certain knowledge about the U process, but no scientific knowledge of, or common language around, sustainability. At the end of the bootcamp, prototypes were aligned with social innovation, leadership and/or technology. But we had no way of testing, mapping or showing that prototypes were aligned with the principles of sustainability as we knew them. Our experience as co-facilitators only reignited a motivation to design a U process that would systematically lead society towards sustainability. Could the next iteration of a u.prototype bootcamp include our suggested interventions for designing for sustainability? How might we accelerate the ripples of change so that, as we learn to live within the means of ecological and social boundaries, we might even begin to look towards a *regenerative* society - a society 5.0?

References

Beltrame, Lucia, Zachary Rootes, and Laurent Serrure. 2013. "Solutions from Below: A Strategic Approach for the Sustainable Management of Organised Community Seed Banks."

Blessing, L. T., & Chakrabarti, A. (2009). *DRM, a design research methodology*. London: Springer.

Collins, J. C., & Porras, J. I. (2009). *Built to last: successful habits of visionary companies*. New York, NY:

Collins.Fink, Arlene. 1995. *The Survey Handbook*. 1st ed. Thousands Oaks, CA: Sage Frensch, P. A., & Funke, J. (1995). *Complex problem solving: the European perspective*. Hillsdale, NJ: L.

Erlbaum Associates. Geels, F. W. (2011). The multi-level perspective on sustainability transitions: Responses to seven criticisms. *Environmental Innovation and Societal Transitions, 1*(1), 24-40. doi:10.1016/j. eist.2011.02.002

Heifetz, R., & Linsky, M. (2002). Leadership on the Line: Staying Alive through the Dangers of Leading. *The Leadership Quarterly*. doi:10.1016/s1048-9843(03)00022-5

Holmberg, J. & and Robèrt, K-H. (2000). "Backcasting — a Framework for Strategic Planning." *International Journal of Sustainable Development & World Ecology* 7 (4). Informa UK: 291–308. doi:10.1080/13504500009470049.

Kates, R. & Clark, W. & Corel, R. (2001). "Sustainability Science." *American Association for the Advancement of Science* 292 (5517): 641–42.

Mintzberg, H. (1994). *The Rise and Fall of Strategic Planning*. New York: Prentice Hall.

Missimer, M. (2015). "Social Sustainability within the Framework for Strategic Sustainable Development." Retrieved from https://www. divaportal.org/smash/get/diva2:852857/FULLTEXT02.pdf

MITx (2015). MITx: U.Lab: Transforming Business, Society, and Self. Edx. Retrieved from: https://courses.edx.org/courses/MITx/15. S23x/3T2014.

Norton, B. G. (2011). The Ways of Wickedness: Analyzing Messiness with Messy Tools. *Journal of Agricultural and Environmental Ethics, 25*(4), 447-465. doi:10.1007/s10806-011-9333-3

Ny, H. & MacDonald, J, P. & Broman, G. & Yamamoto, R. & Robért, K, H. (2008). "Sustainability Constraints as System Boundaries: An Approach to Making Life-Cycle Management Strategic." *Journal of Industrial Ecology* 10 (1-2).

Wiley- Blackwell: 61–77. doi:10.1162/108819806775545349. Presencing Institute Website (2015). Retrived from. https://www.presenc-ing.com/.

Rittel, H. W., & Webber, M. M. (n.d.). Dilemmas in a General Theory of Planing. *Design: Critical and Primary Sources.* doi:10.5040/9781474282932.0015

Robèrt, K,H. & Broman, G. (2015). "A Framework for Strategic Sustainable Development." *Journal of Cleaner Production*, October, 1–15.

Robèrt, K., Daly, H., Hawken, P., & Holmberg, J. (1997). A Compass for Sustainable Development. *International Journal of Sustainable Development & World Ecology,4*(2), 79-92. doi:10.1080/13504509709469945

Rockström, J. (2010). "Planetary Boundaries." *New Perspectives Quarterly* 27 (1). Wiley-Blackwell: 72–74. doi:10.1111/j.1540-5842.2010.01142.x.

Scharmer, C. O., & Kaufer, K. (2010). In front of the blank canvas: sensing emerging futures. *Journal of Business Strategy,31*(4), 21-29. doi:10.1108/02756661011055159

Scharmer, C. O., & Kaufer, K. (2013). Leading from the Emerging Future: From Ego-System to Eco-System Economies. San Francisco: Berret-Koehler Publishers.

Senge, P. M. (1980). The Fifth Discipline: Mastering the Five Practices of the Learning Organization. New Yok: Doubleday/Currency.

Speth, G. (2015, February 13). Living on Earth – Gus Speth calls for a New Environmentalism   Interview by C. Steve Curwood]. Retrieved December 20, 2017, from http://winewaterwatch. org/2016/05/we-scientists-dont-know-how-to-do -that-what-a-commentary/

Xiang, W. (2013). Working with Wicked Problems in Socio-Ecological Systems: Awareness, Acceptance, and Adaptation. *Landscape and Urban Planning,110*, 1-4. doi:10.1016/j.landurbplan.2012.11.006

Note to readers: this chapter is an abridged, re-worked version of our thesis research for the completion of an M.Sc. at the Blekinge Institute of Technology. For further details, our full thesis is available online at the Digitala Vetenskapliga Arkivet (DiVA) portal under the same title.

Biographies

Florentina Bajraktari is an online/offline educator and facilitator of change processes for the Presencing Institute. Her background in politics at the local and international level have given her an understanding of the complexity of traditional systems, and a systemic understanding of the leverage points where change is needed most. She is particularly interested in designing processes that activate individual transformation and collaboration as a starting point for societal renewal in the field of education, workplace innovation and sustainability. She is currently working with her colleagues on hosting a multi-local online innovation journey for teams who are co-shaping more equitable social systems worldwide. Florentina has a Masters in Political Science from the Free University of Brussels and a Masters in Strategic Leadership towards Sustainability from the Blekinge Institute of technology, Sweden.

Kelvy Bird is an internationally recognized graphic facilitator—drawing large pictures as people talk and can see the images unfold—who translates content into formats that aid with reflection and decision-making. Her book, "Generative Scribing: A Social Art of the 21st Century", defines a practice that weaves words, pictures, and energy to reveal a system's potential. As co-founder of the Presencing Institute, Kelvy has helped shape many in person and online offerings for a distributed community of change makers, including the edX course u.lab: Leading from the Emerging Future, for which she contributes extensive visual material. In 2016, she co-edited the anthology "Drawn Together through Visual Practice". She also co-founded dpict llc, a company specializing in scribing to advances social understanding at local and global scales. Kelvy received her BFA in painting and BA in Art History from Cornell University. Her current residence is Somerville, MA. Find more at: www.kelvybird.com

Gloria Bottaro is a PhD student in communication sciences at the University of Vienna. She is part of an interdisciplinary research team in the field of innovation research at the department of Philosophy at the University of Vienna. Her research fields are emotions and group dynamics, collaboration and co-creation (especially in innovation teams), and interdisciplinary didactics with a special interest on teacher-student interfaces. Furthermore, she is developing instructional designs with a special focus on blended learning for higher education settings.

William Brendel is an Assistant Professor of Organization Development and Change at Penn State University and is the CEO of the Transformative Learning Institute. William has over 20 years of experience as an organization development consultant, researcher, author and trainer. His publications on mindful leadership and organizational change span academic journals and popular press. His consultation and workshops have led to measurable transformations in organizational culture and performance across the U.S., China, India and Africa. William has previously held academic positions at Texas A&M, Temple University, and the University of St Thomas, where he has taught graduate courses in Organization Development, Leadership Development, Change Management, Talent Management, Group Dynamics, and Transformative Learning. William received his Doctorate in Adult Learning and Leadership, and Master's degree in Organizational Psychology at Columbia University in New York.

Reilly Dow is a scribe supporting a diverse range of processes in English and Spanish. For the past 10 years, she has used visual facilitation in support of groups looking to share, understand, and act on important ideas. By listening, synthesizing and communicating visually, she helps clients access their creativity with greater depth and engagement. Recent clients include Deutsche Gesellschaft für Internationale Zusammenarbeit (GIZ), International Peace Institute, United Nations and WWF. Reilly holds an MA in Interdisciplinary Studies and is based in Mexico City.

Geoff Fitch is a coach, trainer, and facilitator of growth in individuals and organizations, and a creator of transformative learning programs. He is a founder of Pacific Integral, where he was instrumental in the development of the Generating Transformative Change program, which has been delivered on three continents. Through these programs, he has researched and developed novel approaches to individual and collective growth and has designed and facilitated dozens of residential learning retreats. He has been exploring diverse approaches to cultivating higher human potentials for over 25 years, including somatic and transpersonal psychology, mindfulness, innovation and creativity, leadership, integral theory, and collective intelligence. Geoff also has over 30 year's experience in leadership in business. He holds a master's degree in Transpersonal Psychology from the Institute of Transpersonal Psychology and B.S. in Computer Science, magna cum laude, from Boston University.

Olen Gunnlaugson is an award-winning Associate Professor in Leadership and Organizational Development at Université Laval (Canada) where he teaches MBA courses in leadership, management skills and group communications to managers, leaders and executives. With a research background in Leadership Development, Group Communication and Leadership Coaching, he received his Ph.D. at the University of British Columbia and did his Post-Doctorate at Simon Fraser University, Vancouver. To date, his work has been published extensively in books, articles and chapters in leading academic journals and books. He has presented and keynoted at numerous international conferences, received several teaching awards from universities in Canada and the USA and taught emerging leaders and executives at leading schools in Canada, USA, Austria, Sweden and South Korea. Over the past several years, he has been researching and developing Dynamic Presencing. As the focus of his upcoming book to be released in 2019, Dynamic Presencing introduces five journeys for transforming our existing presencing practices as an orienting way of being. For more information, visit www.dynamicpresencing.com

Martina Hartner-Tiefenthaler is Senior Scientist at the Institute for Management Science (Labor Science and Organization) at TU Wien, Austria. There, she researches aspects on the interface between technology, organization and employees. Drawing on her background in psychology (University of Vienna) and business studies (New College Durham, UK) she is interested how to support individuals and teams to develop their full potential in flexible working arrangements. Thus, her current research lies in the area of new ways of working, flexible teams, and technology affordances. Her most recent research project dealt with smartphone usage in the context of blurred boundaries between work and private.

Abigail Lynam, Ph.D is faculty for Fielding Graduate University's PhD in Human and Organizational Development, and Pacific Integral's Generating Transformative Change program. Her scholarship and practice integrate the interior dimensions of human knowledge and experience (culture, worldviews, psychology, wisdom traditions, etc.) with social and ecological change efforts. An area of emphasis is adult developmental psychology applied to adult learning, organizational change, and leadership development. She works with tools and technologies for transformative change such as Theory U, integral theory and practice, polarity management, social change innovations, and dialogue and contemplative practices. Dr. Lynam has lived and worked internationally in India, Ethiopia, Great Britain, Hong Kong, and Mexico.

Kriyanka Moodley was exposed to Theory U during her doctoral research. She holds a PhD in Leadership from the Graduate School of Business and Leadership, at the University of KwaZulu-Natal, South Africa. In 2017, she started the company Mind

Before Matter, which is an academic and commercial research consultancy. Her professional interests include academia, marketing, leadership, social development, qualitative and quantitative analyses. Her academic and commercial work continue to give her local and international exposure.

Rosamund Mosse is a natural facilitator and a maven of process and experience design. With a bent for facilitation, foresight and servant leadership, she works to co-create participatory, innovative and transformational experiences – embodied and visual. She believes that solving the complex challenges we currently face will involve creativity, a willingness to show up in new ways, and a willingness to be changed in the process. Rosamund has a B.A. in International Development Studies and Spanish, an M. Sc. in Strategic Leadership towards Sustainability, a fellowship in Social Innovation, and now runs Evoke by Design, a consultancy focused on designing processes for systems change: www.evokebydesign.org A lover of language and poetry, she has a fierce respect for the sacredness and power of words. She works to hold dynamic situations with a grounded energy in order to create space for what wants to emerge.

Markus F. Peschl (*1965) is professor of cognitive science and philosophy of science at the University of Vienna, Dept. of Philosophy. His areas of research and expertise include innovation, cognitive science, organizational theory and strategy, design, and spaces for knowledge- and innovation work (Enabling Spaces). Working in the field of radical innovation Markus has developed the concepts of Emergent Innovation and Enabling Spaces which he understands as a form of "socio-epistemological engineering". Furthermore, he is engaged in developing alternative knowledge-/innovation-driven formats of teaching and learning and works in the field of interdisciplinary curriculum development. M. Peschl holds several visiting professorships (Berlin, Bratislava, etc.) and has won various prizes for his innovative approaches to teaching and learning. He has published 6 books and more than 140 papers in international journals and collections. For further details see: http://www.univie.ac.at/knowledge/peschl/

Katharina Roetzer is currently studying cognitive science at the University of Vienna, Austria. She is part of an interdisciplinary teaching and research team in the field of innovation and knowledge creation and a member of the research group OCKO, located at the Department of Philosophy, University of Vienna. Katharina has an academic background in art and design, sociology, and cognitive science. Her research interests revolve around learning and social interaction, and the socio-emotional dimensions of knowledge creation and their applications in learning technologies in particular. Being self-employed since 2013, she has worked with companies from various branches and has several years of work experience in cross-disciplinary, business-oriented research work in the context of innovation.

Jacqueline B. Saldana is a college professor with more than 30 years of experience in program development and strategic management. Saldana is a Faculty Chair and Associate Professor at DeVry University. Saldana is an experienced leader and policy maker; responsible for communication strategies, analysis, and reporting systems with nationally awarded results. Saldana is a writer and peer reviewer for academic journals and research projects, and a regular Guest Speaker for professional associations. Saldana was the first Puerto Rican member of the Society for Healthcare and Marketing Communications of the American Hospital Association (1996-2000), and appointed distinguished Communications Professional by the House of Representatives of the Commonwealth of Puerto Rico in 1997. Saldana has a BA in Communications from the University of the Sacred Heart, an MBA from the University of Phoenix and a Doctoral Degree of Management in Organizational Leadership from the University of Phoenix School of Advanced Studies.

Wilfried Schley studied Pedagogy, Special Education and Clinical Psychology before he was appointed Professor in Special Education at the University of Hamburg in 1982 and, subsequently, Ordinarius of Special Education at the University of Zurich in 1997. He has worked as a researcher, scientist and professional coach. As the Founder of the IOS Schley and Partner

GmbH (Institute of Organisational Development and Systemic Consultancy), which offers consultancy in business transformation, he acts as a consultant in creating coaching cultures in business and education. He is the Founder of the Leadership Foundation for Professional Education and Global Learning in Switzerland and the Co-Director of the Austrian Leadership Academy. One of his main areas of research and development became the INTUS 3 Initiative, a cooperation with the Helga Breuninger Foundation on training concepts to develop competencies on resonance and empathy for education and leadership.

Michael Schratz has been working in the field of education in many countries focusing on system transformation, leadership and learning. He was the Founding Dean of the School of Education at the University of Innsbruck (Austria) and has been Austrian representative for the EU, OECD, Council of Europe. Michael is Co-Director of the National Leadership Academy, Chairman of the Jury of the German School Award and Scientific Director of the European Doctorate in Teacher Education (EDITE), in which five universities work towards *Transformative Teacher Learning for Better Student Learning within an Emerging European Context*. He was President of ICSEI (International Congress of School Effectiveness and Improvement) from 2016-2017 and held the Fritz Karsen Chair at the Humboldt University of Berlin (Germany) in 2018. Michael is also author of many books, partly translated into other languages, and editor of several journals on leadership, school improvement and learning.

Mary Stacey is the founder of Context Consulting, the founder of the Burren Executive Leadership Retreat, and its lead designer. She brings years of collaboration with artists and a depth of experience cultivating forms of leadership that are more systemic, creative, and adaptive. Mary is a founding member of the Action Inquiry Fellowship, scholar practitioners dedicated to practicing timely action inquiry in service of developing personal integrity, relational mutuality, and just and sustainable social systems. She holds an MA in Organizational Leadership and Learning, a diploma in counseling, and is an executive coach certified in a variety of development assessments. She teaches in the Strategic Leadership Advanced Certificate at the University of Toronto, where she also regularly works with delegations from China.

Gabriel Neira Voto is an optimistic system thinker and social entrepreneur. His key interest is in catalyzing social innovation and community engagement in deprived areas with complex social, environmental and economic issues. With a background in Ecology, Gabriel utilizes a systemic perspective to create sustainable local impact; with a sensitivity to the information nodes in the ecosystem to feel how it wants to be changed. He designs and implements social innovation using Theory U amongst other tools, to seize the ecosystem's potential and to open inclusive and generative dialogues. Gabriel has a B.Sc. in Ecology and a M.Sc. in Strategic Leadership towards Sustainability. He is a Lead International Fellow and co-founded Favela Verde, an award-winning NGO in Brazil. Gabriel works as an impact consultant and is currently designing an innovative community development strategy for a historic village in Bristol, UK.

CPSIA information can be obtained
at www.ICGtesting.com
Printed in the USA
LVHW050904030121
675431LV00014BA/2658